The Dialectics of Liquidity Crisis

This book analyses the logic of applying the American Post-Keynesian economist Hyman Minsky's Financial Instability Hypothesis (FIH) to the financial crisis of 2007–08. Arguing that most theories of financial crisis, including Minsky's own, only describe events, but do not actually explain them, the book surveys theories of financial crisis that have been developed to describe instability in the post-WW2 US financial system and analyses them in their historical context.

The book argues that explanation of the financial crisis of 2007–08 should involve interpretation of the concept of 'risk', which guides the construction and pricing of contemporary financial products such as derivatives and asset backed securities, as a form of 'liquidity', the concept that Minsky sought to explain the financial crises of the 1970s and 1980s with. The book highlights the continuing relevance of Minsky's theory of liquidity crisis as 'immanent', in a historical sense, to the products and trading practices of modern finance, because these products were developed to obviate the crisis dynamics that Minsky described. Minsky's FIH can therefore inform historical understanding of the crisis of 2007–08 but is not directly explanatory itself. The book explores explanation of the financial crisis of 2007–08 interpreting 'liquidity', in practical historical terms, as involving a process of development out of prior crisis dynamics.

Seeking to contribute to debates over the causes of the financial crisis of 2007–08 by blending a discussion of historicizing philosophy, economic theory and contemporary financial banking and trading practices this work will be of great interest to scholars of international political economy, heterodox economics and critical theory.

Chris Jefferis is post-doctoral research fellow in the Department of Political Science at Freie Universität's John F. Kennedy Institute for North American Studies. He is also a joint recipient of an Institute for New Economic Thinking (INET) research grant analysing 'Financial Innovation and Central Banking in China: A Money View'.

Routledge Advances in International Political Economy

For a full list of titles in this series, please visit www.routledge.com

22 Transatlantic Politics and the Transformation of the International Monetary System
Michelle Frasher

23 Global Criminal and Sovereign Free Economies and the Demise of the Western Democracies
Dark renaissance
Edited by Robert J. Bunker and Pamela Ligouri Bunker

24 Capitalist Alternatives
Models, Taxonomies, Scenarios
Paul Dragos Aligica and Vlad Tarko

25 International Mobility, Global Capitalism, and Changing Structures of Accumulation
Transforming the Japan-India IT Relationship
Anthony P. D'Costa

26 The Crisis and Renewal of American Capitalism
A Civilizational Approach to Modern American Political Economy
Edited by Laurence Cossu-Beaumont, Jacques-Henri Coste and Jean-Baptiste Velut

27 Globalization and Labour in the Twenty-First Century
Verity Burgmann

28 Emerging Market Multinationals in Europe
Edited by Louis Brennan and Caner Bakir

29 The Dialectics of Liquidity Crisis
An Interpretation of Explanations of the Financial Crisis of 2007–08
Chris Jefferis

The Dialectics of Liquidity Crisis
An Interpretation of Explanations of the Financial Crisis of 2007–08

Chris Jefferis

LONDON AND NEW YORK

First published 2017
by Routledge
2 Park Square, Milton Park, Abingdon, Oxon OX14 4RN

and by Routledge
711 Third Avenue, New York, NY 10017

Routledge is an imprint of the Taylor & Francis Group, an informa business

© 2017 Chris Jefferis

The right of Chris Jefferis to be identified as author of this work has been asserted by him in accordance with sections 77 and 78 of the Copyright, Designs and Patents Act 1988.

All rights reserved. No part of this book may be reprinted or reproduced or utilised in any form or by any electronic, mechanical, or other means, now known or hereafter invented, including photocopying and recording, or in any information storage or retrieval system, without permission in writing from the publishers.

Trademark notice: Product or corporate names may be trademarks or registered trademarks, and are used only for identification and explanation without intent to infringe.

British Library Cataloguing-in-Publication Data
A catalogue record for this book is available from the British Library

Library of Congress Cataloging-in-Publication Data
A catalog record for this book has been requested

ISBN: 978-1-138-84732-3 (hbk)
ISBN: 978-1-315-72614-4 (ebk)

Typeset in Times New Roman
by Apex CoVantage, LLC

Contents

1	Introduction: historicizing economic theories of financial crisis	1
2	Minsky in context: a critique of "liquidity crisis" as an explanatory concept	16
3	Minsky contrary to Monetarism	35
4	Liquidity and abstraction	47
5	Arbitrage as a historical structure shaping the US financial system	60
6	Sociological interlude: calculation or commensuration?	75
7	Recent financial instability in the US mortgage market: the three phases of risk	90
8	Economics, regulation and capital: an assessment of some proposed reforms	109
9	Conclusion	120
	Bibliography	128
	Index	139

1 Introduction

Historicizing economic theories of financial crisis

This book analyses the logic of applying the American Post-Keynesian economist Hyman Minsky's Financial Instability Hypothesis (FIH) to the financial crisis of 2007–08. Key to this project is exploring the "historicity" of Minsky's work asking the question of whether his theory can be applied outside of the historical context in which it was formulated?

Hyman Minsky (born 1919 – died 1996) was a Post-Keynesian economist who developed a theory of the business cycle based on the premise that stability in the financial system is destabilizing because of the effects of financial innovation and debt dynamics on leverage ratios of financial units (Mehrling 1999). He developed his ideas during the 1970s and 1980s, but his work entered the public consciousness again in the lead-up to the financial crisis of 2007–08 as concerns developed about leverage ratios in the mortgage market, real estate investment trusts (REITs), hedge fund and the investment banking sector (the "shadow banking" sector).[1] In the midst of the onset of the crisis of 2007–08, many financial economists and journalists took to debating whether the American financial system was experiencing a "Minsky Moment" (Calomiris 2007, McCulley 2009, Whalen 2008). The "Minsky Moment" connotes the moment in which the market realises that financial units have excessive debts that must be reduced (Whalen 2008:249). The realisation of excessive indebtedness is often followed by a market crash as financial units sell positions in asset markets to make position in the money markets, as actually occurred in 2007–08 (Cohan 2009, Patterson 2010).

The tendency in the use of theories such as Minsky's FIH in the context of crisis is to treat them as "canonical", providing positive knowledge about economic events. Indeed, some economists even argue that events such as the financial crisis of 2007–08 are a testament to the validity and foresight of Minsky's theory (see Keen 2009, McCulley 2009, Toporowski and Tavasci 2010, Wray 2008). These theorists conduct economic inquiry as an exercise in mapping current events onto the theory and vice versa.

This book takes a different approach to explanation of crisis. While the "canonical" approach has some value and is even a necessary and important step towards understanding the financial crisis of 2007–08, this book does not try to reconstruct Post-Keynesian economics as a positive form of knowledge but is instead

2   *Introduction*

structured as a historicizing critique of it, along with other contrasting theories of financial crisis that purport to offer positive forms of knowledge about financial crisis.

The book argues that while Minsky's variant of Post-Keynesian economics can provide some useful insights into contemporary financial crisis, explanation of the financial crisis of 2007–08 cannot be adequately conducted in this framework because Post-Keynesian economics is dismissive of the abstraction of risk. "Risk" is a concept that Minsky did not engage with. Following Keynes, Minsky was more focused on exploring uncertainty (Minsky 1975). Indeed, market "risk" as it is understood today in terms of volatility only emerged as a concern subsequent to the conjuncture that Minsky was focused on with the development of derivatives markets and associated innovations in calculative techniques for managing market volatility (Mehrling 2000).

The book shows how the abstraction of "risk" which conditions trade in financial instruments such as derivatives and asset backed securities can be conceptualised as "liquidity" through a historicizing critique of theories of financial crisis. In particular, the book provides a new illustration of the relevance of Minsky's theory of liquidity crisis as "immanent" to modern finance and the crisis of 2007–08 but not as explanatory in and of itself. The primary value of Minsky's Post-Keynesian economics in explanation of the crisis of 2007–08 lies in providing the grounds for a historically located critique that can illustrate the cause of the crisis through exploring the limitations of the Minskyian explanation of the crisis.

This introduction begins with an outline of an interpretive method for conducting a "historicizing" critique. It provides a critique of the conceptualisation of crisis and history by theories in the Keynesian/Post-Keynesian tradition. It starts by analysing crisis theory in its singular form, as a "universal" form of explanation. This analysis is followed by an exploration of the limitations in the use of crisis theories in plural form as a sequential or heterodox critique of other theories of crisis. Both the singular and plural ways of using theory fail to adequately account for the historicity of the theories they analyse. Hence we need a method for analysing financial crisis in its totality that can move analysis beyond false universalisms (see for example FCIC 2011, Kindleberger and Aliber 2005) or an inadequately reflexive pluralism (see for example Dow 2012) towards a "dialectical"[2] or historicizing analysis of the application of theories of financial crisis.

This introduction does not go into a high degree of detail about particular theories of financial crisis beyond some reference to the terms in which Post-Keynesian and Keynesian theories conceptualise history. The main text of the book will consider in detail some other theories that relate to financial crisis, including Monetarism, the Efficient Market Hypothesis, work from the Social Studies of Finance on financial performativity and Behavioural Finance, contrasting them with the FIH. I include an outline of this contrasting analysis of the causes of the financial crisis of 2007–08 that result from historicizing theories of financial crisis below the following discussion of the nature of liquidity and the treatment of history in the Keynesian/Post-Keynesian construction of the problematic of liquidity crisis.

Introduction 3

Crisis theory – universal and particular

In his history of "manias, panics and crashes", the American macroeconomist Charles Kindleberger and Aliber (2005) sought to popularise Minsky's work. In the opening chapters of his book, Kindleberger and Aliber described Minsky's Financial Instability Hypothesis, arguing that it was typical of most financial bubbles. He argued that financial crisis as typified by Minsky's FIH was a "universal" event (Kindleberger and Aliber 2005:21). Kindleberger, by describing financial crisis as a so-called universal event borrowed a philosophical term from the German Idealists to express how the form of financial crises does not seem to vary with historical circumstances and gives the impression of being an essential feature of capitalism in both its structural dynamics and the pattern of human behaviour – the inherent greed or herd mentality of market participants. Hence financial crisis can be studied by economists using the universalist, idealist and unchanging causative constructions of economic theory.[3]

Kindleberger and Aliber believed that there should be an intellectual division of labour between (a) economists who use models and theory dealing with enduring structural dynamics that shape the economic cycles and (b) historians, who deal with the "particular" – the ephemera of the past, their perceptions, cultures and institutional forms (Kindleberger and Aliber 2005:21). However, this stratification that Kindleberger and Aliber posit between the universal and the particular is itself the problem to be studied. History is not just an attempt at realist preservation of the terms and conditions of the past but takes as its subject the interaction between the universal and the particular. In positing this stratification, Kindleberger and Aliber claim an unwarranted universalism for economic crisis theory in general and Minsky's FIH in particular.

Indeed, the fact that crisis *has a history* actually highlights a contradiction in Kindleberger and Aliber's framework because it suggests that crisis is synonymous with development and is therefore particular in each of its occurrences. For instance, the history of financial crisis implies that the system somehow exists in excess of each particular financial crisis despite the event of crisis being defined in terms of the breakdown of the system as a coherent whole.[4] The ability of crisis to appear to be simultaneously both universal and particular to exist in the system and be of the system as a whole implies development. Otherwise there would be no such thing as a history of financial crises that have a seemingly universal form because crisis would be the end point of the system. Crisis could not by definition exist as a succession unless it also implied subsequent development.[5]

The existence of crisis as development also creates the conditions of theorising while problematising theory itself. As Kindleberger and Aliber argue, the succession of seemingly similar crises gives the appearance of a universal causative logic. However, most theories of financial crisis, not just the Minskyian framework that Kindleberger outlines in his book, brush over the particular details of crisis in order to claim their own universality. The application of a predetermined conceptual framework to the understanding of crisis is problematic because it requires that the identified universal factors that are material to

4   *Introduction*

explanation of an event co-exist in proximity to the "dark matter" of historical development – that which has changed since this type of event last occurred or changed in reaction to its last occurrence. Furthermore, the dark matter has gravity in that it is inherently defined in terms of that which exceeds and obviates crisis. The causative logic is applied to a situation in which it cannot by definition, as a universal form of crisis, be considered to be causative. Crisis theories posit a false universalism.

The implication of development for the understanding of economic history is that the universal form of crisis appears as a result of the breakdown of relations that obviated prior contradictions causing crisis to appear as a kind of return of the repressed. The occurrence of development is instrumental in giving the totality a degree of coherence in that development has a retrospective as well as a forward-looking function. The pre-existing contradictions are continually in the process of being exceeded by the act of development, which if it breaks down, allows these contradictions to become emergent once again. Historical development is what creates the effect of systematic coherence through obviating but not solving the contradictions that can lead to crisis.[6] This illustrates how the moment of crisis is a thoroughly historical event – a crisis from the past is brought forward into the present through the failure of the "future", that is, the process of development.

Without going any further into dialectical logic of history, the point for now is to emphasise the importance of dialectical development in the application of crisis theory. It is easier to make substantive claims towards explaining the relationship between the universal and the particular, about the immanence of phenomena and theory to the occurrence of financial crisis when there is an appreciation of the importance of dialectical development of historical phenomena.[7]

The outline of the limitations of crisis theory thus far distils the question for us pointing towards a way of reconciling the universal and the particular in the application of crisis theory. This is to say that in order to make these claims about the difference between the cause and the appearance of crisis, the application of crisis theory must be grounded in the study of the development of the "form of capital" defined as the regulations, institutions and instruments existing in the financial system whereby the system comes to exceed previous tendencies towards crisis. The existence of the pattern of dialectical development suggests that the development of the form of circulation of value conditions the emergence of crisis. Indeed, the development of the form of circulation determines the appearance of crisis as a recurrent and seemingly universal event. Analysis therefore needs to focus on the growth and breakdown of the most recent forms of capital in order to explain the re-emergence of "universalist historical" forms of crisis such as those which Minsky's FIH seems to apply to.

Crisis theories – subject and object

A testament to the inherent gap between crisis theory and the world it describes is that an accurate theory of crisis would eradicate crisis, so long as we understand "accurate" in terms of "governmentality". This means the theory is able to conceptually grasp and inspire rational control over its object (Foucault 2008). In

Introduction 5

economics the capture of rational control over its object would mean the theory is able to shape development of the form of capital, to be performed or actualised in the world. This type of theory would be aware of the hegemonic terms that influence the historical conjuncture in which it is developed and would be able to be implemented in that conjuncture.

Hardt and Negri (1994:38–45) argue that Keynesian economics once had this type of historical traction. Keynes showed a rare pragmatic genius in the construction of the argument of *The General Theory of Employment Interest and Money* (General Theory) in a way that enabled it as a subject,[8] a set of concepts, to influence its object. However, this is not to say that *The General Theory* somehow also included a solution to the Kantian problem of the gap between subject and object (Beiser 2008:180–210). *The General Theory* did not explain the crisis in-itself, in its particular detail, but rather that its theoretical account resonated with the dynamics of accumulation of the time and provided a new framework under which institutions could be constructed in order to re-route the circulation of value, constituting a new intellectual paradigm and institutional dimension to capitalism that was not subject to the contradictions of the old system.[9]

However, insofar as the controls that formed the Keynesian solution to crisis became contradictory in themselves and these contradictions framed the subsequent development of the form of capitalism (as I argue that they did in Chapters 1 and 2), then we are left without a theory of crisis that is able to address its object in terms that could transform it. The only theoretical tools left to us to explain the contemporary crisis are crisis theories that have been previously developed, though as the historical record shows, these theoretical tools have failed to give us tools to grapple with crisis. The different competing theories of crisis necessarily exist as a catalogue of errors.[10] Crisis theory as a subject is seemingly inherently alienated from its object.

In fact, insofar as the gap between the object of crisis theory and crisis theory as a subject is constituted by development of the form of capital (the underlying object) it creates scope to apply more than one theoretical perspective to the explanation of crisis at the same time. The nature of crisis as development in capitalism generates a particular type of alienation of subject from object that lends itself to pluralism of perspectives applying to an "overdetermined"[11] totality (Althusser 2005:87–129).[12] It becomes possible to tell a number of different stories about the same event insofar as the financial system develops by adding different dimensions that unlock or transcend obstructions in prior forms to enable the flow of value because each crisis theory focuses on explaining the breakdown in circulation on only one of these levels.[13]

The point here is that the diversity of different crisis theories, which appears as a "contest of economic ideas", is a mystification of the process of historical development. For example, insofar as the historical development of the form of capital has added multiple dimensions and processes by which capital flows, the diversity of economic ideas is a characteristic of the form of capital. These theories are not locked in contest in any substantial fashion. In fact, they are not even really separate to one another, but exist as expressions of the development of the

6 Introduction

form of capital through contradiction and crisis into multiple different dimensions and circuits.

Crisis theories are descriptive of prior forms of crisis and often prescriptive of different forms of circulation in terms of the influence, the unintended side effects of the implementation of these theories in spurring new forms of circulation. The development of new forms of liquidity occurs either in terms of more reflexive forms of liquidity, wherein the contradictions of the old forms have been fixed, or in terms of the growth of wholly new alternative forms of liquidity. Breakdowns in circulation or "liquidity crisis", as these breakdowns are called by Keynesian economists, are so hard to understand in theory because circulation or liquidity often exists in material abstraction (innovation) from and theoretical rejection of the institutions and policies that characterised prior historical social formations. Furthermore, this transcendence/rejection is not so much a logical progression, the result of rational new fixes to old problems, as it is a change of subject that naturally follows from the development of the underlying object.

For the study of economics the nature of theoretical progression whereby new economic theories are expressions of the development of the underlying form of capital means that the concept of liquidity can never be "gotten right" on a theoretical level. The reason for this is that liquidity emerges as a succession of forms and changes of subject. There is no logical progression here but the succession of somewhat arbitrary historical developments. Liquidity has no positive theoretical character in itself and is defined retrospectively in terms of the transcendence of obstacles to the expansion of value in the conjuncture. The historical character of circulation means that there can never be any positive definition of liquidity in economics, heterodox or otherwise, but rather only new forms of circulation.

It is always true then, as some post-Keynesian economists such as Mehrling (2000, 2011) claim in relation to the crisis of 2007–08, that liquidity crisis is caused by an absence of a positive definition of liquidity. Liquidity is only present in the alienation of the major theories from each other and from history. The existence of the negative constitutes the positive (Žižek 2012). Indeed, a study of financial crisis must find a way of describing the history of liquidity and addressing the contemporary crisis of 2007–08 in terms of the alienation of crisis theory from its object of study and from other theories of crisis. This is what is constitutive of both the subject and its object.

This means that we need to develop a method of analysing financial crisis that involves historicizing different theories of financial crisis illustrating the contradiction in the terms by which they attempt to explain crisis. By reading the various theories of liquidity crisis against each other and in the context of the historical distance from the context in which they were originally developed, we can begin to show how the result of the development of the US financial system through crisis is a new form of capital that exists as a historical systematic dialectically constituted totality. Furthermore, this system is beset by a retroactive form of breakdown whereby crisis in the most contemporary circuits of capital lead to the appearance of universal forms of crisis in an over-determined totality.

This book

The chapters in this book explore some of the myriad relationships that theory can have to crisis and the form of capital in the economy. The relationships analysed in this book include:

- Crisis as inspiration to theory
- Theories of crisis that are used to influence or reshape the form of capital
- Crisis theories that dismiss developments in the form of capital
- Crisis theories that express developments in the form of capital
- Crisis theory that can interpret capital itself as discursive (especially in light of the prevalence of the second point above in this list)
- Crisis theory as immanent to (infused in) the form of capital
- Crisis theory that unintentionally acts to reproduce or constitute the form of capital

The book begins with an analysis of Minsky's reading of Keynes in Chapter 2 arguing that his work is a form of "hermeneutics". Hermeneutics analyses the intellectual practice of interpretation. The central claim of hermeneutics is that in order to understand a communicative work, be it art or theory, you must have some prior understanding or experience of the underlying concerns communicated by the work. Understanding is not solely a product of the intellect but is also related to some resonance in the conditions of experience between the author and their interpreter (Gadamer 2006, Redding 1996).

Understanding hermeneutics is important for analysing Minsky's work given that it was an interpretation of Keynesian economics (see Minsky 1975 for a systematic account of this interpretation). Minsky invoked Keynes's work as describing a "problematic of liquidity crisis". This was a novel interpretation of Keynes's work designed to make it useful in Minsky's conjuncture for analysing the problem of recurrent liquidity crisis that emerged to afflict the American financial system during the "long 1970s" (1966–1982).[14] However, in taking a hermeneutic approach and adopting the Keynesian problematic, Minsky positioned himself as an idealist. He was seeking to (re)construct an ideal that resonated with his contemporary experience of the conjuncture. For Minsky the recurrent crises of the 1970s was the inspiration or rationale for the adoption of Keynesian inspired economic theory.

Indeed, Minsky's hermeneutic method begs a number of questions. Does Minsky manage to engage with the particular historical details of crisis in his conjuncture, moving analysis beyond description on an abstract theoretical level towards explanation? The first chapter of this book argues that it does not. Minsky's method is largely descriptive of a theoretical problematic as well as of historical phenomena that he feels parallel the Keynesian problematic. This does not constitute explanation of crisis because the real question is what structural changes created the hermeneutic resonance between Keynes's times and his own? What frames the re-emergence of liquidity dynamics as a prevalent concern in the conjuncture?

8   *Introduction*

The exploration of these questions poses something of a paradox. It reveals that liquidity dynamics described in Minsky's work cannot be said to be the causative agent of crisis but rather only an emergent phenomenon. Minsky names the problem as a problem of liquidity crisis but does not overtly and systematically explain what prepared the grounds for the problem to re-appear in the post-war conjuncture. Minsky's use of a hermeneutic method therefore only manages to illustrate how the explanation, as opposed to the accurate description, of the problem of financial crisis is actually external to his Keynesian framework.

Chapter 3 argues that Minsky got closest to overcoming these structural problems caused by his hermeneutic approach with his critique of Monetarism that he published in the *Nebraska Journal of Economics* in 1972. Here we see that it is only as critique that Minsky (1972) manages to give some positive content to the concept of liquidity. Minsky defines liquidity beyond the Monetarist's narrow focus on the central bank's effects on the "money supply", illustrating with a discussion of endogenous debt how the money supply is influenced not only by central bank actions but by newly emergent money market dynamics. He provides a more systematic and reflexive definition of liquidity that incorporates financial innovation by market participants as well as government action in his definition of liquidity. Minsky (1972:43–44) deftly illustrates how Monetarism cannot actually define its object because of a blind spot about how financial innovations affect liquidity dynamics and hence can only be regarded as a limited form of critique of the Keynesian State, perhaps once relevant, but a now surpassed form of historical consciousness about the one-time causes of financial instability.

In this critique Minsky's argument exhibits a latent dialectical structure. Dialectics is an extension, or reflection on, the experience of hermeneutic resonance in that it is focused on "the way in which our particular perspectives on the world must be understood as located within a set of conditions that, although not themselves [directly] experienced, are conditions of that experience" (Pinkard 1998:328, Redding 1996). Dialectics reveals the objectivity behind subjectivity through historicizing subjectivity. It reveals various theories and ideals as determinate forms of historical consciousness that express the historical development of the underlying object that they are focused on.

Chapter 3 reads the concerns and claims of Monetarism as conditions of experience of the FIH. Indeed, this chapter explores how the critique of Monetarism pervades Minsky's work. Minsky's work moves from description to explanation through critique of Monetarism because this is the means whereby the conditions that make the FIH relevant, and that also ground Minsky's idealist vision, can be understood overtly. The critique of Minsky (1972) illustrates how liquidity is historically developing and multi-dimensional in that it is defined by the relationship between the Keynesian state and its effect on market participants and vice versa.

Minsky's critique of Monetarism negates the Monetarist negation of Keynes, thereby re-invoking the Keynesian problematic. But his critique of Monetarism also represents the excesses of history, which suggests that the conjuncture has moved beyond any possibility of a return to the old pattern of implementation of Keynesian principles. This is to say that Minsky's critique illustrates the historical

Introduction 9

nature of liquidity as constant development including plural dimensions to liquidity (state based forms of liquidity and market based forms of liquidity).[15]

The illustration of the dialectical potential in Minsky's work also reveals the difficulty in abstracting Minsky's theory out of the conjuncture and the referents against which it was located to explain the crisis of 2007–08. Indeed, the American economist Gary Dymski (2010) in a recent article in the *Cambridge Journal of Economics* raised concerns about whether Minsky's work could be used to explain the crisis of 2007–08, as some economists have sought to do (Keen 2009, McCulley 2009, Toporowski and Tavasci 2010).

Chapter 4 deals with the issue of abstraction and the logic of applying the FIH to recent financial crises, including the collapse of the hedge fund Long Term Capital Management (LTCM) and the crisis of 2007–08. The application of the FIH in the contemporary context, which is exemplified in a very sophisticated way by Perry Mehrling (2000, 2011), involves universalising the FIH in history, including dismissing as erroneous abstractions some important new calculative processes and forms of capital in the financial system that developed subsequent to formulation of the FIH. I contend in this chapter that they should instead be understood as new forms of liquidity given that liquidity is, in itself, a form of historical development.

Mehrling's application of Minsky's framework to the contemporary conjuncture includes similar errors to Minsky's application of Keynesian economics to the "long 1970s" in that it is another form of hermeneutic idealism that uses crisis as a rationale for a return to theory about liquidity crisis. However, The analysis of this chapter does not dismiss the FIH as immaterial to an explanation of the financial crisis of 2007–08. Although it is easy enough to illustrate its limitations in conceptualising the financial system as a totality, including in its more abstract contemporary dimensions with the derivative risk trading system, I attempt to illustrate how the limitations of the FIH illustrate something formative about the more contemporary conjuncture in which financial calculations and derivatives play a huge role. The limitations we encountered in Mehrling's application of the FIH to modern finance, when understood in dialectical terms, provide insight into the relationship of modern financial instruments to liquidity crisis. The contradictions in the US financial system that the FIH describes provide insight into the structural forces that gave rise to the risk trading system.

Highlighting the conceptual limitations of the FIH in dealing with new forms of capital is the key to illuminating the "historicity" of the FIH as theory. In Chapter 4 I argue how the development of new forms of capital illuminates how liquidity now exists in the historical developments whereby the contradictions described in the FIH have been exceeded and resolved by the development of new components to the financial system. Indeed, I argue that the system of "risk" trading is what exceeds "liquidity crisis" as described by Minsky and this makes it difficult to analyse contemporary crisis in the risk trading system within the framework of a theory of liquidity crisis such as Minsky's FIH. The FIH is a latent component of modern finance in a similar sense to which Monetarism was latent to the FIH – the contradictions described in each proceeding theory explain, or at

10 *Introduction*

least contextualise, the development of the financial processes envisioned in later theory that are held to constitute liquidity.

Chapter 5 contains a key point in the argument of this book, building on this conception of the relationship between theory and developments in the form of capital that generate liquidity. This chapter looks at the FIH as an expression of the development of the US financial system rather than a positive form of knowledge about it. Chapter 5 follows on from the point above about modern finance exceeding the FIH – the risk trading system is a more developed form of capital compared with that which is described in the FIH, looking at the implications of this point for how we should interpret the FIH and indeed the Efficient Market Hypothesis (EMH), which attempts to describe the modern market based financial system, as well.

Chapter 5 looks at the processes of arbitrage in the FIH and the EMH. It provides an historical interpretation of the FIH reconciling risk and liquidity through an analysis of how arbitrage, a key process in the EMH, is historically constructed. Indeed, this chapter argues that both theories – the FIH and the EMH – can be interpreted as illustrations of the structuring, or generative, nature of arbitrage in US financial history.

This interpretation of the relationship between the EMH and the FIH has interesting political economic implications because the EMH theorises arbitrage as having a stabilizing influence on prices in the financial system. Any deviation from "fundamentals" will create incentives to arbitrage these deviations, thereby erasing them. But Chapter 5 suggests that this is an idealist picture of the operations of the financial system that presupposes the existence of instruments such as derivatives and asset-backed securities (ABS) that enable arbitrage to be conducted. The historical development of these instruments actually has a destabilizing effect on prices because these instruments make arbitrage easier, that is, they are a newer and more liquid form of capital. The FIH is immanent to the EMH via the historically located process of financial innovation in arbitrage instruments.

Chapter 6 is a methodological interlude. It outlines some epistemological issues in the social sciences associated with "explaining" financial crisis. This chapter is about financial calculation and the value of financial instruments. It is a critique of discursive sociological approaches to conceptualising value (see MacKenzie 2006, 2009, 2011) in favour of a historicizing approach. This chapter looks at how financial value is calculated and considers whether financial calculations "constitute" value or are themselves constituted by value, understood as the historical process of development of the form of capital described in prior chapters. The central claim is that the value of new financial instruments such as ABS, mortgage backed securities (MBS), collateralised debt obligations (CDOs) and credit default swaps (CDS) is based on their historical materialism as forms of capital that generate liquidity through commensuration rather than through the positivity or even the indirect positivity – that is, "performativity" – of financial calculations (as described by MacKenzie 2006, 2009, 2011).

The next two chapters use the historicizing/dialectical perspective on the financial crisis of 2007–08 to applying the interpretation of risk as liquidity to

Introduction 11

particular issues, including innovation in the sub-prime mortgage market in the lead-up to the crisis and reforms to the financial system designed to mitigate its tendency towards liquidity crisis.

Thus, Chapter 7 analyses the effects of the Hybrid Adjustable Rate Mortgage on liquidity in the US housing market in the lead-up to the crisis of 2007–08. It argues that liquidity dynamics were immanent to mortgage innovation.

Chapter 8 argues that measures such as house price derivatives and pro-cyclical capital buffers that attempt to address the flaws in the financial system that led to crisis by mitigating the build-up of excessive risk could constitute new forms of liquidity and hence reproduce the problem of financial crisis into the future. These measures would constitute a continuation of the dialectics of liquidity.

I conclude by analysing Dodd–Frank legislation to reform the US financial system. I argue that this legislation is interesting for the consistency it displays with the historical dynamics discussed in the book that constitute the dialectics of liquidity. I argue that Dodd–Frank legislation suggests the possibility of a genealogy of forms of risks and is therefore interesting to the extent to which it exists as a testament to the possibilities of a dialectical understanding of forms of liquidity.

APPENDIX A

Dialectics reconsidered

The rest of this book will argue that we need to understand the financial crisis of 2007–08 in terms of a "dialectical" or "historicizing" analysis of how economists and social scientists have used theory to explain past financial crises. But before proceeding with this argument it is important to properly define and consider criticisms of dialectical styles of interpretation in order to defend the argument in this book from the claim that it is just a restatement of anachronistic theoretical methodology.[16]

Dialectics understood as development out of contradiction is controversial amongst social scientists and philosophers (Althusser 2005:161–218, Gibson-Graham et al. 2001). Dialectics as a form of analysis tends to evoke mechanistic view of history as the stage on which some essentialist conflict or contradiction is resolved so that society can progress (Dryzek and Dunleavy 2009:81–82). Social scientists and economists have largely pulled back from claiming to have any insight into the direction and knowledge of structures or cycles that condition history and have focused on understanding the terms in which the notion that history has a direction is constructed. Many social scientists now focus on interrogating terms left over from enlightenment thinking such as rationality, progress, development and high culture along with essentialist notions of identity including race, class and gender, denaturalising them in order to reveal them as part of the constructive apparatus of power.[17]

The critical post-structuralist position is actually similar to the sceptical position of Kantian subjectivism that preceded the development of dialectical logic (Žižek

12 *Introduction*

2012). Kant held that there is an inevitable gap between a "phenomenon" (that which appears) and a "noumenon" (the underlying object). Kant argued that the concepts used to theorise objects are always inadequate to the task because they inevitably exist only in the imagination rather than in the objective world. There is a lacuna between subject and object that cannot be bridged beyond cataloguing "sensations" that the object seems to generate (empiricism), which many philosophers sought to use as the basis of conceptualisation.

The post-structuralist argument proceeds from the viewpoint that in light of our incomplete knowledge, it makes sense to develop a cautious approach to the formulation of knowledge and politics, not making any essentialist claims to privileged knowledge about the nature of any underlying reality beyond appearances and instead developing a critical reflexivity about the terms in which we understand appearances and the power dynamics inherent in these discourses.[18] Critique should look not so much at the object of discourse, which is out of reach, and focus instead on the power relations of discourse which manifest themselves in the terms by which the object is posited (Kelly 2009:13–25).

However, something is also lost in this return to and exclusive focus on Kantian inspired critique. Indeed, Hegel critiqued Kant arguing that philosophy should not only be about critique but also the development, through critique, of speculative knowledge of the underlying object as it exists rather than as it appears in fragmented empirically documented moments (Beiser 2005:163–169).

Hegel's critique of Kant was temporal in that it was based on an observation that Kant ignored history. It is not the case that the only tools we have for understanding the world are concepts and sensibilities but also the history of concepts and their record of error in grasping their object. Hegel defined philosophy as "its own time raised to the level of thought" (Hegel and Houlgate 2008:15). Historicizing the act of conceptualisation helps to illustrate and bring us closer to knowing the object that is, after all, nothing but history itself. Here Hegel is describing how a growing historically re-iterated awareness of the limits of conceptual cognition enable a philosopher (or political economist) to come to know the object through developing a degree of reflexivity about the limitations by which it comes to know the object (Beiser 2005:155–174).

Hegel's genius here lies in the way in which he incorporated Kant's ideas about the limited scope for developing positive knowledge and found a way to define the potential for positive knowledge in terms of the accumulation of negative knowledge. Knowledge is at once positive and negative and develops as a subject becomes aware of the contours and mechanisms of its own alienation – the inherent distance between its concept of the object and the existence of the object itself. The scope to develop this type of knowledge is actually dramatically large (Beiser 2005:163–169). History is actually quite a powerful tool for generating knowledge of an object because it is as broad as it is deep. History happens to a large number of people who can provide sources illustrating the play of the object across geographical, institutional and subjective boundaries as well as through time (Thompson 1978:199).

Hegel never maintained that the process of knowledge formation occurred through the triad of stages from thesis to synthesis to antithesis, as his dialectic

Introduction 13

is popularly summarised (Beiser 2005:161). Rather the contradiction of knowing is that knowledge develops through accumulation of awareness of the limits to knowledge. The development of knowledge occurs through critique and is a "labor of the negative", the revelation and consideration of contradiction as the spur towards the generation of dialectical knowledge of the structure of the underlying object of history (Beiser 2005:167–168).

Indeed, Beiser (2005) and Žižek (2012) argue that the aim of Hegel's work is not to illustrate how history is driven by pure ideas – or take the "inverse" materialist position (which is the common caricature of Marxist dialectics) – but is instead an illustration of a way out of pessimistic subjectivism through a deep form of philosophical and historical reflexivity creating the possibility of knowledge of the "object".[19]

However, the issue with objectivism, which has often been glossed over in caricatures of the Hegelian dialectic and the role of reason in history, is that the objectivity of history is in turn non-essential and thoroughly grounded in the subjectivist framework. Žižek (2012) is very strident on this point, seeking to recover it and place it at the forefront of contemporary readings of Hegel's work in order to illustrate the possibility of "post-structuralist" dialectics. His aim is to move the discussion of the dialectic past its common caricature as describing the march of progress towards the greater manifestation of reason in history, arguing instead that Hegel's notion of reason is anti-essentialist and is defined in terms of the gap between subject and object and does not afford the type of closed certainty about history's endpoint that these caricatures attribute to the dialectic.

Indeed, according to Redding (1996) and Žižek (2012), the dialectic is thoroughly subjectivist for Hegel. Hegel's philosophy has the structure of a *Bildungsroman*, a novel that charts the means of development of experience and perspective (Jameson 2010:16). But Hegel then goes beyond the *Bildungsgroman* and provides a philosophical analysis of the historical conditions under which the development of new forms of reflexivity can be possible in terms of the transformation of the historically existing relationship between subject and object (Beiser 2005:61–65).

These new forms of reflexivity are an expression of history, though Hegel stays true to the Kantian framework of subjectivism by insisting that the "objectivity" of history itself can only be accessed in terms of the structure of this new consciousness as a form of experience of history. The point for Hegel is that new ideas and forms of reflexivity have a degree of "historicity" that illuminates a part of the underlying objectivity of a subject, thereby reconciling subject and object in historical analysis without positing any crude essentialism, idealism or teleology to the process (Beiser 2005:51–76).

Notes

1 See Pozsar et al. (2010) for a comprehensive description of the shadow banking system's operations in America in the lead-up to the financial crisis of 2007–08.
2 Appendix A includes an outline of the philosophical basis of dialectical logic. Dialectics can be understood simply as historicizing critique, and I prefer to refer to it in these

14   *Introduction*

terms because use of the term "dialectics" places a jargonistic term connoting a body of philosophy in front of relatively commonsense consideration of the conditions of historical understanding. Nevertheless, I use the "dialectics" in this book occasionally because it indicates that there is an important body of philosophy that theorises the importance of historicizing critique of theory. The appendix to this introduction provides a thematic summary of this philosophy for those who prefer these principles to be made overt, separate from the argument in which they are contained in this book.

3 Although Kindleberger died in 2003 shortly before the crisis of 2007–08, the subprime crisis spiked sales in his book and it can be safely conjectured that he would have regarded it as a similar event that shared the pattern of previous financial crises.

4 This definition of crisis as inherently holistic is an assumption that underpins the logic of my argument in this section. However, recent experience of the global financial crisis which spread to Europe, China and the rest of the world illustrates that it is a plausible assumption. Indeed, Hegel (see Beiser 2005), Althusser (2005) and Marx (1976) all provide methodologies that assume that agency exists in the totality, the nature of the system, particularly in the event of crisis.

5 Meillassoux (2008) makes a similar point, arguing that the conditions for knowledge of the object via a "speculative realism" lies in the in-itself nature of history.

6 See Žižek (2012:213–240) for a discussion of this process of historical reconciliation that he calls "Hegelian retroactivity".

7 The discussion above is actually an argument made from first principles for accepting the assumption of dialectical development.

8 In this book I generally use the term "subject" in the Hegelian sense, i.e. as akin to "topic" or "discipline of knowledge" rather than the meaning that comes from poststructuralism, where the "subject" is used to mean a person with "subjectivity".

9 The Keynesian critique of the role of the interest rate created an intellectual edifice whereby a new dimension to circulation in big government could be added that went a way towards reconciling the contradictions in the conjuncture associated with the role of labour in capital – that it was both a cost of production and source of demand. The Keynesian state acted to commensurate labour as a cost of production, with labour as a source of demand through industrial arbitration and fiscal policy (Hardt and Negri 1994:38–41).

10 Here I am inspired by Varoufakis et al. (2011:xiii), who conclude that economics as a discipline must be understood and even defined in terms of "inherent error".

11 Over-determination connotes a situation in which there appears to be more than one adequate causal explanation for the appearance of a phenomenon (Althusser 2005).

12 In this book I sometimes refer to Althusser in the context of discussions of Hegel. This would seem to be contradictory because Althusser was a self-styled critic of Hegelian idealism (see Althusser 2005). However, as Jameson (1981) notes, Althusser's criticisms of Hegel were always indirect, about the use of Hegel by other authors, rather than the product of a direct reading and analysis of Hegel. His critique generally applies to the misreading of Hegel. In fact, Althusser's metaphysics are actually quite Hegelian in that structure. Hegel argued that the "abstract universal" is immanent to existence and is only present in terms of its effects (Beiser 2005:144). This is very similar to how Althusser understands the reality of structures as only ever present in their effects (1981:82). The structure/abstract universal is first in terms of the explanation of these effects but second to the determinate/particular in terms of existence (Beiser 2005:144).

13 Explanation of the financial crisis of 2007–08 exemplifies this point in that it can be explained from a variety of theoretical perspectives, including Monetarism (Williamson 2012), Post-Keynesian economics (Mehrling 2011), behavioural economics (Shiller 2008) and asymmetric information (Stiglitz 2009, 2010). Lo (2011) argues that the plurality of explanations is a defining feature of the crisis of 2007–08.

Introduction 15

14 The era I term the long 1970s begins with the central bank intervening in the American financial system as lender of last resort for the first time in post-war history in 1966 and ends with the development and marketing of the collateralised mortgage obligation in 1982 whereby the capital markets came to play a role in consumer debt, beginning a new era of transformation of the structure of the US financial system towards a commodity system involving "risk management" and "risk transfer".

15 The separation of these two approaches of hermeneutics and dialectics is not necessarily a given. Indeed, Redding (1996) interprets Hegel's work as a non-metaphysical hermeneutics. However, Beiser (2005) argues that meta-physics is integral to Hegel's project, which involves not just recognition of the conditions of experience of others but accounting for the nature of this experience in terms of its determinate or particular quality as well as its general or universal character as an expression of a broader development of the totality. Beiser (2005, 2008) therefore sees Hegel's work, and indeed the whole tradition of German Idealism, as providing the ground for an "objectivism". Hegel's work incorporated the sceptical subjectivist perspective of Kant but providing grounds on which to develop an interpretive metaphysics. This is a theme that has influenced the recent development of the speculative realist school of contemporary philosophy, including Meillassoux (2008).

16 Beiser (2005), Jameson (2010) and Žižek (2012) have put a lot of effort into this intellectual project, and I draw on them heavily in this section.

17 Recently, the growth of new abstract financial instruments and their breakdown in the global financial crisis has enticed some social scientists such as MacKenzie (2006, 2009, 2011) and Poon (2009) to attempt to extend these techniques of deconstruction and apply them to finance in order to attempt to deconstruct essentialist neo-liberal constructions of value.

18 Kant seemed to believe in a reference to intuition and the divine as the means of overcoming this gap rather than a focus on discourse (Beiser 2005:34–36).

19 Indeed, Beiser (2005:14) describes Hegel's approach as "objective idealism".

2 Minsky in context

A critique of "liquidity crisis" as an explanatory concept

Many economists analysing the financial crisis of 2007–08, particularly those working in the heterodox economic tradition and central bank economists, have taken a new interest in the concept of "liquidity" (see Baker 2013, Mehrling 2011, Yellen 2009). By looking at the issue of liquidity, many modern economists are choosing a subject of inquiry central to the work of John Maynard Keynes and his more recent interpreter the American economist Hyman Minsky. Minsky is particularly renowned for his emphasis on the importance of the banking sector and the central bank as crucial to the modern US economic system (Mehrling 1998, 2011). The challenge that today's economists are addressing involves developing a way of conceptualising how liquidity dynamics work in the newer parts of the credit system that developed in the decades following the writings of Keynes and Minsky. The so-called non-bank or shadow banking system of institutions that primarily trade in financial instruments such as derivatives and mortgage backed securities, rather than traditional deposit-based banking, is a particularly notable recent development. It often appears that the assumption within the work of today's economists is that understanding liquidity dynamics in this new system is merely a problem of historical refitting, and the conceptual construction of liquidity and use of predetermined theories of financial crisis is not itself problematic.

This chapter challenges this assumption by looking at Minsky's interpretation of Keynes. The chapter argues that the theory Minsky developed through his invocation of Keynes and the problematic of liquidity crisis did not actually constitute a proper explanatory framework for crisis in Minsky's era. There is an inherent tension, or a gap, in Minsky's work between the rich historical detail that he provides in his discussion of the various crises of the 1970s and his use of Keynes to express the problematic of liquidity crisis. The conjuncture that Minsky was writing in was 20–30 years removed from the conjuncture in which Keynes developed his theory, and the conjuncture of the global financial crisis was 30–40 years removed from when Minsky was writing. We will see in this chapter how these critical historical gaps create a need to question whether the categories of the previous era prove adequate to an understanding of the next era.

The historical distance between the event and the theory – the "historicity" of particular financial crises – is a problem that not only contemporary theorists of liquidity crisis are dealing with but is actually endemic to the Keynesian tradition

Minsky in context   17

and the way it treats the history of financial crises. What is the significance of this? The problem with positing the problematic of "liquidity crisis" is that it suggests that all liquidity crises are variations on a theme, whereas they could be conjuncturally quite distinct. The critical issue is to find out how conjunctural distinctiveness matters, for it is always possible to "force" new evidence into outmoded categories, but whether the categories are indeed outmoded and the evidence is indeed being "forced" is a matter of judgment for which there are no clear rules.

This chapter focuses on addressing the issue of the "historicity" of the problem of liquidity crisis by bringing the rich historical detail about structural change and liquidity dynamics that Minsky often alluded to in his work to the foreground of analysis in order to illustrate Minsky's "hermeneutic idealism" – his invocation of the Keynesian problematic of liquidity crisis. I argue that emphasising the hermeneutic qualities of Minsky's work captures the problem of the historicity of theory, more adequately preparing the grounds to reconceptualise liquidity in a way that is historically grounded in the next chapter.

This chapter begins to address the issue of historicity by providing a short description of Minsky's Financial Instability Hypothesis (FIH) before moving on to look at the problems in Minsky's use of Keynes and the tension in his work between his use of Keynes and his attempts to develop his own specifically historically located analysis. The chapter draws on the philosophical work of Hans Georg Gadamer (2006) and his ideas on hermeneutic interpretation in order to understand the unresolved issues with historicity that Minsky exhibits in his referencing of Keynes. The chapter then looks at ways of historicizing Minsky's work to show how the structure of his argument, including the problems in his use of Keynes, express structural developments in the form of capital.

The FIH in context

Hyman Minsky's work explores the structural transformation of the US financial system not only on a theoretical level as a reconstruction of Keynes's work but also via a description of the importance of financial innovation (Minsky 1982:v). Financial innovations that helped the US financial system generate credit began to spread throughout the financial system in the late 1960s and 1970s. The growing use of innovative money market instruments led to instability in the price of capital assets and institutional breakdown of the post-war regulatory structure erected to stabilise the US economy during the Great Depression (Minsky 1982a). Minsky was writing in the context of the collapse of one system of capital, which governed by price and quantity controls on credit, and the emergence of a new form of capital, manifested in a growing market for credit instruments that were priced by the market rather than government regulation controlling interest rates. These new markets for credit instruments challenged the efficacy of government controlled monetary flows as the dominant means of credit creation in the financial system. Money market credit instruments were designed to have floating interest rates that moved up or down according to market demand for capital and

18   *Minsky in context*

were developed to work around the existing New Deal regulatory controls that governed what rates borrowers and lenders could expect to receive on bank loans and deposits (Silber 1983:90).[1]

I argue that we need to read Minsky's work as being a critique of the development of the new system of money market credit highlighting how financial innovation made the fundamental nature of funding relationships underpinning American capitalism more precarious. Contemporary events, generally the meltdown of a corporation or bank which had overextended itself in the trade of these instruments, would become new examples which Minsky used to update his impression of the maelstrom of modern finance – that commitments of money now for money later, the creation of debt contracts, were continually being warped, by the turnings of the business cycle, which was itself defined in Minsky's era by the development of new financial instruments (Mehrling 1999:137).

Minsky theorised the problems associated with developments of money market credit instruments in terms of the issue of liquidity (Minsky 1982). In this vein Minsky is best known for his illustration of his cash flow typologies, the hedge, speculative and Ponzi financial units. Minsky writes:

> Hedge financing units are those which can fulfill all of their contractual payment obligations by their cash flows: the greater the weight of equity financing in the liability structure, the greater the likelihood that the unit is a hedge-financing unit. Speculative finance units are those that can meet their payment commitments on 'income account' on their liabilities even though they cannot repay the principal out of income cash flows. Such units need to 'roll over' their liabilities; i.e. issue new debt to meet commitments on maturing debts. Governments with floating debts, corporations with floating issues of commercial paper and banks are typical speculative units. For Ponzi units the cash flows from operations are not sufficient to fulfill either the repayment of principal or the interest due on outstanding debts. . . . Each unit that Ponzi finances lowers the margin of safety that it offers the holders of its debts.
>
> (Minsky 2011:203)

Minsky constructed this cash flow taxonomy to show how a financial unit or system could transit from robust finance to fragile finance through the steady accretion of risk as a result of an increasing weight of optimistic commitments to pay future income streams which, made in good times on the basis of buoyant expectations, would not be realised. Under these circumstances, Minsky argued, hedge financing units could change into speculative financial units and speculative financial units transform into Ponzi units if they experienced an unexpected shortfall in income or an increase in interest rates. Hence, the economy tended towards instability as part of its normal operation of creating debts as income levels and interest rates varied, sometimes rapidly, through the business cycle.

Minsky thought of his work as a theory of the interaction between funding liquidity and market liquidity and how this interaction could become irrational

Minsky in context 19

contrary to equilibrium thinking (Minsky 1975:67–91). Minsky envisaged the interaction between funding liquidity and market liquidity as working via an initially virtuous but then vicious spiral. An increase in funding liquidity through financial innovation would increase the prices of capital assets, that is, cause a corresponding increase in market liquidity. This would, in turn, increase the value of collateral in the financial system, inspiring bankers to lend more freely, creating an increase in funding liquidity. The virtuous spiral is largely self-referential and generated bubbles in capital asset markets and funding liquidity markets, causing financial instability. The "thrust towards Ponzi finance" as Minsky (1986:233) referred to it, would eventually cause asset price falls when these bubble dynamics were recognised. At this point financial units would have to sell position in asset markets in order to make position in the money markets.

The propensity towards instability had very practical ramifications for central bank operations. The central bank was required to counter instability through lender of last resort interventions on a number of occasions in the long 1970s. Indeed the lender of last resort interventions of the 1960s and 1970s appear clearly displayed in stock market prices such as the Dow Jones Industrial Average (see Figure 2.1). The Federal Reserve halted slides in 1966, 1970, 1974–5, 1978 and 1981–82 (Minsky 1986:16–75, Wojnilower 1980). The pattern of asset prices from these times shows the economy moving in sync with the cycles that Minsky described whereby the financial system would transit from a robust to a fragile financial state according to runs on various different sources of funding liquidity. These instruments included certificates of deposits (CDs) in 1966, commercial paper in 1970, and real estate investment trusts (REITs) and Eurodollars in 1974[2] (Minsky 1986:16–75, Wojnilower 1980).

Keynes and the conjuncture

The effects of financial innovation on instability therefore spoke quite strongly to Minsky, inspiring him to invoke and update the work of Keynes. Minsky called his FIH an interpretation of Keynes's General Theory of Employment Interest and Money, which he worked out in his book first published in 1975 called *John Maynard Keynes*.

An important aspect of Minsky's work is the way it connected to the particular conjuncture and structural transformation of capital. The use of Keynes's work, written at least 20 years before Minsky began to write on the theme of liquidity crisis,[3] is therefore a paradox – how did Minsky reconcile his application of Keynes to the conjuncture he was writing in and use Keynes's work in his method? We need to ask basic questions about what it means to be a "Keynesian" – whether Keynes can be extracted from his context of the 1930s and 40s and 'elevated' into an ahistorical theory. Indeed, how did Minsky's use of Keynes fit with Minsky's interest in contemporary financial developments?

Contrary to the current incorporation of Minsky into the Post-Keynesian camp of political economy, we would do better to re-interpret Minsky's method and conception of liquidity crisis in a way that admits some historical distance from

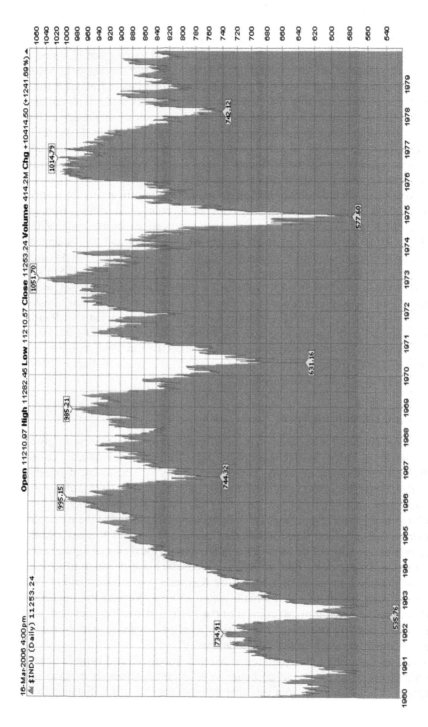

Figure 2.1 Dow Jones Industrial Average from 1960 to 1980

Minsky in context 21

Keynes whereby crisis is, very importantly, *not driven by expectations*, but material institutional and instrumental developments in the economy.[4] In fact, a big obstacle to understanding Minsky and the economic dynamics of the time in which he was writing stems from this association with Keynes and the construction of the FIH as a theory of liquidity crisis rather than as a materially grounded analysis of underlying structural change.

The question is: how to begin to render Minsky's work as relating to structural change? While Minsky's work is idealist in his use of Keynes, it is worth paying attention to the fact that his work is also peppered with interpretation of material phenomena. Indeed, Minsky criticised the treatment of finance in Keynes's *General Theory* as idealist. He argued that the discussion in *The General Theory*, Keynes's most famous work, was inferior to the detailed description of financial markets in his earlier work the *Treatise on Money* because the *Treatise on Money* included more concrete detail about how the financial markets and financial units actually worked rather than dealing in abstractions such as "liquidity preference" (1975:8–11). Minsky (1975) advocated a focus on financial units as fixing some key problems in Keynes's work that Neo-classical economists used to incorporate Keynes's work into the investment saving/liquidity money (IS/LM) Neo-classical synthesis, thereby aborting the revolutionary potential his work posed.

I argue that there was a better way for Minsky to stay true to his goal of anchoring the use of Keynes to Minsky's own particular conjuncture. The question for Minsky should not have been to revisit Keynes in order to purge him of the potential to be neutralised in a contest of economic ideas but rather about the extent to which his own use of Keynes occluded the "material" interpretation of the processes of structural change that gave rise to the resonance of Keynes's work.

However, despite apparently misdirecting analysis away from the object at issue in his own times, Minsky's interpretation of Keynes is significant to understanding the Minskyian conjuncture because the use of a prior conceptual framework introduces a historical question – what is it that delivers contemporary relevance while at the same time requiring interpretation of traditional texts? The practice of interpretation presupposes a mixture of historical change with some form of historical continuity.

A useful way of addressing this question comes from the work on the philosophy of interpretation by Hans Georg Gadamer (2006), who addressed the question by theorizing the "hermeneutic circle". The idea of the hermeneutic circle describes a feeling of resonance that is derived from some prior understanding that seems to bridge historical distance when reading and interpreting a text. Gadamer argues that in the hermeneutic circle, understanding and interpretation are the same things and that tracing the correlations and differences between the contextual factors that generate resonances is the substance of history (Gadamer 2006:258–274). Hermeneutic interpretation therefore poses questions about the historical materialism of a work of art or theory.

Minsky's work on Keynes can usefully be understood as an example of hermeneutic thought. What Minsky derives from Keynes is a conceptualisation of economic change as led by investment and fraught by uncertainty (Minsky 1975).

22 *Minsky in context*

At its core there is a tension in Minsky's work because despite his use of Keynes to present his theory, the type of investment Minsky is talking about is investment undertaken via new financial innovations that emerged as structural developments rather than, as in Keynes's work, a matter of psychological expectations and preferences (Minsky 1975:8–11).

Various passages of Minsky's writing make it clear that he understood that instability stemmed from a "material" source, i.e. structural systemic change. For example, Minsky writes:

> Financial fragility is an attribute of the financial system. In a fragile financial system continued normal functioning can be disrupted by some not unusual event. Systemic fragility means that the development of a fragile financial structure results from the normal functioning of our economy; financial fragility and thus the susceptibility of our economy to disruption is not due to either accidents or policy errors. Therefore a theory of systemic fragility endeavours to explain why our economy endogenously develops fragile or crisis prone financial structures. . . . Once fragile financial structures exist, the incoherent behaviour characteristic of a financial crisis can develop.
>
> (Minsky 1977:139–140)

Here Minsky clearly identifies "materialist" historical processes as the engine of change. The key signifiers are the repeated use of the word "systemic" and the phrase "the development of a fragile financial structure that results from *the normal functioning of our economy*; financial fragility and thus the susceptibility of our economy to disruption is not due to either accidents or policy errors." Minsky evokes a semi-natural evolution of the system according to its own internal or, as he puts it, "endogenous" logic. Hence, Minsky's work alludes to a "buried materialism", a focus on historical change of phenomena according to the internal structural contradictions of a phenomenon. This materialism needs to be excavated in order to understand the real agent of financial crisis that he is theorizing by reference to Keynes.

Minsky's "buried materialism"

The point for Minsky (1975) in interpreting Keynes was to highlight the potential for liquidity crisis. Whereas Keynes posits an "idealist" catalyst to liquidity crisis through the idea of the liquidity preference, new possibilities arise if we give Minsky's work a fully fleshed out materialist basis involving conceptualizing the transformation in the "form of capital" that re-invoked the problematic of liquidity crisis – something that Minsky headed in the direction of doing in his study of Keynes but could not properly complete because he addressed the issue as a matter of updating theory rather than confronting the problem of the relationship between theory and history.

Minsky begins his analysis of liquidity by adopting Keynes's view of how money emerges in the conjuncture. Minsky outlines what he calls the "banker's view" to convey a feeling for the constraints on action and underlying concerns of those who make financial contracts regarding debt[5] (Minsky 1977). He borrows this perspective from Keynes, who used the idea of the money veil to describe the banker's view of the economy and to describe his concept of liquidity preference and the role of expectations in determining future output (Minsky 1982b:61). This is the "original position"[6] of finance for Minsky – the situation from which the logic of the system stems. Minsky writes:

> money is not just a generalized ration point that makes the double coincidence of wants unnecessary for trading to take place; money is a special type of bond that emerges as positions in capital assets are financed. . . . This conception of money, as a financing veil between the "real asset and the wealth owner," is a natural way for a banker to view money and is fundamental to understanding both Keynes and our economy.
>
> (1982b:61)

Hence, from the banker's point of view, money in a capitalist economy is merely a means to knit together the different parties to investment into a profitable relationship. Minsky encouraged Keyensian economists to interpret money, as a systemic phenomenon that emerges as a representation of the spread of relationships that facilitate investment in capital assets.[7]

Minsky's adoption of the Keynesian money veil here is actually a very insightful definition of the "systemic form" of capital if we make the leap (that Minsky doesn't quite attempt) towards exploring it as embedded in the conjuncture and the operation of the various governing and stabilizing institutions that enable this bond to be upheld. His adoption of this idea moves analysis beyond viewing money as in itself token or in terms of its most direct function in exchange towards viewing money as part of the reproduction of a system of relationships based on the "circulation of value" (Postone 1993).

The perspective on money as a relationship implies that value does not inhere solely in money but also exists in capital assets and the set of institutions that enable capital assets to perform their role in generating a yield for the asset manager. Hence, Minsky and Keynes provide some insight into how the creation of money is not an isolated act or mere investment decision but needs to be understood in a historical and structural context of the relationships that enable the real asset and the wealth owner to fulfil their roles.

Unfortunately Minsky, after adopting this starting point, does not pursue this avenue of inquiry in a way that could help him to conceptualise the form of capital and money's location within this whole-of-system form of capital. Instead, Minsky is interested in the way the need for money illustrates the problem of liquidity. Minsky adopts the whole-of-system view in order to focus on the case in which it breaks down and value moves from existing in the system of relationships that facilitate investment to inhering mainly in money. Liquidity crisis was a problem in the breakdown of the value form wherein value would become singular rather than systemic.

24 *Minsky in context*

Minsky maintains that it is the act of investment in assets that underpins the generation of money that on a systemic level underpins the liquidity, and hence value, of potentially illiquid capital assets throughout the economy. In Minsky's view of liquidity, there is a hierarchy of different forms of capital assets of varying liquidity involved in investment, that is, money, bonds, factories and property. The liquidity of these assets is related to each other via the successful performance of the debt/investment contract. If the relationship between the real asset (manager) and the wealth owner (banker) experiences a systemic breakdown because the capital asset base of the economy fails to generate enough income to fulfil the debt contracts underpinning investment, there will be a form of backwash as liquidity rushes back down the hierarchy towards the more liquid stores of wealth, reducing the value of the less liquid capital assets and leaving them stranded "high and dry". The market for illiquid capital assets can evaporate under these conditions (Mehrling 2000).

Contrary to the established Neo-classical wisdom of his time that maintained that markets tended to utilise all available resources such as capital, or in other words, that supply created its own demand, and hence all the stock of capital would tend to be invested, Keynes held that investors could have a "liquidity preference", a desire to hold money at hand, if they felt that the cost of capital, the interest rate, would increase in the future and they could therefore achieve a better yield through withholding investment in the present. These expectations had the effect of choking off investment in projects that would yield an amount below the threshold at which the rate of interest was expected to increase to. Hence liquidity preference tended to be a self-fulfilling prophecy driving up the rate of interest by creating a scarcity of capital and hence investment. This outcome led to a reduction in employment and demand for output, leading to economic depression (Argyrous 2011:175–179). Investors could have a particularly strong liquidity preference in the wake of a speculative bubble where they felt that returns on investment were likely to be low because enterprises would be focused on paying down heavy debt loads, and consumers for new products would be scarce.

Yet this is not the scenario that Minsky felt characterised the conjuncture in which he was writing. Rather, he was seeking to illuminate a theory more rigorously tied to the contemporary institutional dynamics of his time by describing his cash flow taxonomy. For example, in a slight adjustment to Keynes, Minsky argued that with the development of the short-term money markets, starting in the late 1950s with the Fed funds market but beginning in earnest in 1961 with the creation of the secondary market for term deposits, expectations had their most significant effect on the market valuation of capital assets via the relationship dynamics that placed bankers in a position to accept the cash flow forecasts of managers and hence *roll over, assure and extend short-term debts* (Minsky 1982a:61–62). The markets for short-term debt came to form the nexus between different levels of the liquidity hierarchy of capital assets including money, bonds, factories and property.

A change in expectations could run through the whole gamut of effects outlined by Keynes and hence lead to depression but, in the context of the post-war environment and the growth of the welfare state, this was not a certainty given that big government could ameliorate uncertainty to some extent through a variety of means that instigated effective demand. The development of the money markets, however, ensured that the rupture would be felt by bankers as an increased demand for money or liquidity and cause an ensuing financial crisis that would generally manifest itself as a run on the money markets (Mehrling 2000). Debtors would seek to sell position in capital assets to make position on their floating debts to bankers who now required a higher interest rate to guard against future uncertainty. This tended to necessitate a "lender of last resort" intervention by the Federal Reserve Banks to prop up existing liability structures. Indeed, this is largely the argument of Minsky's collection of articles published in the volume *Can 'It' Happen Again?* (1982c).

These "slight adjustments" that Minsky made to Keynes indicate some significant differences in context. Minsky's early writings on liquidity were separated from Keynes's by a period of more than 20 years (1936 versus 1957–1994) wherein the US state had assumed a degree of control over the financial system and the price of capital, before losing it again in the face of the emergence of the short-term money markets (Krippner 2011, Wojnilower 1980). The New Deal system, developed in the mid-late 1930s, managed expectations about future credit conditions to facilitate investment by using state regulation to impute the price of credit (as well as labour). These measures controlling the price of credit were particularly prevalent and strong in the area of housing finance in the USA but also extended to the commercial banking sector. In the mid-1930s Roosevelt intervened to indirectly anchor mortgage interest rates, guarantee mortgage contracts and guarantee deposits in thrift building and loan institutions that were the source of mortgages, as well as to provide liquidity backing for building and loan institutions. In the commercial banking sector the government created the Federal Deposit Insurance Corporation (FDIC) to prevent runs on banks, and mandated the interest rate that banks could pay to depositors using Regulation Q ceilings to prevent ruinous competition for deposits between banks and thrifts (Mason 2004).

In the post-war period the state enjoyed a monopoly position in the provision of secondary sources of liquidity outside of the deposit base of banks. Banks were generally limited to lending on the basis of their deposit base given that the interbank market had evaporated in the Depression. The state guaranteed the flow of investment in the housing sector and to a lesser extent the commercial banking sector and formalised its control over the flow of capital into different sectors and between banks through the Glass–Steagall Act of 1933, adherence to which determined a bank's access to the Federal Reserve System. Glass–Steagall (via Regulation Q) gave the American state control to toggle the respective interest rate ceilings that covered the deposits and lending of the savings and loan associations, commercial banks and investment banks in order to direct capital into a chosen area of the economy should the need arise (Hardt and Negri 1994, Mason 2004). The government could cause a credit crunch in a certain sector by enforcing Regulation Q ceilings on deposits if they persisted in increasing the deposit rates they offered to savers to increase the quantity of capital that they could lend.

26 *Minsky in context*

This drastically reduced the incidence of credit bubble dynamics in the various markets for capital assets (Krippner 2011).

The role of the US state is important to note because much of Minsky's work is cast against the background of "pre-modern"[8] US financial relations between the years 1945 and 1965 before the emergence of the money markets. In a sense Minsky is exploring the reopening of the void at the heart of finance as the state relinquished its role in connecting the present with the future for the purposes of investment. His analysis is an exploration of the re-emergence of flux and uncertainty in financial relations as a normal state of affairs.

It was actually a series of historical changes involving the government's desire for economic growth, the New Deal regulatory system, financial innovation and consequent deregulatory action to manage the effects of financial innovation that generated the spate of financial crises that afflicted the US financial system in the long 1970s. These changes shifted the credit system from being a quantity-constrained system to being a price-constrained system. Henry Kaufman (1986) and Albert Wojnilower (1980) – both former Federal Reserve Bank economists working in the investment banking sector at the time they wrote books on this topic – describe this situation in more detail than Minsky (1986) does. Wojnilower in particular succinctly captures the contradictions inherent in the post-war system of capital that gave rise to the problematic of liquidity crisis, outlining a situation whereby the banking sector had developed the perception that regulators were scared of applying Regulation Q ceilings because they did not want to cause a credit crunch that would shake confidence in the economy. From 1945 to 1965 the government was keen to guarantee growth, creating a situation where banks discounted liquid holdings that could easily be sold should the bank need cash to cover a shortfall in cash inflows, such as Treasury bonds, in order to take positions in capital assets, believing that the government would facilitate future credit growth in the economy. When the government decided to implement its controls over concerns about inflation and instability, it caused a credit crunch to occur as money flowed from the banking sector into the Treasury Bills market, which was not covered by Regulation Q and could continue to offer higher interest rates. The government would immediately take fright at the downturn it had instigated and allow banks to develop a new method of funding loans – through financial innovations – and institute permissive regulatory adjustments "so as to prevent the recurrence of that particular form of credit supply interruption" (Wojnilower 1980). Hence, the sequence of crises in the 1970s was caused by a series of structural changes. The stop-go pattern of economic growth in the long 1970s actually characterised the origins of contemporary forms of capital that emerged from structural change.

Kaufman (1986) and Wojnilower (1980) provide an interesting contrast to Minsky because they are not idealists engaged in theoretical battles and approach structural change in the financial system with a concern for practical questions of coherent governance located in a particular historical conjuncture within which they were active. Their writing is more concerned with how it was actually the collapse of the integrity of categories at the heart of the New Deal system of

Minsky in context 27

financial regulation and permissive approach to financial innovation that generated the tendency to crisis that expressed itself in terms of financial instability.

Minsky's return to Keynes actually occurs at the precise moment in US financial history at which it becomes impossible to return to Keynes as a source of governance solutions given the internal breakdown of the New Deal system of financial regulations. Minsky's theory is therefore somewhat contradictory in that it is formulated during a moment in history characterised by crisis on the level of the political power of the state to guarantee the integrity of the categories and regulation that enabled it to control the form of capital. Yet Minsky does not overtly admit this and does not explore what these historical developments mean for his efforts to formulate a theory derived from Keynes's work that construes the dynamics of the financial system in terms whereby the solution is the legitimation of the state form and its ability to shape the form of capital.

Negri (Hardt and Negri 1994:24–51) provides grounds for making sense of this contradiction in the Keynesian tradition. We can use Negri's work to derive a definition of the Keynesian form of capital and its contradictions that can help us to see how Minsky's work was an expression of the transformation of the form of capital.

Negri (Hardt and Negri 1994) argues that the original intention of Keynes's theory of liquidity crisis was to incorporate labour into capital via the development of a new state form. The flash of genius in Keynes's system of thought was his realisation that the root cause of the Great Depression was the role of labour *in capital*, not capitalism per se, but the category of capital itself understood as a set of socio-political economic relations that facilitated the expansion of values. Negri (Hardt and Negri 1994) argues that when Keynes developed his theory of effective demand and liquidity preference, he developed a conceptualisation of the role of labour in capital in terms of the language of economics.

The conventional wisdom up to this point was deeply flawed in that it did not account for the dual role of labour in capitalism as a cost of production and source of demand. For instance, the previous construction of economics prior to Keynes's intervention conceived of labour as only a cost of production. Say's law stated that decreasing labour costs in a competitive market would flow through to lower prices enabling consumption to be maintained (Argyrous 2011:167–169).

Similarly there could be no problem of sourcing investment capital either, because capital markets would deal with a scarcity of capital by driving up the interest rate, enticing the market to provide more savings. It is implicit in Say's law that an increase in the cost of capital signals an increase in the marginal efficiency of capital, implying that investment will lead to cheaper methods of production and more competitive prices. This would ensure that what was produced using new capital would be consumed.

It must be noted that Say's equilibrium is dependent on the interest rate serving as the cost of capital (Argyrous 2011:168). Keynes excised these elements of Say's law from conventional theory with his theory of liquidity preference that linked the cost of capital (the interest rate) to investors' expectations that

28 *Minsky in context*

were largely conditioned by the levels of demand in the economy. Keynes therefore linked the cost of capital to the conditions of labour, providing a platform to incorporate labour into capital, muting class conflict and generating financial stability by pointing out the limitations in leaving investment decisions up to the individual judgments of capitalists and rentiers whose short-term horizon and lack of systemic perspective on investment tended to incentivise them to cut labour costs, which when conducted on a systemic level by capitalists as a whole group, tended to lead to crisis of effective demand and underconsumption (Hardt and Negri 1994:36–41).

Keynes's system of thought therefore created a historically grounded framework to conceptualise of capital in its totality, including the dual role of labour, creating commensuration between its component parts through managing expectations on two fronts – by socializing the determination of the cost of capital as well as the cost of labour. This ensured systemic commensuration between aggregate investment levels, yield and demand, including on the level of the social/political/economic consensus among labour, capital and the state (Hardt and Negri 1994:42–43).

Reading Minsky in the context of a materially grounded theory of capital, we can see the limitations in his hermeneutic appropriation of Keynes and invocation of liquidity crisis. On the simplest level, his interpretation should be taken to indicate that there is a breakdown of commensuration in the system in terms of these social phenomena but not as an actual description of the mechanics of crisis. The level on which the breakdown in commensuration occurs must be conceptualised in terms of the historical pattern of social relations and is not evident on a purely technical level of debt processes and folly (expectations). The failure of commensuration occurs in the pattern of relationships and the means whereby capital commensurates its component parts. We therefore need to find a way of conceptualizing the breakdown of the old forms of capital described by Kaufman (1986) and Wojnilower (1980) and buried in the theory of Minsky (1986), and the generation of new forms of capital in terms of the transformation of social relations similar to the fashion in which Negri (Hardt and Negri 1994) reads Keynes.

The meaning of the money markets: a structural interpretation

The regulatory system that incorporated labour into the form of capital via the state became problematic as labour started to invest more directly in the capital markets. One of the pillars of labour's incorporation into capital was the use of labour's savings as funding liquidity guaranteed by the state. The New Deal system, given its commitment to generating effective demand, encouraged workers to save in order to smooth out future consumption rather than for reasons of thrift or profit.

This system gave the banking sector some degree of stability too. This system incorporated labour into the form of capital more effectively than the pre-Depression economy by recognising the role of labour as demand and hence supporting wages growth as well as recognising the role of labour as a source of

Minsky in context 29

funding liquidity to the commercial banks and home loan sector, thereby guaranteeing bank deposits to prevent runs on the bank. Furthermore, Regulation Q prevented banks from competing with one another to attract capital on the basis of price, thereby delivering stable funding liquidity conditions to the banking sectors (Hardt and Negri 1994).

In contrast to savers, investors tended to be people and institutions with a larger store of capital that were interested in using it to generate a yield by taking some risk – *the search for yield*. The investment banks selling stocks and bonds catered to this market. The yield of stocks and bonds could vary dramatically in excess of Regulation Q rates because their price was set by forces of supply and demand which were not managed by the state in the way that general consumer demand and housing and corporate investment were underpinned by the New Deal system. Investors could also lose all of their money in a way that savers could not, given the system of government guarantees. The funding for investment could consequently be subject to runs, i.e. liquidity crises, whereas savings funding was more stable given that it was guaranteed by the state.

It was the breakdown of the differentiation between the categories of savings and investment that eventually jeopardised the state's ability to perform the systemic commensuration of investment rates. New financial innovations that promised "consumer savers" (labour) a higher growth rate than bank accounts rose to prevalence in the long 1970s (Krippner 2011). These instruments promised consumer savers a higher yield than both savings and loan bank or commercial bank deposits (see Appendix B for a detailed description of this historical process drawing on Krippner [2011]).

In this way *Labour became the source of new forms of investment capital* intermediated via financial innovations. The *search for yield*, which typically characterised investment, came to characterise how consumer savers (labour) engaged with the financial system. This shift was a watershed moment that transformed the form of capital. On a direct institutional level it was a profound change because it afforded the commercial banks that created the new products access to a new source of capital the price of which, as an investment good rather than a form of savings covered by FDIC or the Federal Home Loan Bank Board (FHLBB) guarantees, floated according to demand rather than being fixed by Regulation Q. A commercial bank could therefore offer a higher yield to consumer savers if it could find borrowers willing to pay a higher cost for capital because they were confident of taking advantage of a profit opportunity that could deliver the yield.

The introduction of floating rate instruments ushered in an era whereby volatility management was privatised and managed by individual financial institutions rather than systemically addressed through state regulation. With the development of the money markets, banks became directly responsible for matching the rate that they paid to depositors with the rate that they earned on their lending.

Perhaps startlingly, given the prevalence and widespread acceptance of volatility in the contemporary financial system, this means that there was a period where volatility was constructed, or built into the US finance system, as a constitutive discourse of American financial institutions and credit instruments. The logic

30 *Minsky in context*

behind this shift was that the development of financial innovations solved the problem of volatility in credit volumes (disintermediation or credit crunches) by creating the problem of volatility in the price of credit. Floating rate instruments, which developed as investment products, obviated downward volatility in the quantity of credit that stemmed from the restrictions on credit growth that were developed during the New Deal (Krippner 2011, Wojnilower 1980). The move towards deregulation that permitted floating rate instruments lifted the restrictions on credit creation, enabling banks and thrifts to create credit by buying it at a market rate in the money markets or from offering investors higher yields on new financial products and lending this money to borrowers at higher rates. Banks using this channel sidestepped the requirement to source their funding from deposits that tended to ebb and flow between the various sectors of the banking system and the market for Treasury Bonds.

Some economists were excited by the development of floating rate instruments heralding a new age of 'financial innovation'. The economist William Silber kept a database tracking the proliferation of new financial instruments and technologies, noting in 1983 in his paper "The Process of Financial Innovation" to the Fifth Annual Meeting of the American Economic Association that out of 38 notable financial innovations that arose during the period 1970–82, including technological advances such as the development of debit cards, 23 were floating rate instruments, many of which had been designed to escape interest rate controls under Regulation Q (Silber 1983:91–94) . Indeed, Silber argued that most "new financial products are designed to sustain financing flexibility for the firm" (Silber 1983:90).

Conclusion

Many prominent critically minded economists such as Henry Kaufman (1986), Hyman Minsky (1977) and Albert Wojnilower (1980) held the view that the move towards floating rate instruments meant that there was no longer a "guardian of credit" in the American finance system (Kaufman 1986:52) and the new floating rate structure encouraged debt creation and instability because floating rate debt transformed a lender's objective into simply maximising total assets by lending under high interest rate conditions because the lender could always pass on the cost of funding to the borrower, so long as the borrower could pay the interest rate (Wojnilower 1980).

Hence, the US financial system developed a tendency no longer towards credit crunches but towards debt creation and asset price bubbles. The effect of this transformation was to move the system away, at least in the initial stages of the business cycle, from being constrained in terms of the quantity of capital to being constrained in terms of liquidity, i.e. the business cycle as described by Minsky.

The importance of Minsky's work, then, is in expressing through his hermeneutic reading of Keynes the development of a new form of capital. He described an increasing instance of fragility in the financial system that stemmed from the effects that volatility in funding liquidity instruments, that is, the volatility of investment as opposed to the stability of savings, had on capital asset prices. The changing nature of funding liquidity re-introduced the possibility of "runs on the bank" as money market finance was withdrawn in the face of uncertainty or over government action to control financial innovations that generated funding liquidity.

APPENDIX B

The incorporation of labour into capital

The first tensions in the New Deal form of capital emerged as the Savings and Loans banks (S&Ls), which were not initially covered by Regulation Q ceilings, increased their savings rates above Regulation Q levels that covered commercial banks. In the period 1945–1961 the S&Ls provided significantly better deposit rates to savers (Hester 1981:149). However, after sustained regulatory pressure from the FHLBB on thrifts to curb "destructive competition" – that is, greedily high interest rates compared with the commercial banks, and under pressure from commercial bank lobbyists, the American government brought the S&Ls under Regulation Q, though at a slightly higher ceiling in 1966 (Mason 2004:182–183). By this time the commercial banks had already begun deploying innovations that circumvented Regulation Q and allowed them to offer higher rates to claw back market share of deposits. This led to a phase of credit crunches, disintermediation and financial innovation throughout the 60s and 70s (Krippner 2011, Wojnilower 1980).

Labour became the source of new forms of investment capital through a series of policy dilemmas that occurred in reaction to the 1959–60 credit crunch. In 1959, in the face of significant inflation, the US government refused to lift the regulated ceiling on deposit rates, leading to a significant credit crunch centred in the commercial banking system that spread to the S&Ls. Deposit funding in both the commercial banks and the S&Ls flowed into the capital markets, where Treasury Bill rates had soared above Regulation Q ceilings in the face of inflation given that in 1959 US Treasuries could be purchased in small denominations (Wojnilower 1980:283–284).[9]

The commercial banks responded to the 1959 crisis by taking a number of measures to strengthen their funding position, at least in relation to the S&Ls. The commercial banks introduced the "negotiable certificate of deposit" – a term deposit account with a higher interest rate than a regular deposit account to compensate the depositor for the loss of liquidity. These instruments were initially only offered to corporate customers with large accounts. In the mid-1960s, as the commercial banks faced funding liquidity difficulties, however, they were offered in small denominations to attract household savings, providing a new source of competition to the S&Ls (Krippner 2011:66). The regulators eventually responded to the emerging gulf between the rate of interest that S&Ls could offer and the consumer CD accounts that commercial banks offered by lifting Regulation Q ceilings on S&Ls and creating ceilings to cover small denomination CDs in 1966 (Krippner 2011:68).

32   *Minsky in context*

Policy makers began to realise that they were increasingly faced with a situation whereby in the context of growth and financial innovation, financial regulation based on the New Deal system "cut unevenly across the economy", falling most heavily on the S&Ls, causing fragility in housing finance (Krippner 2011:72). Although regulators could adjust the Regulation Q ceilings on deposits and loans, this no longer had the universal and equitable effect of making capital unavailable to both commercial banks and S&Ls because the large commercial banks had developed alternative sources of funding through the secondary market for CDs.

Regulators were increasingly unable to control the channel by which commercial banks secured funding. Throughout the late 1960s and 1970s a number of other innovations emerged that expanded the funding flexibility of commercial banks, including bank holding companies, Eurobranches, repurchase agreements, money market mutual funds, futures markets and the growth of the secondary market for mortgages (Hester 1981). These developments posed a similar problem to the development of CDs in that they enabled commercial banks to secure funding at a price and potentially continue lending, without any contraction in the availability of capital as the price of credit exceeded Regulation Q deposit levels.

The S&Ls, given their smaller scale and sophistication of operations, did not enjoy the same flexible funding arrangements. Furthermore, American mortgages had traditionally been set at a fixed rate ever since the Great Depression, which meant that S&Ls were effectively prevented from purchasing credit at a price and transferring it to borrowers using financial innovations. As the government increased Regulation Q ceilings and hence interest rates, the S&Ls were left in the position of paying more for credit "but their fixed rate assets would still be yielding the old interest rate that was agreed upon back when they were acquired" (Kaufman 1986:21).

Krippner writes of the policy dilemmas this posed:

> Either policymakers would need to return to a world in which credit restraints bound all borrowers tightly, or housing and other similarly constrained sectors would have to be unshackled from these restraints. The former choice would place policymakers in the position of continually having to decide how to allocate the burden of restraint across competing sectors. The latter choice meant that, at least within certain limits, the market could do the choosing – even as the generally higher cost of credit excluded some classes of borrowers from access to credit altogether.
>
> (Krippner 2011:72)

The move towards floating rate instruments jeopardised institutional functional specificity between the commercial banks and the S&Ls – the institutions would become more homogeneously structured according to the need to pursue yield rather than social concerns and personal relationships with borrowers and lenders, if their funding were linked to the capital markets. The cost of credit for all institutions would be determined by the market price rather than by political choice.

In the context of politically demarcated rates of return on deposits it was actually the invocation of the interests of small savers that policy makers used to

Minsky in context 33

justify deregulation of interest rates and the introduction of floating rate instruments that were linked to the cost of funding (Krippner 2011:74–82). For example, Citicorp restructured itself into a holding company, an organisation outside of the regulatory jurisdiction of the Federal Reserve, issuing $850 million of its own debt at market rates of interest directly to consumers through its branch network (Krippner 2011). Krippner writes:

> Policymakers again faced a choice between bringing errant market innovators back under the umbrella of regulation and further liberalizing the regulations that constrained Citicorp's competitors. The first course of action was difficult given strong public enthusiasm for the issue. "It is hard to believe that responsible people would seriously advance the thesis that large investors are somehow entitled to a higher return on their money than the consumer," Citibank complained loudly invoking the consumer saver.
>
> (Krippner 2011:75)

Citicorp's issue of debt ushered in a new principle to consumer finance. Krippner writes that "the most remarkable feature of the Citicorp issue was not the relatively high rates of interest that it offered savers, but the fact that the value of the security floated with the market. The implication was that if one side of the balance sheet fluctuated with the market, the other side should fluctuate as well" (Krippner 2011:76). Citicorp did not publicise that this means of consumer savings was not covered by FDIC deposit guarantees.

The commercial banks continued to look at developing financial innovations that priced credit at floating market rates, and these innovations continued to eclipse fixed rate products. Consumer savers were increasingly frustrated with the small range of investment products offered them. In 1977 a commercial bank developed a money market fund that included a checking account, though regulators eventually placed a minimum denomination of $10,000 on the account to help thrifts retain deposits. This led to a consumer-saver campaign to lower the ceiling for money market mutual funds to $500, which the thrifts held would lead to capital flight. A number of government inquiries were held, with President Carter urging that interest rate ceilings be phased out and that variable rate mortgages be introduced to help thrifts ensure that they would not be caught borrowing short at high rates and lending long on mortgages, which tended to be a 20–30 year contract, at low rates. In 1980 the Depository Institutions Deregulation and Monetary Control Act (DIDMCA) was passed to introduce these changes (Krippner 2011:80–82).

Notes

1 I provide a detailed description of the development of floating rate instruments drawing on the work of Krippner (2011) and Wojnilower (1980) in Appendix B at the end of this chapter.

2 The 78–79 crisis also displayed in Figure 2.1 was an international crisis in the role of the dollar.

34 *Minsky in context*

3 Minsky's first iteration of the theme of financial instability appeared in his article on Fed funds in 1957, "Central Banking and Money Market Changes" in the *Quarterly Journal of Economics*.

4 Though Minsky did self-nominate as a Post-Keynesian, that doesn't mean that this is the best way to understand him for our purposes of historicizing his work rather than idealising it as these labels tend to do.

5 There is some evidence that he was successful in capturing the conditions of banking in that many notable former Reserve Bank economists and investment bankers, such as Henry Kaufman (1986) and Albert Wojnilower (1980), were supporters of Minsky's outlook

6 To borrow a term from John Rawls's modernising exploration of contract theory in *A Theory of Justice* (1971).

7 Capital assets are assets that give their owners a yield either through generating income or through capital gains.

8 Pre-modern in the sense that we consider the period Minsky (1986) was writing about as modern.

9 The Federal Reserve took a number of measures to prevent outflow of capital from the banking system by increasing the minimum denomination of Treasuries in 1970 (Krippner 2011:79). However, this regulation inspired the creation of money market mutual funds in the 1970s to enable consumers to access higher rates (Hester 1981:161).

3 Minsky contrary to Monetarism

Monetarism is important to consider in this study of the dialectics of liquidity crisis because of the extent to which the debates over Monetarism were important context to the development of the ideas of Minsky (1972, 1975, 1986), who saw the policy changes that Monetarists urged as having profound effects on the development of the form of capital styling his Financial Instability Hypothesis (FIH) as a theoretical challenge to Monetarism.

The value of looking at Minsky's critique of Monetarism is in the methodological advances that Minsky made in his critique. These methodological advances are relevant to the application of the FIH to contemporary financial crisis. This chapter argues that Minsky moved beyond idealist description of financial crisis (the last chapter characterised his work in these terms) towards developing a historically located explanation of financial crisis via his critique of Monetarism.

Establishing that Minsky's work can have explanatory power would seem to be a basic first step towards giving legitimacy to the use of Minsky's work to explain the crisis of 2007–08 (which we will deal with in the next chapter). But before engaging with these issues, I would like to explore the terms in which Minsky's critique of Monetarism is successful and enables him to explain the roots of the financial crises of the late 1960s and early 1970s. This chapter therefore explores the Monetarist epistemological methodology before moving on to an interpretation of how Minsky's critique of Monetarism constituted a critique of this epistemology and an important methodological advance towards a dialectical understanding of the development of the form of capital and the historically grounded explanation, rather than idealist description, of financial crisis.

Two components of Monetarism

There were two dominant intellectual components of Monetarism – Theoretical Monetarism and Empirical Monetarism (Palley 1993:71). Both were oriented towards a critique of the Keynesian system of controls in the US financial system, particularly in relation to monetary policy. As Palley (1993:71) notes, Theoretical Monetarism was conducted within a pre-Keynesian intellectual framework based on Irving Fisher's Quantity Theory of Money. However, the Theoretical Monetarist criticism was consistent with the logic and terms of expression in the IS/LM

36 *Minsky contrary to Monetarism*

framework insofar as the IS/LM model represented a re-incorporation of Keynesian ideas into the Quantity Theory of Money framework (Palley 1993, Snowdon and Vane 2005:202–203). This begs the historical question of how to understand the rise of Monetarism if it was not a theoretical advance. The consensus now is that the conceptual debate associated with the rise of Monetarism was a refraction of the central political economic issue; the preferential use of fiscal policy versus monetary policy for stabilisation purposes (Mehrling 1998:295).

Empirical Monetarism was complementary to Theoretical Monetarism, though it used a different style of positivist empirical argument and expressed its political objectives more overtly. Empirical Monetarism sought to illustrate, using statistical correlation, how the US Federal Reserve held primary responsibility for causing the Great Depression and subsequent financial crises through its misapplication of monetary policy (Palley 1993:74). Its zenith was in the early 1970s, when it was seen to provide a coherent response to 'stagflation', itself a Keynesian *non sequitur* that brought post-war Keynesianism into disrepute.

Empirical Monetarism became less influential in the 1980s when the relationship between the volume of money and the velocity of money, the correlation of which enabled the Monetarists to draw a causative link between the price level and the volume of money for the purposes of curing inflation, began to become erratic, deviating from its historical correlations. These deviations occurred in the wake of the increasing globalisation and financial innovation problematising the causative link that Monetarists posited between the money supply and nominal incomes and economic activity (Hafer and Wheelock 2001:16–18). As these relationships broke down, it meant that Monetarists could not define their object.[1] This meant that Monetarists could no longer claim that their models represented real processes.

Friedman's positive economics

The question that arises about the meaning of Monetarism, given the "degeneration" of the core propositions of Theoretical Monetarism and Empirical Monetarism, described above, is: what was substantive about it as a form of knowledge about the economy other than its role as ideology championing the priority of monetary policy over fiscal policy? Blaug (1975) states that Friedman's scientific approach, including comprehensive empirical surveys, was part of the reason his work was so influential in that it constituted an epistemological advance in economics which was otherwise argumentative and political rather than scientific. Indeed, Friedman opens a famous book of his essays, *Essays in Positive Economics* (1966), by citing the value of scientific method in cutting through the heat generated by these other forms of "normative" discourse (Friedman 1966:3–6).

The possibility that part of the authority of Monetarism stems from its methodological sophistication suggests that in order to mount a successful critique of Monetarism it is not only enough to point out its limitations. Critique of Monetarist economics also needs to not only point out its limitations but also make sense of them on an epistemological level, offering an alternative framework of

Minsky contrary to Monetarism   37

knowledge as well as critiquing the Monetarist framework. The absence of epistemological critique has enabled Monetarists to claim that any apparent error in the
application of their framework was not due to deficiencies in the framework itself
but due to inherent limits of knowledge. Indeed, this is the measure by which I
suggest that we need to judge Minsky's critique of Monetarism.

The two strands of Monetarism, Theoretical and Empirical Monetarism, corresponded with Friedman's definition of "positive economics". The two types of
Monetarism existed not just as sympathetic styles of scholarship but actually
stemmed from Friedman's epistemological outlook. Friedman wrote in his book
Essays in Positive Economics (Positive Economics) that

> [t]he canons of formal logic alone can show whether a particular language
> is complete and consistent, that is, wherever propositions in the language
> are right or wrong. Factual evidence alone can show where the categories of
> the analytical filing system have a meaningful empirical counterpart, that is,
> whether they are useful in analysing a particular class of concrete problems.
> (1966:7)

Friedman contended that his monetary economics had a history of yielding more
accurate predictions than the fiscalist explanations of the business cycle that
relied on a particular and erroneous experience of the failures of monetary policy
during the Great Depression (Friedman and Goodhart 2003:80–81). Snowdon and
Vane (2005:204) note that Friedman was also regarded to have predicted the onset
of inflation in the 1970s with his paper in the *American Economic Review* called
"The Role of Monetary Policy" (1968).

The epistemological groundings to Friedman's positive economics were similar to Karl Popper's theory of falsifiability in that the value of a theory was held
to reside in its ability to generate predictions of higher empirical accuracy than
previous hypotheses (Snowdon and Vane 2005:209–210). Popper maintained that
a theory can never be proven but can be disproven. Here Popper adopts Kant's
dictum that there is a natural gap between the concepts we have of the world
that necessarily exist primarily in the mind and the world itself, which has its
own independent objectivity. Hence the split between Empirical Monetarism and
Theoretical Monetarism is a natural corollary of the process of explanation in that
its two components represented the two-step process towards knowing via falsifiability, that is, the formulation and the testing of hypotheses.

Many critics of Friedman have ridiculed his scientific aspirations, seizing on
his statement that the realities of assumptions in a theory are irrelevant to the
veracity of a theory (Stilwell 2002:291, Varoufakis et al. 2011). Despite how
counter-intuitive this sounds, it is actually quite consistent with some forms of
rigorous scientific scepticism. As Kant and Popper maintained, the assumptions
underpinning a theory are always necessarily abstractions divorced from the
world. What matters to Popper is not the connection of these assumptions to the
world, because we can never have any confidence about this and should retain
our scepticism in this regard, but their instrumental value in enabling us to know

38 *Minsky contrary to Monetarism*

how the world behaves. This is the only level on which we can come to know the object for Popper and Friedman.

Scientific practice, as described in the work of Friedman (1966) and Popper (Snowdon and Vane 2005:170 & 209–210), is not focused on conceptualisation of the world but rather correlation. The process of conceptualisation is left unaddressed as a "black box". Leaving conceptualisation in a "black box" is problematic because it means that this process does not really lead to any substantive knowledge about the nature of the underlying object in-itself but rather only a catalogue of correlations between objects, the nature of which is assumed.

The ability of this process to generate "objective" knowledge is therefore debatable because the process does not provide any interrogation of the nature of the "object" itself. Indeed, although various studies of empirical monetarism indicated that the money supply had some determinacy, other studies indicated that credit, not just money, had similar levels of predictive power and correlation with nominal incomes (see Modigliani 1988 for a survey). The suggestion of this work was that the Monetarist focus on the money supply and monetary policy was, scientifically speaking, somewhat arbitrary.

In fact, Minsky's (1972) prediction of financial instability and the tendency of financial units to move from being hedge to speculative to Ponzi units had quite a lot of empirical evidence to support it predicting the path of funding liquidity and asset price movements even though its tenets were harder to formulate as determinate quantitative relationships but tended to describe the course of events.

The methodological difficulties in Minsky's expression, which have been noted even by sympathetic interpreters (see Mehrling 1999:130–137) compared with the succinct expression of the epistemological basis to Monetarism are interesting to consider because the issue illustrates how the critique of Monetarism was a central structuring principle in Minsky's work beyond his stated political objectives including informing the very terms in which he formulated and structured his arguments. The very language by which Minsky connotes his theory as a "hypothesis" speaks to the language of scientific inquiry in the spirit that Friedman described in *Positive Economics* (1966), that is, in terms of the formulation and testing of hypotheses that have predictive power. Minsky's use of this language suggests that he was concerned to claim this status for his own work.[2]

Despite appropriating the language of Positive Economics and taking aim at the same issues of inflation, growth in the money supply, crisis and the role of the central bank, Minsky employed a different logic when talking about the inherent character of the system, including its contradictions. Indeed, as I will explore in this chapter, Minsky's method of economics was not only epistemologically orientated but also had a metaphysical perspective (a focus on the nature of causation) that included ontology and phenomenology as grounds for developing a contrary epistemology to Monetarism.

In this chapter I argue that Minsky's critique of Monetarism has a latent and undeveloped dialectical structure that could have been used to give his work an explicit epistemology and metaphysics he could have used to engage with Monetarism beyond just imitating its language in order to enjoy its status while dismissing its politics and epistemology.

Minsky contrary to Monetarism 39

To develop this proposition, I contrast Minsky's "An Evaluation of Recent Monetary Policy" (1972) from the *Nebraska Journal of Economics and Business* with Milton Friedman's paper in the *American Economic Review* called "The Role of Monetary Policy" (1968).[3] The interesting thing about these two papers is that although they are from opposing schools of economic thought they describe the problems with the US financial system in terms of very similar processes. They both focus on the interaction between capital asset prices and funding liquidity. Both writers were, in the first instance, at least in these two articles, grappling with the recent history of how the US financial system operated and fell into crisis.

Although these authors highlight the same problem – the vagaries of the business cycle – the problem these authors analysed appeared to be caused by different components of the US financial system. Friedman (1968) sees the problem located in central bank action. Minsky (1972) sees it located in the money markets. This is not a question of right or wrong identification of empirical processes, that their observations are a purely ideological selection of processes determined according to their political program, although there were undoubtedly elements of this in both of their arguments, but rather that the way capital flows through the US financial system developed through time in reaction to crisis. The objects that these theorists were analysing, despite the relatively close period in which they were writing, was different. They were looking at different objects due to the rapid evolution of US political economic structures in this period.

We can now see through this contrast that the debate was about the "object" (liquidity) as it existed in history. The significance of this is that as Frederic Jameson (1981) argues, different theories need to be periodised and understood as determinate expressions of capital and its development rather than as timeless ideals that capture all the relevant circumstances of the operation of the financial system that exist and can possibly ever exist. Historicizing the work of Friedman (1968) and Minsky (1972) can help us to develop a definition of liquidity that reveals it as a historical phenomenon.

Monetarism and the development of the business cycle

Friedman (1968) highlighted the problems with "fiscalism" in terms of its lack of consciousness about the negative effects of interventions to control interest rates and the business cycle. Under fiscalism, economic growth often necessitated the central bank to act to keep interest rates low in order to protect the banking system and prevent a credit crunch. In doing this, however, the central bank unwittingly increased the money supply. As the central bank bought government bonds to keep interest rates below Regulation Q levels, the value of these bonds would increase, expanding the quantity of reserves which banks that had significant holding in government bonds could leverage or liquefy by selling (Friedman 1968:5–6, Wojnilower 1980:281). Friedman writes that, following these actions,

> [t]he more rapid rate of monetary growth will stimulate spending, both through the impact on investment of lower market interest rates and through

40 *Minsky contrary to Monetarism*

the impact of other spending and thereby relative prices of higher cash balances than are desired. But one man's spending is another man's income. Rising income will raise the liquidity preference schedule and the demand for loans; it may also raise prices, which would reduce the real quantity of money. These three effects will reverse the initial downward pressure on interest rates fairly promptly, say, in something less than a year. Together they will tend, after a somewhat longer interval, say, a year or two, to return interest rates to the level they would otherwise have had. Indeed, given the tendency for the economy to overreact, they are highly likely to raise interest rates temporarily beyond that level, setting in motion a cyclical adjustment process.

(Friedman 1968:6)

The fiscalist solution to the problem of the business cycle (credit crunches) also constituted its cause according to Friedman. Friedman concluded that there was no way to adjust the growth path of the economy without introducing these kinds of distortions.

Friedman framed Monetarism as a kind of "Hippocratic Oath" for central bankers and treasury officials. The imperative was to do no harm. Friedman wanted the central bank to vacate the field as far as it could by adopting "publicly the policy of achieving a steady rate of growth in a specified monetary total. The precise rate of growth, like the precise monetary total, is less important than the adoption of some stated and known rate" (Friedman 1968:16). The point of monetary targeting was to tie the growth rate of the monetary aggregate to the growth rate of the economy to ensure the neutrality of money. In this way central bankers could help to achieve an equilibrium wherein the "average level of prices will behave in a known way in the future – preferably that it will be highly stable" (Friedman 1968:13).

Friedman was guilty of not observing the way the conjuncture was developing in reaction to the problems that he had identified, and he prematurely draws conclusions about solutions that suited his ideological commitments. For example, Friedman's most fundamental assumption that the central bank could control the monetary aggregate was, by the time Friedman made the above statements about monetary growth in 1968, no longer able to be assumed: a point well recognised by Minsky. According to Minsky (1972), banks were in the process of developing the capacity to issue liabilities that increased the volume of credit outside of the central bank's control. These new forms of credit included commercial paper, Eurodollars and certificates of deposit – forms of what is often referred to by Post-Keynesians in their critiques of Monetarism as "endogenous" bank created debt. These forms of credit were developed in order to resolve the contradictions for financial units in the inherited regulatory regime, namely the quantity constraints imposed by the New Deal system of credit controls such as Regulation Q and the consequent tendency in the US financial system towards disintermediation (Wojnilower 1980). Importantly, they were not directly held to be forms of M1 money (bank deposits), even though US Monetarists tended to target M1 as its proxy for the overall money supply (Minsky 1972).

Minsky (1972), writing slightly later than Friedman, was able to observe how the private sector had developed solutions to the form of credit supply interruptions and expansions that characterised the "fiscalist" paradigm[4] rather than relying on Monetarist policy fixes. Minsky conducted his analysis in the Post-Keynesian tradition and was equally critical of the fiscalist paradigm as Friedman but also deeply critical of Monetarism and simple models of the financial system working in the tradition of the Quantity Theory of Money. Minsky had worked briefly at the US Federal Reserve and had experienced firsthand the way in which banks innovated in order to create money, witnessing the development of the federal funds market (Minsky 1957). Minsky's work factored in the transformation away from fiscalism that characterised the "long 1970s" and contributed to the development of "Post-Keynesian" economics, an intellectual program dedicated to revolutionising macro-economics in a way that was true to the spirit of Keynes eschewing the Neo-classical synthesis inherent to the IS/LM models that formed the basis of fiscalism (Minsky 1975).

Minsky (1975) held that market based forms of liquidity, developed through financial innovation, tended to constitute, on the level of a single organisation, the solution to the vagaries of the business cycle. At the same time, market based forms of liquidity cause at a systemic level – as multiple organisations adopted these solutions – the cause of a new form of an endogenously created credit cycle that disrupted price levels, especially in capital asset markets. The development of financial innovations tended to necessitate central bank action to eventually expand the money supply as a stabilizing measure to mitigate the vagaries of money market dynamics by swapping these instruments for loans in the event of their liquidity crisis (Minsky 1980:31–32). From 1966 onwards, when the central bank was forced to conduct its first lender of last resort action in the post-war period, monetary expansions by the central bank were no longer only conducted as a means of supporting fiscal policy by preventing disintermediation but as an accompaniment to lender of last resort interventions to mitigate liquidity crises and the expansion of government deficits to mitigate subsequent recessions that occurred as a result of endogenous credit growth (Minsky 1975:160; 1980, 1986).

The intensification of the capacity of the banking system to create money endogenously, which Minsky highlighted, was theoretically significant in that it rendered the Monetarist policy solution obsolete at precisely the same time as its critique seemed the most intellectually appealing and its policy agenda developed its greatest political traction in the midst of the breakdown of fiscalism and associated New Deal regulatory structures. The development of these innovations problematised fiscalist regulatory structures. The new forms of endogenous money that Post-Keynesians were focused on made it harder for regulators to control the business cycle and direct capital into the sectors of the economy that needed it using interest rate controls that formed the core of the use of fiscal policy. This could have added weight to the Monetarist critique that fiscalist regulation was inappropriate to the goal of stability. But these same developments also problematised the assumption of Monetarism that the money supply could be conceptualised as exogenous, that is, controlled by the central bank.

42 *Minsky contrary to Monetarism*

Minsky's critique of Monetarism was important for the way in which it problematised the "objectivity" of Monetarism by illustrating how the concept of the "money supply" had recently come to be divisible into component processes that were defined by the way the financial system reacted to and was transformed by financial innovations. According to Minsky (1972, 1975), these innovations generated pervasive uncertainty across the business cycle. The conditions of economic activity, Minsky (1972, 1975, 1986) believed, were therefore more effectively understood within a Post-Keynesian framework. Minsky showed that historical developments in the form of capital negated the coherence of the "money supply" as an object of Monetarist policy. Minsky showed how Monetarism was an intellectual edifice containing a hollow core.

Indeed, Monetarism, understood in terms of its positive policy prescription that the central bank should target growth in the money supply, allowing it to expand at a preordained rate, never really became a hegemonic discourse (Hafer and Wheelock 2001). Only the negative solutions that Friedman advocated – decoupling of monetary policy from fiscal policy and a relaxation of interest rate pegging to potentially free up this tool for pragmatic policy use to control inflation – were eventually adopted. Monetarism influenced the policy consensus, moving it towards an "immanent" incorporation of Monetarist principles. Central banks tended to act on Monetarist principles one step removed from directly controlling an imprecise "money supply", focusing instead on the less precise though more actionable proposition that excessive growth in the "money supply" was the source of inflation.

Minsky contrary to Monetarism

Having reflected on how Minsky revealed Monetarism to be a form of historical consciousness about state-determined liquidity, it is pertinent to ask: what can we then say about Minsky's work as a historically determinate form of critique? Is it the case that the FIH was to Monetarism what Monetarism was to Fiscalism?, that is, each of these theories is an exploration of the effects of complex capital flows in causing crisis and a critique of prior, partially developed and less historically reflexive theories of crisis. The implication, which all of these theories contain, is that the later contrary theory contains an analysis of historical developments that is more coherent and allows a greater degree of understanding about both the object of study and the historical conditions of theorising than is present in prior theories.

Minsky's work would deserve these positive implications if it succeeded in illustrating a new way of knowing the object in economics beyond Friedman's positive economics. Indeed, Minsky's article "An Evaluation of Recent Monetary Policy" (1972) can be interpreted as positing a critical methodology in contrast to Friedman's Positive Economics. Although his critique was insightful, it was also problematic in its formulation as an intervention in the contest of economic ideas. In adopting an idealist approach to history, Minsky's criticism of Monetarism attempted to assume its status as a positive form of knowledge by dismissing

Monetarism rather than supplanting Monetarism. By this I mean that Minsky additionally needed to develop a countervailing epistemology on which he could situate his critique of Monetarism's flawed claims to scientific objectivity in light of his observations about the ignorance of Monetarists towards the historical development of their object (the money supply/liquidity).

We can begin to develop Minsky's critique into a more overt critical methodology by focusing on the way he dealt with history in contrast to Friedman. In some ways the most important difference between the Monetarist view of crisis and Minsky's view was conjunctural. The mechanisms of crisis in both theories related to the reflexive dynamics between asset prices and the amount of credit. It was just that the location and participants in the reflexive loop were different. Friedman (1968) viewed reflexive dynamics as stemming from central bank actions, while Minsky (1972) held that it was the development of the money markets.

Minsky's description of crisis here is worth quoting in order to measure against Friedman's statement above:

> In today's economy after a crisis, income, employment, and business profits are maintained by government deficits, so that business profits increase relative to business investment. This decreases the weight of external financing of capital-asset positions, even as refinancing operations at lower post-crisis interest rates fund short-term debts into equities and long-term debts. Simultaneously, because of the deficit, government debt is fed into the portfolios of banks and other financial units, which decreases the exposure of the banking and financial systems to default. The economy emerges from a recession that follows a financial crisis with a more robust structure than it had when the crisis took place. . . .
>
> In a world . . . in which little value is placed on liquidity because it is so plentiful, the interest rate structure yields profit opportunities in financing positions in capital assets by using short-term liquid liabilities. This interest rate structure will exist if the inherited asset structure is heavily weighted by money or liquid assets or if the government deficit is large enough to generate high quasi-rents relative to the current expenditures on capital assets. . . . [T]he interest rate on short-term money-like liabilities of firms and financial institutions will be lower than on the longer-term liabilities used in hedge-financing positions in capital assets. There are profit prospects that induce units to engage in speculative finance [leverage].
>
> (Minsky 1986:234–235)

This quote is taken from a passage where Minsky is explaining the typical path of interest rates as a conjunctural factor determining "the thrust towards Ponzi finance". There are parallels here with the Monetarist view of crisis in that Minsky accepts that the state influences the business cycle, creating the grounds for reflexive dynamics to develop.

Despite the commonality, there were important differences in the Monetarist view and Minsky's view of the business cycle. The theory of Monetarism that

44   *Minsky contrary to Monetarism*

Friedman and Schwartz (1963, 1968) posited favourably viewed the use of monetary policy to control the money supply. However, Minsky maintained that under the influence of Monetarist thought:

> The standard analysis of banking has led to a game that is played by central banks, henceforth to be called the authorities, and profit-seeking banks. In this game, the authorities impose interest rates and reserve regulations and operate in money markets to get what they consider to be the right amount of money, and the banks invent and innovate in order to circumvent the authorities. The authorities may constrain the rate of growth of the reserve base, but the banking and financial structure determines the efficacy of reserves.
>
> (Minsky 1986:279)

Monetarist policy, Minsky held, tended to create incentives towards the transformation of the system away from the one in which its tenets were formulated, as endogenous sources of money and non-bank financing structures, highly responsive to asset price gains, were developed. Monetarism was instrumental in the formation of unstable financial structures.

In this context, Minsky held that monetary policy could not fulfil the role that Monetarists envisaged for it. With the growth of new forms of market liquidity, demand for capital was becoming largely inelastic to price except when the price of capital reached such high levels that it jeopardised systemic stability by affecting capital asset prices, thus precipitating liquidity crisis (Minsky 1986:240, Wojnilower 1980, 2001). This is to say that interest rate rises, which were the favoured tool of Monetarists to minimise inflation and control the money supply, and growth of capital asset prices that influenced the "money supply" were not mutually exclusive. Price movements in capital assets tended to determine investments rather than interest rate conditions so long as the combination of the yield on the asset and capital gains exceeded the cost of debt. Interest rate increases above this point would then tend to necessitate fire sales that could threaten to turn into systemic liquidity crisis (Minsky 1986:238–239).

The telling factor in Minsky's critique which illustrates its latent dialectics is the way that Minsky absorbed Monetarism itself into the historical phenomena, the landscape and dynamics of the economy that are to be explained by theorising how the adoption of Monetarist policy gave rise to development in the form of capital and associated uncertainty and crisis. He illustrated how the problem of financial crisis, as he understood it in the conjuncture in which he was writing, was a deeply historical problem associated with the historical materialism of Monetarism itself. Minsky did this by painting a picture of disequilibrium that incorporated Monetarism, critiquing not so much the logical content of the Monetarist's hypotheses, as focusing on Monetarism itself, as it was being implemented in the conjuncture spurring the spread of unstable financing structures not covered by the Federal Reserve system.

In his critique of Monetarism in his book *John Maynard Keynes*, Minsky (1975) reiterated that Keynesian uncertainty about liquidity dynamics determined the

Minsky contrary to Monetarism   45

path of the business cycles. However, Minsky (1975) sought to revise Keynes's work by focus on financing structures and the dynamics of capital asset prices as determining liquidity instead of the interest rate and liquidity preferences. Minsky hoped to moved Keynes's insight beyond incorporation into the Quantity Theory of Money by making it non-marginalist, suggesting instead that developments in the form of capital that affected these aspects of the financial system should be the main focus of an historically aware approach to applying Keynesian economic analysis.

Minsky built on this perspective in his later book *Stabilizing an Unstable Economy* (1986) by linking Monetarism with the development of unstable financial structures, implicitly suggesting that to adopt Monetarism was to perform the Keynesian object, insofar as it gave rise to inherent uncertainty in the financial structure as a result of the spread of fragile liability structures. Minsky therefore highlighted how Keynesian economics was immanent to Monetarism in the way that Monetarism shaped the conjuncture and there could be no substantive break from the problems of financial history in any turn towards Monetarist policies.

Indeed, Minsky (1980) defined the problem of liquidity in terms that were cognisant of the effects that these historical and theoretical contradictions had on the form of capital, particularly in the operation of the central bank. In 1980 he wrote, "The Federal Reserve is locked into a dismal cycle whereby what it does to halt inflation can trigger debt-deflation, and what it does to prevent that debt-deflation increases inflation" (Minsky 1980:30). He noted that if the Federal Reserve acted as Monetarists prescribed it should, then it would be increasing interest rates in the context of a low-yielding asset base historically inherited from fiscalists who had sought to keep interest rates low to facilitate investment growth. This would set the scene for a credit crunch and debt deflation to occur by constricting liquidity. When it then acted to counter debt deflation, as Keynesians prescribed by injecting liquidity into the system, it would be setting the stage for inflation that Monetarists abhorred. These liquidity dynamics were indeed a good example of a mutually constitutive dialectical relationship whereby contrasting economic theories invoked their opposite as a result of the adverse effects that their prescriptions had on the economy.

Conclusion

Minsky went some ways towards demonstrating how Monetarism, as a critique of Keynesian economics, had come to be part of the constitution of the historical phenomena of inflation and liquidity crisis that it had taken as its reason for being. Minsky could have used this type of historical analysis to illustrate the problems in the pursuit of "positive economics" by showing how a scientific approach focused on correlation could mistake subject and object in history. In doing this he could have developed a definition of liquidity that illustrated how the historical development of the form of capital gave liquidity a multi-faceted systematic dimension that interpreted debates in monetary economics as an expression of the form of capital, thereby paving the way towards a greater understanding of the

46 *Minsky contrary to Monetarism*

inherent problems and contradictions in the form of capital. Minsky did not do this overtly but we can interpret his work, in the structure of its argument and the way it uses history and theory, as expressing these types of methodological points about the dialectics of liquidity crisis.

Having explored how Minsky's FIH is tenable as historicizing critique of Monetarism but not as theory in itself (this latter point was outlined in Chapter 2), Chapter 4 then goes on to explore the implications of this analysis for how economists are currently using Minsky to explain contemporary financial crisis. The next chapter argues that current use of Minsky's FIH as heterodox economic theory is not a viable approach to explaining contemporary financial crisis. Chapter 5 then returns to look at how Minsky's work can be usefully reinterpreted as critique, not of Monetarism this time but of contemporary equilibrium based financial economics, that is, of the Efficient Market Hypothesis (EMH) in a way that can help to explain contemporary financial crisis, including the crisis of 2007–08.

Notes

1 Monetarism was concerned about prices not liquidity. The loanable-funds perspective and the "New Monetary Theory" let them think that liquidity was everywhere (see Fama 1980). However, leaving the matter of formal theoretical construction aside, this chapter is based on a Monetarist text by Friedman where he closely aligns Monetarist arguments with the concept and historically characteristic processes of liquidity. I interpret Friedman (1968) as seeking to highlight how the state is creating a "problem of liquidity" expressed as inflation. Friedman is seeking to argue how the liquidity measures of the New Deal system were inadequate according to their own rationale in guaranteeing stable liquidity. I want to stay close to this argument, rather than provide an exhaustive discussion of Monetarist theory, because it speaks to the broader point of the book about the historical difficulty of defining liquidity – a point which Monetarism itself failed to account for in its ignorance about the implications of the developments of the money markets and the possibility of creating "endogenous" money which problematized the Monetarist assumption that the "money supply" could be easily defined and controlled.
2 Indeed, the last chapter in his book on Keynes was an alternative explanation of "inflation", the prediction of and ministering to which was the key to much of Monetarism's influence. Minsky (1975:159–166) conducted this discussion in terms of a Post-Keynesian understanding of economics.
3 Paul Krugman called this paper "the most influential paper ever published in an economics journal" for the role it had on shifting the debate on the appropriate use of monetary policy towards targeting inflation over fiscal objectives (Snowdon and Vane 2005:173).
4 Though the problem of credit crunches in the post-war US financial system are described most lucidly by Wojnilower (1980) rather than Minsky (1986).

4   Liquidity and abstraction

The argument in the previous two chapters illustrated the methodological difficulties Minsky had in adapting a Keynesian analysis to explain the tendency towards crisis in his conjuncture. There are similar difficulties associated with abstracting Minsky's theory out of the conjuncture and the referents against which it was located to explain contemporary crisis. Indeed, the American economist Gary Dymski (2010) in a recent article in the *Cambridge Journal of Economics* raised concerns about whether Minsky's work could be used to explain the crisis of 2007–08, as some economists have sought to do (see Keen 2009, McCulley 2009, Toporowski and Tavasci 2010). Dymski (2010) as well as Kregel (2008) have argued that the financial system has changed drastically from the system that Minsky was analysing, including through the development of new practices such as risk calculation and new instruments such as derivatives and asset backed securities.

This chapter deals with the logic of applying an analysis of liquidity crisis inspired by Minsky's work to recent financial crises, including the collapse of the hedge fund Long Term Capital Management (LTCM) in 1998 and the crisis of 2007–08. I analyse the work of Mehrling (2000, 2011) as a proxy for Minsky, who died in 1996 and therefore provided no analysis of these events.[1] Mehrling uses Minsky's framework to analyse financial crises such as the collapse of LTCM and the crisis of 2007–08. Mehrling (2000, 2011) is an economic historian as well as a financial economist and is seeking to recover Minsky's work, update it and illustrate how Minsky's discussion of liquidity provides insight into the shortcomings of the conceptualisation of the financial system by modern financial economists (who according to Mehrling (2000) tend to work in the tradition of the Efficient Market Hypothesis [EMH] and see risk trading as leading to equilibrium and stability to the exclusion of considering crisis tendencies in the financial system).

The work of Mehrling (2000, 2011) is important to consider because it has advanced the possibility of developing a Minskyian analysis of contemporary financial crisis in very important ways. This chapter focuses on Mehrling's hermeneutic reading of Minsky's ideas rather than Minsky's ideas alone. Indeed, Mehrling (2000, 2011) found a way to begin to interrogate "risk", which is the central concept of modern finance and the constitutive discourse of the derivatives market, and a concept that has risen to prominence prior to Minsky's development

48 *Liquidity and abstraction*

of the FIH, in terms of liquidity. As the introduction to this book outlined, the relationship between risk and liquidity is the central question that those seeking to apply a Minskyan analysis to contemporary financial crisis need to address. Hence, Mehrling's (2000, 2011) analysis of this issue via a very insightful analysis of the activities of broker dealers, that is, derivatives traders, in terms of liquidity, is extremely valuable to the overall argument of the book.

This chapter provides a description of how Mehrling (2000, 2011) and other banking economists (such as Adrian and Shin 2010, Borio 2009, Brunnermeier 2009) who are working within a similar Minskyan inspired framework to Mehrling interpret the activities of derivative risk traders in terms of liquidity. I argue that while Mehrling's work (2000, 2011) is insightful to the extent that it does important work in updating Minsky's FIH and locating how it could be applied to the contemporary financial system, I argue that Mehrling still applies the FIH to contemporary financial crisis in a way that does not adequately account for liquidity as a historical phenomenon.

Indeed, Mehrling (2000, 2011) is more cautious in his work on liquidity than Minsky. Instead of seeking to develop a hypothesis of the operations of the whole business cycle and explain the recurrent and contradictory nature of accumulation, as Minsky (1986) did, Mehrling (2000, 2011) is seeking rather to highlight a neglected dimension, that of liquidity, to contemporary financial economics. His Minskyan analysis works as a description of the moment of crisis and its typical dynamics but not an explanation of the business cycle. Mehrling does not explain how the development of risk trading appeared to obviate the tendency towards liquidity crisis for a time, generating significant profits for risk traders and dampening systemic volatility in the years 1982–2000, before breaking down.

What then is the value of Mehrling's Minskyan analysis of contemporary financial crisis if it only captures a moment in the operation of the financial system while ignoring or even occluding the dynamics that lead to the development of this moment? Is a focus on liquidity, as opposed to the analysis of risk, useful in explaining the gestation of contemporary financial crisis in the way that Minsky sought to explain the historical development of financial crisis in his conjuncture? This chapter outlines how the historical and explanatory shortcomings of Mehrling's Minskyan analysis can actually help us understand liquidity as a systemic and historical phenomenon and, somewhat paradoxically, the role of liquidity crisis in generating new forms of liquidity.

Risk trading and liquidity

Financial economists have quite a simplistic view of liquidity as the depth of exchange in the market. There is no theory of funding liquidity crisis in modern financial economics (Mehrling 2011:4–10). Mehrling (2000) sets out to address this occlusion by illustrating how the activities of derivative traders, who normally consider themselves to be overtly involved in the calculation and exchange of risk, can be understood in terms of the concept of liquidity as inspired by Minsky (1986). This chapter will describe Mehrling's work on this problem but before

Liquidity and abstraction 49

looking at this issue, analysing it is useful to consider the conceptual framework many derivative traders use to understand their own activities in terms of risk trading in order to give us a grounding on which we can judge whether Mehrling's work to characterise risk trading in terms of liquidity is successful.

Modern financial economics assumes largely efficient, rational and liquid markets (Fox 2009). Indeed, the EMH describes how market liquidity emerges as a result of the possibility of making profits from arbitrage and therefore needs little consideration in itself (Barberis and Thaler 2002). Market participants seek to detect when two stocks with similar fundamentals are mispriced relative to one another. After identifying this type of pricing discrepancy, they will buy the cheaper stock and short sell the dearer stock until the value of the stocks reaches a comparative equilibrium reflecting fundamentals. In financial markets and especially with high speed electronic trading, this process could be thought to happen almost instantaneously as traders react to the release of new information in the news or by companies. The prevalence of arbitrage in the financial system forms the core of the EMH, which states that arbitrage tends to perform a rationalising function on prices, so that there are "no free lunches" in the financial markets and neither should there be much scope for damaging price bubbles to occur (Fox 2009).

Quantitative traders conduct an even more subtle form of arbitrage than the description above. They attempt to abstract from the noise of small-scale stock price reactions to news and information. Quantitative analysts use the assumption that although specific price movements are difficult to predict, in general, these types of reactive price movements will follow a "random walk" pattern. Quantitative analysts use this insight as the basis on which to construct statistical models of the range of stock price moves and the correlation of different stocks and bonds to one another in relation to certain market movements to construct a measure – "risk" that is defined in relation to normal market range of volatility (Fox 2009).

The activities of quantitative traders, often colloquially referred to as "Quants", are now a central part of the US financial system, particularly the "shadow banking system" which developed in the 1980s and 1990s with the development of securitisation and derivatives markets (Pozsar et al. 2010). Quantitative trading has recently been implicated in a number of financial crises despite its elegant rationale and supposed commitment to generating equilibrium in the financial system.

Perhaps the most infamous exercise in quantitative trading was conducted by the hedge fund LTCM. In 1994 two economists who had won a Nobel prize for their work on pricing options started LTCM with the aim of pioneering a form of trading using derivatives to arbitrage small price discrepancies to generate yield. LTCM continuously assessed multiple different correlations between the price movements of different bonds in relation to various market risks and bought options on them to gain exposure to any correlation they identified that looked like it could generate a yield. They would gain exposure to these correlations by hedging against all other market risks and then waiting for the identified risk to come about. LTCM often had to wait for long periods of time for these correlations to

50 *Liquidity and abstraction*

make money, hence the hedge fund's namesake, but the wait appeared to be worth it because it was a low-risk way of making profits according to LTCM's calculations (Mehrling 2000:84).

It is telling that in 1998 LTCM experienced a liquidity crisis and had to be rescued by a coalition of banks organised by the Federal Reserve. This event came to symbolise the hubris of financial engineering and risk trading. Many reports of LTCM's collapse emphasise how LTCM put too much faith in financial modelling while taking an aggressive approach to leverage, posting the derivative positions they had purchased in the repo market to fund them. This enabled LTCM to generate high yields, well in excess of the cost of debt in the repo market for holding these positions. However, an increase in the interest rate in the repo market made it difficult for them to roll over their funding, eventually overwhelming them. Indeed, their use of leverage turned their collapse into a potentially systemic event necessitating the involvement of the Federal Reserve in orchestrating their rescue (Lowenstein 2000, MacKenzie 2003).

Mehrling (2000) offered insight into the nature of LTCM's hubris, observing that financial economics seems to "abstract" from dealing with the problem of liquidity (leverage) by focusing instead on risk. Indeed, Mehrling (2011) later argued that the collapse of LTCM – which traded in early sub-prime mortgage-backed securities (MBS), and whose collapse, as Goodman et al. (2008:11) note, set back the development of this market for a number of years – was a dress rehearsal for the liquidity crisis of 2007–08. According to Mehrling (2000, 2011) these two crises illustrated the importance of liquidity by proving that trading units cannot hedge against a run in the money markets because the money markets are what enable trading units to hold hedge positions.

The need for dialogue on liquidity

Given this tendency towards liquidity crisis at the heart of the system of risk transfer, Mehrling has repeatedly called for a dialogue between modern financial economics and Minskyian economists, first in the wake of the collapse of LTCM and reiterated in his recent book *the New Lombard St* (Mehrling 2000, 2011). Mehrling's call for dialogue has been prescient in that liquidity has indeed come back into view for economists, particularly banking economists, in the wake of the crisis that afflicted the US financial system beginning in earnest in 2007 and continuing until November 2008 with the bailout of AIG and the release of the Troubled Asset Relief Program (TARP) by the US government in partnership with the US Federal Reserve. A number of economists appear to have rediscovered the work of Hyman Minsky and his method of descriptive exploration of funding conditions to inform the analysis of liquidity crisis. Whether it be overtly in the case of Claudio Borio (2009) from the Bank of International Settlements or implied in the case of Tobias Adrian and Hyun Song Shin (2010) from the Federal Reserve Bank of New York and Markus Brunnermeier (2009) from Princeton University (formerly Federal Reserve), many economists are currently exploring

Liquidity and abstraction   51

the mechanics of liquidity in similar terms to Minsky (1986), seeking to understand the endogenous build-up of risk in the credit system.

Given the nature of the global financial crisis, which was located in markets for new financial instruments such as asset-backed securities (ABS) and credit default swaps (CDS), banking economists are now grappling with a different system and different instruments than the ones Minsky (1972, 1986, 2008) addressed. These instruments are not directly linked to the banking system but rather are traded in capital markets whose liquidity is defined in terms of market liquidity rather than cash flows in the banking sector. Furthermore, the capital markets are predominantly global derivative markets where decisions are based on calculation about volatility and risk so that liquidity dynamics, which were something of a national phenomenon, should not be so prevalent.

The location of the financial crisis of 2007–08 in markets for new financial instruments poses the question of how to define liquidity and understand liquidity crisis in the modern conjuncture? Does it make a difference that the current system is characterised by risk based derivative markets rather than monetary flows? The banking economists, including Mehrling (2000, 2011), have addressed these questions by developing the theory of liquidity crisis to account for the fact that the financial crisis of 2007–08 occurred in the market for asset-backed securities. The banking economists therefore focus on the crisis dimensions of market liquidity for these securities, where Minsky primarily focused on funding liquidity problems associated with the development of the money markets. This does not mean that they are abandoning the Minskyian framework and its analysis of funding liquidity. Instead they have refocused their Minskyian analysis to place greater emphasis on how financial units take positions in these new types of financial instruments, that is, how funding liquidity underpins market liquidity.

Indeed, the collapse of LTCM in 1998 illustrated how funding liquidity could influence market liquidity. Mehrling (2000) explains the collapse in these terms. He maintains that hedge funds act as dealers in various bond markets using borrowed money and equity to take positions. For instance LTCM ran a statistical arbitrage strategy involving fixed income securities. This involved making similar bets to those of a "dealer" relying on the likelihood of convergence in the price of various bonds. Mehrling writes that

> ordinary security dealers make markets by buying and selling securities to absorb fluctuations in the balance between fundamental demand and supply. In the short term, they make money on the bid-ask spread. In the longer term, they make money by absorbing securities when prices are weak and disgorging them when prices are strong. Dealers finance their fluctuating security holdings primarily by borrowing in the money market using repurchase agreements. Thus, in their ordinary business they are long securities and short money, which is to say that their long positions are less liquid than their short positions.

(Mehrling 2000:85)

52 *Liquidity and abstraction*

In conducting its trading operations LTCM behaved like a dealer helping to make "illiquid securities more liquid", spreading liquidity in the funding market across securities markets and generating market liquidity (Mehrling 2000:86).

This interpretation explains how dealer/brokers make profits in terms of liquidity dynamics. Dealing in securities markets is profitable so long as the income a dealer makes in the market through arbitrage exceeds the costs of maintaining their position through borrowing in the money markets. Similarly any position in convergence trading is profitable so long as the profits from playing the spread are larger than the cost of borrowing. This is remarkable because it illustrates how clever risk calculation is only a secondary driver of profits. The real source of profits is the ability to generate what Minsky (1982b) called a "liquidity yield".

The reliance on the money market to fund trading positions also illustrates how trading units are still, in a fundamental sense, engaged in the activity of borrowing short and lending long to generate a "liquidity yield" – a practice which Minsky (1982b) held generated financial instability. The activities of quantitative traders can be made explicable in terms of liquidity dynamics.

The inattention of LTCM to its liquidity dynamics did eventually backfire. It became difficult, in 1998, for LTCM to roll over its loans in order to refinance its security holdings because the interest rate ("haircut") on overnight and monthly repo funding had increased in response to a glut of positions in statistical arbitrage convergence trading. Over the years the success of LTCM's strategy had created a number of imitators who were able to infer their techniques and copy their models. Hence, there were a number of trading units reacting to similar stimuli and therefore amplifying the effects of these stimuli. When the Russian government defaulted on its bonds, the homogeneity in the market stopped contributing to a virtuous spiral of growth in asset values and created a vicious spiral of asset price deflation as many trading units sought to sell their positions at the same time as LTCM. This created a crisis in market liquidity for LTCM (Brunnermeier and Pedersen 2005:1826, MacKenzie 2003).

The crisis in market liquidity could have led to fire sales where LTCM would have had to liquidate its market position at vastly reduced prices to make position in the money market. This would have threatened the solvency of LTCM, which was counterparty to a large number of positions in the Treasury Bills future markets. The Federal Reserve stepped in to prevent contagion in the Treasury Bills future market, which was a central market in terms of global capital flows and the value of the US dollar organising a bailout of LTCM. It organised for LTCM's trades to be distributed to other institutions which enjoyed a larger degree of funding diversification and were therefore able to hold LTCM's positions on their books until they became profitable (Borio 2009:3, Mehrling 2000:86).

A similar problem emerged in the market for ABS in 2007–08, though this time the major investment banks were caught up in the problem, having steadily grown their proprietary trading desks, their in-house hedge fund operations, in the intervening period. Indeed, many of these units were used as warehouses for ABS collateralised debt obligations (CDOs) that the investment banks had created by securitising the sub-prime mortgages of sub-prime mortgage companies that they owned (Lewis 2010, Muolo and Padilla 2010, Patterson 2010). The practices at the heart of the LTCM collapse had become widespread and mainstream, drastically expanding in quantity from what LTCM was involved in (see Pozsar et al. 2010 for a thorough description of the growth of the shadow banking sector).

Mehrling argued that the collapse of LTCM showed that dealers such as hedge funds and proprietary trading desks at investment banks play a key role in creating liquidity in securities markets and are therefore, whether it is recognised in the theories they use to guide development of their trading strategies or not, generally part of a set of hierarchical linkages that guarantee liquidity in the financial system. Dealers need to have backup lines of credit with deposit taking banks that, in turn, are generally eligible to borrow from the Federal Reserve. If these linkages do not exist prior to the event of crisis, then they must be hastily constructed during a bailout to prevent systemic contagion (Mehrling 2000:86).

Dialogue or dialectic?

What type of dialogue between modern finance and banking economists does Mehrling and those who seek to develop a contemporary position on liquidity crisis believe is possible? Does Mehrling's call for theoretical dialogue stand in contrast to the actual historical relationship between modern finance, which has inspired such a concerted program of financial innovation over the last 30 years,[2] and liquidity dynamics? This question is important because there are many levels on which theories can relate to each other, including in conceptual dialogue or in terms of how they influence and condition the financial system, that is, in terms of their historical materialism.

While financial innovations such as ABS and derivatives are deeply implicated in the liquidity crisis of 2007–08, financial innovation has historically played a role in resolving structural tendencies towards liquidity crisis in the US economy in the 1980s and 1990s, suggesting that the valence of the relationship between risk trading and liquidity crisis has shifted over time.

The Savings and Loan (S&L) crisis, which was brewing all throughout the 1970s and into the 1980s, constituted perhaps the prime example of the central problem in the US financial system lucidly described by Minsky's FIH (Minsky 2008). Savings and Loan banks were commonly caught borrowing short, relying on demand deposits for funding while lending long on mortgages and hence were exposed to liquidity crisis. Furthermore, they relied on 30-year fixed-rate mortgages for income. These mortgages were issued in a low interest rate environment and had a low yield. Hence, the inherited capital base of S&Ls did not allow them to pay high deposit rates that would have enabled them to compete in the competition for funding liquidity that characterised the US financial system of the 1970s (see Krippner 2011, Minsky 2008).

Securitisation, the creation of securities based on the credit risk of a pool of borrowers, appeared to fix this problem in housing finance by shifting the source of credit for housing from the funding liquidity of S&L banks towards market liquidity for ABS (Lewis 2010, Minsky 2008, Ranieri 1996, Wojnilower 1985).

54 Liquidity and abstraction

With the development of securitisation of MBS, Ponzi units (typically S&Ls in the late 1970s and early 1980s) no longer had to freeze loan issuance when they were unable to attract deposit funding with competitive rates. They could sell the low yielding debt to be packaged into securities into a secondary market. Indeed, the initial creation of the Government Sponsored Enterprise, Freddie Mac, as an adjunct of the Federal Home Loan Bank Board, was largely conducted in recognition of the need to find a solution to instability in the Savings and Loan sector in this regard.[3] The US government gave additional support to S&Ls to do this in 1981 by giving them tax breaks on their losses on the mortgages they sold into the secondary market (Lewis 1989:121–122).

The development of securitisation in the context of liquidity crisis is relevant to the discussion of the historical applicability of the FIH because secondary markets for underlying capital assets influence liquidity dynamics by affecting the scope for reflexive dynamics between funding liquidity and market liquidity – the very mechanism by which Mehrling and other banking economists identify liquidity crisis as occurring in modern derivatives markets. The FIH is a theory that focuses on the reflexivity of asset prices to funding liquidity, that is, the interaction between market liquidity and funding liquidity. For instance, an increase in funding liquidity enables a larger number of financial units to take positions in an asset such as MBS. The increase in funding liquidity eventually drives up the price of the capital market asset, creating capital gains for its owners in addition to its yield. This gives lenders more confidence to lend to them. This further second increase in funding liquidity and demand for the capital asset drives asset prices and leverage up, further moving the market into increasingly fragile territory (Borio 2004, Brunnermeier 2009, Minsky 1986:249–283).

In fact secondary markets for a capital asset, such as the market for MBS that globalised access to the yield of the capital assets, would seem to mitigate the second reflexive movement in instability dynamics whereby increases in asset prices generate an increase in funding liquidity. In Minsky's era, part of the increase in funding liquidity came from collateral effects of an increase in market liquidity on the portfolio of lenders and was therefore self-referential (Minsky 1986:249–283, Soros 1994:81–89). However, if the pool of funding liquidity is larger, it would be harder then for growth of a pool of asset values to create collateral effects that would significantly influence funding liquidity unless the pool of assets was very large. This is to say that unless the secondary market for the capital asset is so large that growth in asset values is likely to increase global funding liquidity, then the growth of globally accessible secondary markets for capital assets tends to dampen instability dynamics by preventing reflexive funding dynamics from setting in (Greenspan 2000).

Consequently, the recent crises in market liquidity of derivatives and MBS stand in stark contrast to the fact that the development of market liquidity for these products was actually a development in reaction to financial instability in US housing finance. The abstraction from liquidity that Mehrling identifies as occurring on a theoretical level in financial economics is a matter that exists on the part of the historical record as well. This reveals how Minsky's FIH is part of a particular historical moment in the growth of US finance wherein the limited extent of globalisation and the relative size of funding markets compared with asset markets, facilitated instability dynamics by enabling funding liquidity to influence market liquidity via collateral effects.

The possibilities of dialogue between Post-Keynesianism and modern finance must therefore be assessed in light of the fact that these discourses, or at least their respective objects of liquidity crisis and financial innovation, have a history of interaction that has resulted in the formation of the current conjuncture. The tendency towards liquidity crisis has been mitigated through restructuring the financial system in light of the obviation that financial innovation has enabled from liquidity crisis.

Risk as abstraction

The role of the concept of risk in the financial system is integral in the broadening of the market described above. Indeed, Bryan and Rafferty (2006) outline how the function of risk is to provide an abstract language in which different forms of capital from stocks and bonds to currencies to commodities can be made commensurate with one another and their underlying value made more mobile. The creation of risk trading therefore generates a larger, fungible pool of capital that would seem to be, in its very nature, given that it is composed of practices whereby different forms of capital are made commensurate and hence global, somewhat resistant to the reflexive dynamics that Mehrling (2000) and Minsky (1986) describe.

In this light, Mehrling's call for a dialogue between modern finance and Post-Keynesians is suggestive but somewhat problematic. Indeed it is worth considering again Mehrling's comments (quoted above) about how financial economics "abstracts" from considering the issue of liquidity. Mehrling believes that given the recurrence of liquidity crisis in the risk trading system, this occlusion of liquidity is problematic. However, the historical discussion above suggests that the purpose of the risk trading system is to occlude the necessity of accounting for liquidity dynamics. Mehrling's construction of the importance of liquidity dynamics over consideration of risk ignores the historical development of the risk trading system in obviation of liquidity crisis.

Taking this history into account suggests that Mehrling's reinterpretation of the activities of derivative traders in terms of liquidity is descriptive of crisis rather than explanatory. If the risk trading system is what obviates liquidity crisis, then the re-emergence of liquidity crisis is exemplary of the breakdown of the risk trading system. The more abstract and less visible, breakdown should then be the object of analysis that is held to explain the re-emergence of liquidity crisis rather than using Minsky's FIH as a proxy for doing an analysis of the historical materialism of risk.

The problem of focusing on a Mehrling-like theoretical dialogue rather than privileging a focus on historical change is that analysis systematically shies away from the question of the materiality of asset values across the business cycle.

56   *Liquidity and abstraction*

Mehrling is forced to describe how the cells of modern finance, the innovations it enables, are largely "performative" of market liquidity. From this perspective the values that new risk models allegedly discern are determined in a circular fashion given that there is no other standpoint from which to discern fundamentals than the actual operation of the market as a plebiscite on fundamental values (Mehrling 2000:84).

The problem is that given the fundamental epistemological circularity in financial modelling, it has the capacity to create an illusion of value. Mehrling views the modern financial system as characterised by trading units that vie to develop the most accurate technique for modelling risk and hence discerning the "Truth" of asset prices. But there will eventually be problems in the veracity of this illusion:

> When a substantial fraction of investors come to view the world in this way, and come also to agree on what is the most fine asset pricing theory, we are well on our way to what Minsky in another context calls "the economics of euphoria". In Minsky's view of the world, there is no beautiful Truth toward which we are converging. It's an illusion, and we are in the most danger when the largest number of us come to believe in the illusion.
>
> (Mehrling 2000:84)

The calculations of modern finance appear to give its adherents greater capacity to confront the future by devising accurate means of pricing with volatility but instead tend to move the market towards their prescriptions and lead to a build-up of cash commitments on a largely arbitrary basis inevitably leading to liquidity crisis. Modern finance therefore lacks a materiality.

This perspective is insightful to some extent, mirroring the terms of recent sociological analysis of financial crisis as "performative" (MacKenzie 2006, 2009), though it dismisses modern finance as idealism. This neglects the fact that the conjuncture has been profoundly shaped by financial innovation.

In fact, although Mehrling is quick to be critical of the concept of risk, as the previous two chapters argued, the concept of "liquidity" that Mehrling relies on is itself not that well defined. What is defined as "liquidity" has a degree of historical contingency about it, especially given that liquidity crisis is often a spur to create institutional arrangements that guarantee the liquidity of certain markets by bringing them under the auspices of central bank lender-of-last-resort (LOLR) coverage (Mehrling 2011, Minsky 1980:31–32). Nominating a certain instrument, market or institutional constellation as the determinant of liquidity is therefore likely to be anachronistic in the face of a transformation in the means by which value is mobilised and circulated in the financial system. Hence, Mehrling's critique (2000, 2011) merely replaces one idealist concept with another idealist concept that shares the same underlying lack of materialism (as an abstraction) that Mehrling sees in modern finance.

Ascribing cause and giving order to the financial system in terms of the concept of liquidity may just be an act of language attempting to bring into being some of the causes and links that the theory itself attributes to the system, i.e. an act

Liquidity and abstraction 57

of rationalisation necessary in order to justify a certain remedial policy program involving central bank intervention. The Post-Keynesian theory justifies central bank LOLR and liquidity provisions by highlighting the sole culpability of the banking and finance sector in liquidity crisis through the theory of endogenous money. In this way it justifies the substitution of a set of commodity relationships oriented around value and risk calculations in the market for a set of institutional relationships brokered by the central bank oriented around guaranteeing liquidity flows and hence systemic stability in the event of crisis. The discourse of liquidity crisis understood in this way is a similarly "performative" discourse to modern finance in that its structure operates to change the world as well as acting to explain it (Austin 1965, MacKenzie 2006).

Part of the problem in orchestrating dialogue between the two theories considered in this chapter is that both theories tend to present as closed logical loops that cannot admit contrary perspectives. This has been explored above in relation to the Post-Keynesian understanding of the role of modern finance in the world. However, modern finance has a similar structure in this regard based on the equilibrium thinking of Neo-classical economics. Indeed, they deploy their own type of totalizing thinking based on a hierarchy of metaphysical processes where even in the context of crisis the tendency towards equilibrium retains priority as the fundamental tendency of the economy (Greenspan 2007). For instance, Joseph Schumpeter (1928) looked at economic instability as not a structural feature of the system but only local and temporal interruptions of transformation of the system through innovation towards a new, more visibly perfect system of price discovery – part of a process of "creative destruction". He viewed any disruptions as crises *in* the system not crises *of* the system (Schumpeter 1928:363). The movement towards equilibrium is always something yet to be realised in the world.

We need to move forward by developing an understanding of the debate between "Post-Monetarist" and "Post-Keynesian" (Mehrling 2000) accounts of the financial system from the perspective of the disjuncture between the two theories. Indeed, as we saw Minsky (1980) do in the last chapter in relation to fiscal Keynesianism and Monetarism, it is useful to frame the concept of liquidity in terms of theoretical disjuncture because it helps us to understand the historical dynamics that tend to define liquidity dynamics.

The hoped-for dialogue that Mehrling is calling for but which can never be realised actually illustrates the nature of the system and the historical dimension of liquidity. This is to say that the theory of liquidity crisis serves as a plausible idealism that is expressive of the practice of central banking in that it can be used to resolve the crisis after the fact by bringing the instruments at the centre of the crisis into the ambit of central bank evaluation through its function as the LOLR. The dynamic and historical nature of the definition of what is liquid means that although the discourse of liquidity crisis cannot actually be used to explain the cause of crisis and is unlikely to be able to be used to intervene in accumulation, as it actually occurs through financial innovation, it still provides a way to address any new crisis through remedial practices. Its main significance is as an ideological rationale to enable the central bank to resolve these types of problems

58 *Liquidity and abstraction*

in practice without having to contest the practice of accumulation that gives rise to these contradictions.

The discourse of liquidity crisis is therefore part of the dialectic of liquidity whereby what is liquid is contingently determined according to historical necessity after the event of crisis. The theoretical interpretation of financial crisis in terms of liquidity dynamics now needs to be historicised and understood as part of the historical process whereby liquidity is constituted in all of its composite moments.

Conclusion

The perspective on Mehrling's work outlined in this chapter highlights how the very paradigm in which Mehrling calls for a dialogue between liquidity theorists and modern finance is unbalanced given that liquidity crisis is no longer used as a rationale to justify regulation of capital accumulation but to justify remedial action in light of the self-annihilation of capital in the context of the realisation of its own contradictions. Governments and central banks remain sideline players in shaping the dynamics of financial markets supporting their expansion and development in new abstract dimensions, including by providing a safety net to market participants engaged in the construction of the world in terms of risk through financial innovation.

The illustration of the relationship between the FIH and contemporary liquidity dynamics outlined in this chapter shows how the FIH appears to have lost its critical edge. It needs to be reassessed and reinterpreted in a way that engages with the way in which liquidity is a historical phenomenon. In fact the contemporary definition of liquidity now exceeds Post-Keynesian frameworks seeking to highlight the importance of liquidity in terms of endogenous money processes. These frameworks have a limited ability to understand how abstract risk calculation now constitutes the form of capital. Indeed, the argument above suggests that in order to define contemporary liquidity dynamics, including recovering the possibility of not just a dialogue, but a critique of modern financial economics as inspired by Minskyian analysis depends on further conceptualisation of the historical materialism of risk. The next chapter pursues these leads and seeks to reinterpret Minsky's FIH as providing a structural account of the drive towards risk trading also recasting it as a critique of the EMH. In doing this Chapter 5 seeks to explain contemporary financial crisis, including the crisis of 2007–08 in terms of the historical materialism of risk.

Notes

1 Although the efforts of Kregel (2008) and Wray (2008a) may be closer to Minsky's approach (especially Minsky [2011]) than Mehrling's work, I chose Mehrling as the "Minsky of the present" because he has the same level of awareness as Minsky about the problem of history for theory. The significant changes that Minsky made to Keynes indicate that he is aware of the problem that history poses for theory. Mehrling deviates from Minsky and is not the faithful adherent of Minsky's ideas that those from the Levy

school may be. However, I think Mehrling is trying to do something similar for Minsky, as to what Minsky did for Keynes. He is therefore engaged in the same type of intellectual endeavour as Minsky in the same spirit as Minsky and is therefore perhaps not a pure Minskyian but is on some level more faithful to Minsky's efforts in that he displays a similar vision of financial instability combined with historical awareness.

2 See Miller (1992) for an account of the influence of financial theory on financial innovation.

3 See, for example, the US League of Savings Associations submission to the Committee on Banking, Housing and Urban Affairs United States Senate (1976:126).

5 Arbitrage as a historical structure shaping the US financial system

The previous chapters illustrated how the problem of explaining financial crisis relates to finding an epistemological basis from which to make sense of how to apply a necessarily universalizing theoretical framework (Minsky's FIH) to an inherently historically particular event. The last chapter analysed the attempt of Mehrling (2000, 2011) to do this in relation to Long Term Capital Management (LTCM) and the crisis of 2007–08. It argued that Mehrling's work suffers from the same problem as much of Minsky's work, as explored in Chapter 2, in that it is a form of hermeneutic idealism using crisis as a rationale for why we need heterodox economic theory rather than consideration and explanation of the historical event of crisis and the historical forms in which it manifested itself.

The question then is how to bridge the gap between theory and event. This chapter addresses this question in the application of Minskyian analysis, seeking to underpin it with a structuralist epistemological basis. Structuralism, as outlined by Jameson (1981), switches the metaphysical priority around between subject and object (as explored in the second dialectic titled "crisis theories – subject and object" described in the introduction of this book). Instead of exploring the problems of theory in terms of addressing the question of whether the subject can grasp the object, structuralism sees the subject itself (or its invocation in relation to certain historical events) and its inevitable errors in conceptualising its object as a projection of the object. The object causes the subject. The task is then to find a way of interpreting the subject in terms of the logic of the object that expresses it. This can be done through historicizing the act of theorizing. Indeed, Jameson (1981:9) urges us to "Always historicise!"

This chapter explores a structuralist reinterpretation of Minsky's (1972, 1982a, 1982b, 1986) work in light of the development of a structure of "arbitrage". This reinterpretation is an attempt to use Minsky's ideas to help explain contemporary financial crisis and critique modern finance. Arbitrage is prevalent in contemporary finance. Indeed it is central to equilibrium thinking outlined in the Efficient Market Hypothesis (EMH). This chapter argues that it is also of central importance to interpreting the contemporary relevance of the Financial Instability Hypothesis.

The practice of "arbitrage" connotes the generation of profits not from an increase in productivity but instead by buying one thing in a particular market

Arbitrage as historical structure 61

and selling another thing which is fundamentally composed of the first thing, into another market where it raises a higher price. Liquidity is arbitraged by banks, which in the 3/6 model seek to borrow from depositors at 3 per cent and lend to borrowers at 6 per cent. Risk is arbitraged by hedge funds that assess correlations on the risk of volatility affecting the value of a stock or bond and whether this is appropriately reflected in the price of the asset compared with other, similar assets.

In this chapter I interpret Minsky (1972, 1982, 1986) as describing the development of a structure of arbitrage in the US financial system in terms of the development of new forms of funding liquidity in the US financial system. The interpretation of Minsky in terms of the practice of arbitrage provides a common denominator with the discipline of modern finance, which places arbitrage processes at the centre of its vision of how equilibrium develops in financial markets (Barberis and Thaler 2002, Fox 2009). The focus on arbitrage gives us a common standpoint from which we can explore how Minsky's FIH and the EMH can be said to relate to each other, even though the two theories are derived from different historical epochs and in relation to analysis of different financial instruments. Articulating the common standpoint between the FIH and the EMH enables us to develop a framework that illustrates a way to understand how risk and liquidity are related: the common denominator enables us to interpret risk as a form of liquidity.

The second part of this chapter provides an analysis of the financial crisis of 2007–08 as a crisis in this structure of arbitrage in the US financial system in terms of a critique of the EMH. This chapter is the first in a series of chapters in this book (Chapters 5, 6, 7) that seek to explain the financial crisis of 2007–08 by illustrating how "risk", although an abstraction, can also be considered to be a form of liquidity and how this makes liquidity dynamics, as described in Minsky's FIH, immanent to risk trading.

Arbitrage as a structure underpinning the generation of liquidity

This chapter contends that Minsky's FIH, when historicised, can be read as describing the development of a structure of arbitrage. This perspective is useful because it illustrates how risk can be interpreted as a form of liquidity and hence the FIH can be extended to explain more contemporary financial crises in risk calculation and trading.

The first three sections of this chapter seek to illustrate how Minsky's FIH, whereby financial units would transit from hedge to speculative to Ponzi units under the influence of liquidity dynamics, can be re-interpreted in terms of the more fully developed processes and forms of arbitrage of the current financial system that the historical developments that Minsky was analysing eventually resulted in. Although this attempt at re-interpretation may at first appear teleological,[1] it is still a tenable proposition because at the heart of the development of the US financial system and the liquidity dynamics that Minsky was analysing is a process of financial innovation whereby financial units arbitraged new, more

62 *Arbitrage as historical structure*

flexible forms of capital against prior less fungible forms of capital (Wojnilower 1980:278). This important historical insight illustrates how the development of financial forms therefore tended to occur in a structured way according to the need to find more streamlined ways of arbitraging prior forms of capital.

Here I am expanding on the meaning of arbitrage as understood by financial economists who subscribe to the EMH and see arbitrage as an isolated trading practice (buying shares of cheap companies with a certain risk profile and shorting more expensive companies that have the same risk profile). I see arbitrage as having three dimensions: (1) arbitrage is a practice conducted by financial units; (2) arbitrage is a practice that needs to be historicised, in that its contemporary practice needs to be understood in terms of its contemporary manifestations, which exist as a result of a historical process whereby the techniques and instruments of arbitrage were created; (3) arbitrage is also *history itself* in that arbitrage, understood as a form of accumulation, was generative. Arbitrage was generative of financial forms and practices that facilitated making profits through arbitrage. Arbitrage was the principle of modernisation of the US financial system, hence arbitrage occurs through development of the form of capital to further the scope for arbitrage.

The multiple components to the practice of arbitrage, particularly the last one, have significant theoretical ramifications that I will explore later in this chapter. The EMH affirms the first isolated and immediate instance of arbitrage as having a stabilizing influence on the financial system creating incentives towards more correct pricing, but the EMH can only do this by denying the other two more historical dimensions to the phenomenon of arbitrage.

Before exploring these theoretical issues associated with the conceptualisation of arbitrage in the EMH, it is useful to describe in fuller detail the additional two rarely theorised aspects of arbitrage in relation to Minsky's FIH. How is arbitrage history? Minsky's FIH, when historicised, can be interpreted as illustrating how arbitrage was a structural feature of the US financial system: arbitrage was the form of crisis as well as the principle of development shaping new forms of capital. The growth dynamics described in Minsky's FIH are an expression of the historical structuring principle of arbitrage in that the development of arbitrage opportunities conditioned liquidity dynamics, turning hedge units into speculative and eventually Ponzi finance. The transition of financial units through these states of varying fragility occurred not so much as a result of expectations, but it corresponded to a pattern whereby financial units innovated in order to arbitrage new, more flexible forms of capital against prior less fungible forms of capital.

Indeed, a summary of this historical process could start with a consideration of the work of Wojnilower (1980), who writes that the financial dynamics of the long 1970s were defined in terms of the transformation of the form of capital by a process whereby various financial innovations emerged that removed the "speed limits" on credit growth. The speed limits were generally quantity and price controls (such as Glass–Steagall, Regulation Q) governing the flow of credit into a particular market, that is, limitations on the mobility of capital. Financial units developed financial innovations to help them arbitrage these limitations taking

Arbitrage as historical structure 63

positions in assets using less restricted sources of funding liquidity. This tended to increase asset prices, inspiring further investment. This meant that financial units moved from being hedge units to being speculative units as described in Minsky's FIH.

In the context of innovation around these limits, regulators would often intervene to reimpose these speed limits, extending them to cover the new instruments, causing a credit crunch (Krippner 2011, Minsky 1986:16–76, Wojnilower 1980). When the government acted to restrict the flow of new forms of credit via innovation, these restrictions would turn speculative units into Ponzi units which could no longer afford to hold all of their positions on their books. These units would then sell position to make position precipitating a systemic crisis. The prospect of crisis then tended to cause regulators to reverse course and "deliberately reshape the financial structure so as to prevent a reoccurrence of that particular form of credit supply interruption" they had orchestrated (Wojnilower 1980:277). This often involved legitimising the financial instrument associated with the credit crunch, adding it to the stock of guaranteed instruments that the Central Bank would loan against (Minsky 1986:16–76, Wojnilower 1980:277). In this way, liquidity crises came to be the means of development of the new form of capital. Liquidity crisis was exemplary of a historical structure of arbitrage.

Three stages in the development of arbitrage

In developing this proposition about a structure of arbitrage in US finance, it is useful to think in terms of three stages in the development of arbitrage that can be identified. Although these stages are not necessarily totally distinct and the forms of arbitrage characterising each stage also occur in later and prior stages to some extent, the stages capture the pattern of systemic dynamics and are illustrative for the purposes of analysing the structure of arbitrage and its effect in US financial history. These stages are suggestive of the generative historical role of arbitrage.

Pre-arbitrage (1945–1961)

In the post-war era there was disintermediation as the form of financial crisis rather than liquidity crisis (Krippner 2011, Wojnilower 1980). Disintermediation was endemic to the post-war form of capital but was transcended by arbitrage.

Disintermediation occurred as investment increased, creating competition for funding liquidity among US financial units, including the US government. The US government would often find it hard to fund its activities without increasing the interest rate on bonds above the levels that regulators permitted the banking system to offer. When the interest rate moved above Regulation Q levels, money would flow out of the banking system into the bond market to chase higher yields there. The outflow of money from the banking system would create disintermediation in the banking system leading to a credit crunch. The US financial system was afflicted by this problem a number of times throughout the 1950s and early 1960s (Krippner 2011, Wojnilower 1980).

64   *Arbitrage as historical structure*

Minsky (1972) observed how the commercial banking sector in particular developed solutions to these credit supply interruptions. The private sector developed financial innovations that arbitraged funding liquidity sources that were constrained by Regulation Q. These financial innovations provided the private sector with less price constrained short-term cheaper sources of funding liquidity. The commercial banks could continue to supply capital using these new instruments, such as the certificate of deposit when the price of capital exceeded Regulation Q (see Mehrling (2011:89–90) and Wojnilower (1980) for further description of the arbitrage as the spur to financial innovation in the US financial system).

Institutional and instrumental arbitrage (1966–1982 or the "long 1970s")

The development of new financial innovations, which Minsky (1972, 1986) gave significant attention to analysing, involved arbitraging new, more liquid instruments against prior forms of capital. What Minsky was not historically placed to recognise but that we can now see is that in this role arbitrage came to be the principle of institutional and instrumental development as well as accumulation. The tendency to liquidity crisis that Minsky (1972, 1986) identified in the US financial system was a result of a re-evaluation of the value of capital assets in the economy in light of the emergent possibility of using cheaper short-term funding in the money markets to hold these assets, that is, the result of the development of new techniques of arbitrage on asset price values.

Minsky (1986:230–245) described how the problem was that the new system of evaluation was somewhat reflexive. The emergence of the money markets transformed the capacity of the US financial system to generate credit. The allocation and cost of credit which had previously been politically determined and directed came to be a matter of value determined by the search for yield, that is, making position in an asset which would enable its owner to reliably pay the floating cost of debt back to the financial unit lending to it. Lenders innovated in the extension of short-term, cheap, money market debt to financial units borrowing from them. Funding was often purchased from other financial units rather than sourced from the lender's own deposit base and was therefore not immediately constrained by Regulation Q price controls. The transformation of the capacity to create debt in the context of a hitherto quantity constrained low interest rate environment tended to increase capital asset prices, generating reflexive bubble dynamics.

The contradictions described in the FIH generated a new round of financial innovation in the US financial system that became prevalent in the 1980s. In the context of an increasingly high interest rate environment, the funding liquidity of the thrifts (that after all relied on an asset base of 30 year low interest rate mortgages for income) became compromised. The development of securitisation enabled the thrifts to substitute funding liquidity (deposit capital) for market liquidity (investment capital) in the capital markets (Minsky 2008). Securitisation markets developed throughout the 1980s to include commercial property and eventually other forms of debt, such as student loans so that most capital assets

Arbitrage as historical structure   65

were brought into comparison with one another through funding via more liquid capital markets (Ranieri 1996).

Hence, capital assets given their now homogeneous form as securities were exposed to evaluation of their comparative yield by long-term investors via the capital markets in the first instance and then short-term money markets interested in the liquidity yield between the cost of short-term debt and long-term rates in the second instance as hedge funds began to borrow to take positions in these assets (Wojnilower 2001).

Arbitrage through abstraction (1982–2008)

The processes characterising this era are closest to the idealised process of rational development of pricing financial risk as described in the EMH (which will be discussed in more detail below). These processes involve the development of the abstraction of risk by which all capital assets come into comparison with one another according to the volatility of their yield (Bryan and Rafferty 2011). This era is also characterised by incentives towards financial innovation and more risk calculation in order to get a more fine grained calculation of the level of risk in order to profit through calculative sophistication (Mehrling 2000). This epoch is characterised by intensification in the evaluation of assets through arbitrage (Bryan and Rafferty 2006).

The development of derivatives markets makes this era distinct from the prior eras in that the intensified evaluation process occurs in terms of the market liquidity of assets, beyond consideration of funding liquidity dynamics, through the abstraction of risk transfer (Bryan and Rafferty 2006). The derivative plays an integral role in hedging against market risks (interest rate risk, currency risk, credit risk, operational risk, etc.) in the global economy. For example, a derivative gives its holders a means of diversifying risk inherent in ownership of a certain capital asset such as a US government bond. Buying a derivative introduces an element of abstraction into the portfolio because the purchase of the derivative to hedge ownership of an asset allows the owners of the derivative to transform their potential yield from being the bare yield of the capital asset to being a function of the yield they get through holding capital asset A, minus risk A, minus premium A. The resulting portfolio therefore constructs the potential for yield according to the abstraction of risk transfer with the objective of securing a greater yield through accurately calculating and hedging risks.

These were processes that Minsky could not have been expected to have foreseen and which transcend Minsky's own framing of the FIH. Minsky's FIH is a historically constrained study of liquidity dynamics associated with the transformation of the US banking system from a system where arbitrage was expressly prohibited by interest rate ceilings (Regulation Q) towards a system that by necessity permitted arbitrage. The more fully developed processes and forms of the current financial system which the historical developments that Minsky analysed eventually resulted in relate to Minsky's theory in terms of explaining the development of the current form of capital out of the context and contradictions that

66 *Arbitrage as historical structure*

Minsky describes with his FIH. Minsky's work is therefore immanent to modern finance in that it helps to explain the development of the contemporary form of capital and the re-occurrence of liquidity crisis in the context of the breakdown of the abstraction of risk that constituted this form of capital.

Arbitrage through abstraction as a critical lens on the EMH

The previous chapter analysing the work of Mehrling (2000) explored how he viewed abstraction in finance in negative terms, dismissing it as immaterial. This chapter and the rest of the book refer to abstraction as a historical process. From this perspective an idea/abstraction can have a degree of historical materialism or agency in shaping the conjuncture. This section focuses on exploring the historical materialism of the idea of risk in finance.

However, before moving on to an analysis of the role of arbitrage through abstraction in the financial crisis of 2007–08, it is useful to revisit the theoretical implication of the above analysis of arbitrage as conditioning the form of capital for equilibrium thinking about the financial system that tends to idealise arbitrage. This type of thinking about risk played a role in allowing the crisis to occur and deserves a critique that illustrates the historical problems associated with it.

Indeed, the EMH seeks to illustrate how arbitrage in financial markets enables the more efficient allocation of capital, therefore negating further opportunities for arbitrage. The negation of arbitrage opportunities occurs as market participants seek to detect when two stocks with similar fundamentals are mispriced relative to one another. After identifying this type of pricing discrepancy, they will buy the cheaper stock and short sell the dearer stock until the value of the stocks reaches a comparative equilibrium reflecting fundamentals (Barberis and Thaler 2002).

The EMH therefore views financial markets as a discounting machine that works to internalise information about the fundamentals of a company's operations into its stock price. The practice of arbitrage binds stock prices to fundamentals so that stock prices will tend to follow a random walk reflecting the release of information about the conditions of supply and demand in relevant markets that the company operates in (Fama 1970, Malkiel 1987).

Although there is some empirical evidence for this proposition, many economists have critiqued this view on the basis that it contradicts the contemporary reality wherein many market participants are involved in arbitrage of one form or another and price movements exhibit less stability than the EMH predicts (Barberis and Thaler 2002, Lo 2005). These types of criticisms moved the debate to focus on whether the evidence supported strong or weak versions of the propositions in the EMH before the debate was rendered absurd in the wake of the financial crisis of 2007–08 that revealed systemic mispricing of risks (Fox 2009).

Mehrling (2000) notes that traders such as those at LTCM tended not to concern themselves with these empirical debates but rather treated the EMH as describing a set of incentives towards the development of better risk calculation techniques. Practitioners tend to see a potential for arbitrage that is then eventually negated

Arbitrage as historical structure 67

through a historical process of calculative development in the markets (see MacKenzie 2003 for an example of this process). The discovery of mispricing will create incentives to arbitrage and those with more efficient pricing models will prosper at the expense of those who are unable to grapple adequately with how to price risks in the market. In this way the capacity of financial units to deal with risk is continually increasing. Practitioners therefore treat the EMH as a philosophy of rationalisation rather than a description of reality as it actually is.

Whether this rationalising process results in any actual form of rationality has been vigorously contested. The EMH has been criticised by both Keynesian economists and behavioural economists in terms of its conclusions about the rationality of markets. Keynesians argue that investors can have a liquidity preference that will drag the economy into a downturn, and behavioural economists have illustrated how bubbles can be rational given the limits to the rationalising process of arbitrage. Indeed, in some circumstances the limits to arbitrage are framed by the liquidity preference of lenders who retract funding, forcing rational arbitragers such as LTCM to dump their positions or seek bailouts (or similar arrangements) that enable them (or a more liquid proxy) to hold their position for the duration of the mispricing (Barberis and Thaler 2002).

However, to dismiss the EMH in terms of the irrationality of financial markets is therefore to engage with the EMH on its own terms given that it is a theory about how to construct rationality in the world. The EMH is a theory of financial development where crisis borne of irrationality drives development of rationality. This means that the prescriptions of the EMH, its affirmation of market processes, have a peculiar ubiquity no matter whether the initial assumption is that financial markets are rational or irrational. The EMH incorporates the apparent failure of its prediction of rationality in that the fact that investors can be observed to have behaved irrationally and succeeded in making money provides informational feedback that should further the development of the techniques used to calculate asset prices by providing new precedents and scenarios that illustrate how asset prices can move and value is constructed.

This discussion about the effects of arbitrage on the form of capital above indicates that there is another dimension to the assumption of rational markets that is outside of the capacity of the EMH to deal with so easily as it does with the critique stemming from the apparent irrationality of financial markets. Although it is probably easy enough to find examples of the rationalising function of arbitrage in the history of financial markets (as Fama 1970 does), this leads us to a prior question about the transformation of the financial system into a system where it is possible for arbitrage as described in the EMH to serve a central rationalising role. There is a need to explain not only the rationality of isolated instances of arbitrage, as the EMH does, but the emergence of arbitrage as a central practice in the financial system, including instruments that can facilitate rational arbitrage. Ideas such as the EMH need to be evaluated not only for the internal logic of their prescriptions, which can be incredibly gripping, but also in terms of the logic of their actualisation in the world in terms of the instruments and institutions that shape the conjuncture in which they are being deployed.

68 *Arbitrage as historical structure*

The subject in need of consideration, when we talk about the failure of the market for asset-backed securities (ABS) in 2007–08 is not only the theoretical failings of arbitrage-based theories of rational markets that informed and rationalised the trade in these instruments, but the historically determinate development of arbitrage as a financial practice and its material effects on the world. An understanding of the crisis therefore involves the development of a somewhat paradoxical understanding of the economy not in terms of the logic of economic theory itself but in terms of the gap between economic theory and the world – the effect of economic theory on the world and the actions that bring the prescriptions of economic theory into being in an inevitably changed form to what the ideal suggests.

The historical emergence of arbitrage as a practice does not necessarily have a neutral or rationalizing effect on asset prices, contrary to what the EMH suggests in relation to arbitrage as a discrete financial practice conducted by individual institutions. The act of arbitrage as it is historically constructed implies that trading units are bringing a capital asset into the orbit of a larger, more fungible pool of capital for evaluation. Arbitrage is premised on constructing a *commensuration* in forms and valuation techniques and hence the possibility of arbitrage between previously segmented (national, sectoral, etc.) forms of capital. The real "efficiency" of markets is that more and more things are made commensurable, not that claims can be made about the Pareto optimality of prices.

The process of market extension can make it look as if the adoption of new financial instruments and pricing techniques create an increase in value of the capital asset because of an increase in the integrity of valuation techniques, what is commonly called risk management or diversification; however, the source of value lies in their constructive dimension, in the historical transformation of the form of capital and growth of a new mode of evaluation through the extension of markets for risks.[2] For instance, the development of securitisation in particular is a telling example of the story of the construction of arbitrage opportunities. In this case, it occurred through the creation of a secondary market for the underlying capital assets, housing, which in itself could not be easily arbitraged with other capital assets or traded in the financial system given the peculiarities of the mortgage contract (Wojnilower 1980:301–302, 1985:351–352). The creation of mortgage-backed securities (MBS) involved a process of abstraction whereby what came to be commodified was not so much the underlying asset, the house itself, as the mortgage borrower's ability to pay the mortgage, that is, the yield on the asset (Bryan, Martin and Rafferty 2009).

ABS were first developed by the American investment bank Salomon Brothers, which developed a way in the early 1980s to bundle mortgages together into a form of risk that resembled US government bonds. By bundling mortgages together in this way, Salomon Brothers ensured that the paper they created included a government guarantee and was structured in a form that facilitated its commensuration with other established assets, including Treasury bonds that enjoyed a large market as a relatively "safe" and liquid financial asset. The bankers at Salomon Brothers hoped to do this to help increase the amount of credit flowing into mortgage finance to take advantage of the difference in yield on mortgages above Treasury

Arbitrage as historical structure 69

bonds while only taking on similar levels of risk (Lewis 1989, Ranieri 1996). This transformation marked the beginning of a significant increase in volume of investment in housing in the US economy that coincided with a dramatic increase in asset prices (Wojnilower 1985). This indicates how arbitrage considered in terms of its historical dimensions as commensuration between forms of capital rather than in its idealised state as risk management can create liquidity and economic growth.

This picture of the generation of liquidity through commensurating different assets can take us beyond a critique of the EMH towards an insight that is conceptually useful in resolving the paradox of the build-up of the apparent inaccuracy of financial calculations of risk underpinning instruments such as derivatives. It helps to explain how these instruments and the calculations underpinning them could have veracity for a time but lose it in liquidity crisis. We can gain a new perspective on the puzzle of the materialism (or agency) of financial calculations, which I argued in the previous chapter that Mehrling (2000, 2011) framed but failed to solve, if we interpret the agency of financial instruments not so much in terms of the veracity of the calculation, but rather in terms of the role that calculation plays in the integration (or commensuration) of markets and capital assets to extract value from instrumental and institutional silos. As alluded to in the section above titled "Arbitrage through abstraction", financial calculation should be understood as a development in the form of capital.

The paradox of financial calculation is that its value stems from the role it plays in the commensuration of different types of capital assets rather than actual positive risk management. But the practice of calculating risks could not serve as a proxy for liquidity if it was understood that it was the introduction of calculation (as commensuration) into the system itself that generates a wave of liquidity. This would mean that the system of liquidity was understood to be inherently self-referential. Recognition of this fact constitutes the form of crisis of risk calculation. If the calculation was not held to be a legitimate approximation of actual risk, it could not serve as a form of commensuration whereby market liquidity (and hence funding liquidity) is actually generated, apparently giving accuracy, at least for a time, to the prescriptions of the EMH whereby risk calculation and arbitrage are said to lead to the more efficient allocation of capital. The EMH cannot according to its very nature provide an account of how liquidity dynamics rendered by arbitrage processes work in a way that subverts its prescriptions. Yet it is the effects of the actualisation of the EMH, the historical construction of arbitrage, which ultimately generates liquidity in the contemporary financial system, giving the EMH the appearance of a positive epistemology with traction on the governance of financial risk.[3]

Arbitrage in the era of derivatives: a novel approach to explaining the financial crisis of 2007–08

The reading of Minsky's FIH and the EMH above illustrates how there is a tendency towards the expansion of the field of liquid and commensurable instruments in the US financial system as a means of furthering the expansion of

70 *Arbitrage as historical structure*

arbitrage-based value forms. These developments can be interpreted as having been integral to the growth dynamics in the US financial system. In our era, which has recently been subject to the largest liquidity crisis since the Great Depression, the exploration of the crisis can usefully be conducted in terms of looking at how the creation of new financial instruments to further the practice of arbitrage experienced a systemic breakdown in 2007–08.

The previous chapter explored the implications of how, quite paradoxically, Post-Keynesians such as Mehrling take liquidity crisis as a testament to their theories about the irrationality equilibrium models of financial processes without providing a description or even a method for discerning the systemic nature of liquidity beyond Keynes's focus on the concept of liquidity preference and associated concepts of uncertainty and expectations. It is more useful to interrogate the relationship between modern finance, financial innovation and the conjuncture, all of which have combined to constitute the contemporary form of capital, in order to gain an understanding of liquidity than a reference to Keynesian economic theory. The liquidity crisis of 2007–08 should be explored as some sort of end point to, or at least an historical event within, a process involving the structuring and transformation of capital via the process of securitisation and the creation of new derivatives that facilitate the transfer of risk associated with these securities in order to conduct arbitrage on an abstract level.

The imperative of the language of 'risk' as a system governing capital accumulation is not, as it is commonly understood, to always give a right and accurate prediction of future yields. The systemic role that it plays lies in oblique relation to its overt technical function of quantifying market risk. Systemically speaking, derivatives and the discourse of risk calculation provide tools of comparison to commensurate the value of different assets against one another in order to facilitate exchange and generate liquidity. The previous system of liquidity relied on a system of loans. In contrast the new system of liquidity relies on a system of comparisons and arbitrage processes whereby volatility can be managed and any deficits offset. Hence, volatility is rationalised according to deft use of the tools of risk management and market processes. The new system of commensuration processes facilitates the "self-transformation" (Bryan and Rafferty 2013) of capital, enabling movement of value across a myriad of asset classes in the context of volatility (this relationship between the concept of risk and liquidity will be discussed in greater detail in Chapter 6).

The new system of liquidity of risks "across asset forms" has come to replace the older system of liquidity of monetary flows. This means that investment in a capital asset that is expected to generate a high yield in the future may not preclude investment in a venture that will give a short-term yield. Often the capital asset can be posted in the repurchase agreements market for cash. A financial model will be used to assess the risk associated with a financial asset and determine its price accordingly (Derman 2011:193–194). The asset can then be posted in the repo market to borrow funds that can then be deployed at short notice in a higher yielding short-term venture. Once the short-term venture is completed and the financial unit is liquid again, it can repurchase the original capital asset.

Arbitrage as historical structure 71

The description above of liquidity in terms of commensuration corresponds with the recent work of Robert C. Merton, co-inventor of the Black-Scholes-Merton formula for pricing derivatives, who sees derivatives as a tool for expanding the amount of capital that companies can mobilise to generate value. He argues that derivatives are "tools that enable companies to free up [equity] capital and get it working to create value" (Merton 2005:1). Derivatives enable a company to transfer risks that add no value, ensuring that they use equity capital more exclusively to insure against risks that the corporation is best placed to generate value by managing. The 'unbundling of risk' expands liquidity and lowers the discount against the future (the interest rate) on borrowed capital (Greenspan 2000).

The liberation of liquidity from instrumental and institutional categories via its abstraction as risk was at least partially responsible for the "giant pool of money" phenomenon that intensified the search for yield in the lead-up to the crisis (Blumberg et al. 2008, Lysandrou 2011b). The "giant pool of money" represented an historic development of a system whose logic was novel and was very effective at generating liquidity. A decade earlier, the now infamous hedge fund Long Term Capital Management, with Robert Merton and Myron Scholes at the helm, pioneered this approach to the generation of liquidity before going bust in 1998 (MacKenzie 2003, Mehrling 2000). A decade later a new generation of hedge funds investing in ABS, such as collateralised debt obligations (CDOs) and credit default swaps (CDS) pursued a similar strategy of liquidity creation up until August 2007 before their collapse. These hedge funds collapsed as a run on the money market funding of these financial units occurred when the concept of risk, the fulcrum of this new form of abstract formless risk-based liquidity, lost coherence in relation to ABS (Patterson 2010).

Before drawing conclusions from this analysis of the historical dimension of arbitrage, it is interesting to summarise the picture of how the creation of liquidity through abstraction can work in order to exemplify the various roles that derivatives play in the financial system ranging from a risk management tool for individual financial units such as hedge funds and how this can become contradictory to the role that derivative markets play in constituting a new abstract form of liquidity.

The following illustrative description below of the implications of abstract forms of arbitrage for liquidity dynamics is informed by the work of Adrian and Shin (2009), Borio (2004, 2009a) and Brunnermeier (2009) on liquidity dynamics in risk trading systems. The picture of liquidity dynamics provided by these authors is familiar. The development of new markets for financial innovations (which are typically secondary markets in derivatives or MBS for some underlying asset) goes through a gestation period where there is not much liquidity for the instruments and hence premiums are high in order to borrow to hold these instruments. However, after a period in which the markets show some resilience, more trading units enter the market, increasing its liquidity. These trading units sometimes use these markets for speculative purposes and other times use them for hedging and insurance "like" purposes or as an alternative source of liquidity. Whatever the intention of the trading unit, the result of the increase in activity is

72 *Arbitrage as historical structure*

increased market liquidity, giving lenders who finance trading units to hold positions in these markets some confidence that these units will be able to smoothly enter and exit their positions. Hence market liquidity tends to lower funding liquidity prices, which increases the size of the position that trading units can maintain and consequently increases their profits. This tends to lead to capital gains and further profits and leverage as more trading units vie to hold these positions.

The inherent error in derivatives, their contradiction, lies in relation to the contrast between arbitrage as a discrete practice conducted by financial units (the object of analysis of the EMH) and the historical dimension of arbitrage as liquidity. Indeed, the functioning of derivatives markets in constructing new, more abstract forms of evaluation can catalyse credit cycle dynamics by generating increased market liquidity for securities by allowing the transfer of their risks. The practice of transferring risks to other units better able to hold them could reduce the cost of funding liquidity to that unit which would increase the "liquidity yield"[4] – the spread between the cost of borrowing to hold these securities and their yield.[5] When this occurs on a systemic basis, it generates capital gains for securities holders because there is typically, with a drop in funding costs, an expansion of demand to hold these types of positions. This would further decrease the risk profile of these securities.

However, this virtuous cycle contains a paradox. It must be noted that what is actually being capitalised through the use of derivatives here is the liquidity of the securities, not their efficacy for transferring risks. Financial units are using derivatives to generate a liquidity yield, which is actually an indirect form of income not directly linked to the function of the derivative in risk management, that is, assessment of the performance of the security, but rather stems from the reflexivity between market liquidity and funding liquidity market dynamics. The liquidity yield is not an inherent property of the securities, even though it is accounted for as such by risk models in the measure of implied volatility of derivatives and securities.

This contradiction is a reflection of a systemically reflexive process – the deepening and broadening of commensuration in the system through risk transfer. The use of derivatives and other instruments of risk transfer such as ABS CDOs (which will be described and explored in detail in the next chapter) as a form of insurance for an individual financial unit is therefore fraught because their use is also a key practice at the centre of a new system of liquidity generated by the integration of markets through the construction of arbitrage opportunities, via risk transfer.

This contradiction between the use of derivatives as a risk management tool on the level of the individual financial unit and as a means of commensuration bringing an asset into the orbit of a larger, more liquid pool of capital poses a paradox. The paradox is that the meaning of the use of derivatives is not determined on the level of the individual financial units despite their instrumental function in risk management but is externally attributed according to the development and extension of the relations of risk transfer in the surrounding financial system according to the possibility of making money through a "liquidity yield".

Arbitrage as historical structure 73

There is an emerging body of empirical evidence that describes how financial innovation was used to generate a "liquidity yield" in the lead-up to the financial crisis of 2007–08. Adrian and Shin (2010) have provided a series of brilliant research papers exploring the pro-cyclicality of the balance sheets of investment banks, looking at them as amplifying mechanisms that created what they call, using a term adopted from Claudio Borio (2008), the "risk taking channel". The risk-taking channel emerged as a result of increases in liquidity yield and capital asset values on MBS and ABS CDOs that enabled banks to take on a number of marginal loans[6] (Adrian and Shin 2009:7).

Adrian and Shin argue that the pro-cyclical nature of investment bank and trading unit balance sheets, which were heavily involved in purchasing MBS and ABS CDOs, largely explains the liquidity and hence the credit crunch of 2007–08, writing:

> The supply of credit is the outcome of increased leverage of the banking sector as a whole. As balance sheets expand, new borrowers must be found. In other words, new assets must be generated that will fill expanding balance sheets. When all prime borrowers have a mortgage, but still balance sheets need to expand, then banks have to lower their lending standards in order to lend to sub-prime borrowers. The seeds of the subsequent downturn in the credit cycle are thus sown. . . . This explains two features of the sub-prime crisis – first, why apparently sophisticated financial intermediaries held the bad loans on their own balance sheets, rather than passing them on to other unsuspecting investors. Both facts are explained by the imperative to use up slack in balance sheet capacity during an upturn in the credit cycle.
>
> (2009:12–13)

As asset prices increased, the balance sheets of investment banks achieved a state of self-sustaining accretion, sucking in more and more loans to be added to the balance sheet, the capital gains on which generated an enlarged space for new credit creation. The crisis appeared to occur when it became obvious that capital had been allocated in an arbitrary way according to these hidden dynamics and the income on the underlying capital assets would not support their stated yield and hence value of the securities and their price collapses.

Conclusions on the historical construction of arbitrage and the EMH

In this chapter, the reading of the historical materialism of arbitrage, drawn from historicizing Minsky's FIH, gives us new grounds for reflection on the central role of arbitrage and developing a historicizing critique of the EMH. The analysis here has revealed new critical potential of the FIH in relation to contemporary financial crisis. The EMH describes a functionalist process of modernisation where rationalisation via arbitrage aids the integrity of the whole. However, if we treat arbitrage as a structuring agent, then its results are not functionalist, as in

74 *Arbitrage as historical structure*

the EMH, but rather phenomenological. The practice of arbitrage is part of what Žižek (2012:459) calls the "self-preproduction of capital", which I interpret here as a process whereby the search for yield is conducted through the construction of new financial instruments and business models according to the need to generate yield via arbitrage. The realisation of value through arbitrage occurs through the reproduction and development of the form of value in instruments that enable arbitrage to be conducted more effectively.

The process of financial growth then is self-referential, defined in terms of the generation of financial forms that expand the scope and intensity of arbitrage. This is a form of rationalisation that goes beyond rationality understood merely as a framework for understanding the world towards being an active agent in the constitution of the world in its own image. Rationalisation proceeds on a self-referential and phenomenological level rather than as an expanded field of logical operations.

The EMH therefore should not be read as a theory of the operations of the financial system, but rather the apparent relevance of the EMH should be explained as a result of the dialectical process whereby the US financial system was given its form in a response to the growth of pricing discrepancies between different forms of capital that increased the scope for arbitrage (see Krippner 2011, Wojnilower 1980). The apparent relevance of the EMH is an expression of the structuring nature of arbitrage in the US financial system. The EMH is a symptom of arbitrage as modernisation and liquidity crisis as the means of development of new forms of capital. The EMH is part of the dialectics of liquidity crisis.

Notes

1 This may be considered "teleological" analysis because this interpretation is attributing a purpose to apparently contingent developments as informed by the final form in which these developments resulted. It is based on interpreting a theory developed in the main to explain the US financial system of the 1970s from the perspective of what these developments resulted in as of the early 2000s.
2 A number of mainstream financial economists with iconoclastic tendencies such as Brown (2006) and Edmunds (1996, 2003) admit that the extension of more liquid risky forms of capital creates a wealth effect, arguing that this is a desirable side effect of financial innovation.
3 This illustrates how this form of liquidity is tied to a particular type of science which has been rendered moribund by the collapse of the underlying historical process of transformation that gave some veracity to the abstractions that the science posited. In this sense liquidity needs to be theorised in terms of different forms of historically emergent rationalities.
4 This term was first described on page 52 in Chapter 4.
5 For an interesting discussion of this process in relation to the US financial system circa 2000, see remarks by Chairman Alan Greenspan on technology and financial services before the *Journal of Financial Services Research* and the American Enterprise Institute Conference, in Honor of Anna Schwartz, Washington, DC, April 14, 2000, http://www.federalreserve.gov/boarddocs/speeches/2000/20000414.htm.
6 Adrian and Shin (2009) argue that the basis of the risk-taking channel is a gap between long-term interest rates and short-term interest rates. This gap is explicable in terms of the growth of market liquidity enabling financial units to increase their reliance on short-term finance.

6 Sociological interlude

Calculation or commensuration?

The development of securitisation has meant a shift from banks as the main intermediaries that provide liquidity towards the derivative form to generate liquidity (Mehrling 2011:79–91). The analytical significance of this development is that the question of the form of capital assets is no longer separate from the question of how liquidity is generated in the credit system. Banks were institutions that made profits on the spread between the cost of their borrowing and the cost of their lending. Liquidity management was a means to make profits guaranteed by state underwriting. Should individual financial units mismanage their interest rate spreads in a way that jeopardised systemic stability, the state guaranteed their book. However, in a commodified credit system with securitisation and derivatives, liquidity is, as we have seen in the financial crisis of 2007–08, seemingly determined via the veracity of the calculations involved in the construction of commodified credit risk instruments such as mortgage-backed securities (MBS), collateralised debt obligations (CDOs) and credit default swaps (CDS) and the profitability of holding these instruments (MacKenzie 2011).

Indeed, a new school of sociological analysis, the social studies of finance, has sprung up around the observation that liquidity now has an abstract conceptual dimension to it in hyper modern financial markets which trade financial instruments whose value is calculated using risk models (Beunza and Stark 2010; MacKenzie 2006, 2009, 2011; Poon 2009). This shift from the institutional focus on banks to the abstract construction of risk products opens up new approaches to liquidity. These studies generally focus on the epistemology underpinning liquidity, commenting on the ever-increasing scope and hence material importance of calculative knowledge. Calculation appears to have agency in finance. MacKenzie (2006, 2009; MacKenzie, Muniesa and Siu 2007) even claims that financial calculation is to some extent "performative" of financial market dynamics. Hence there is a consequent need for a reflexive sociological understanding of the nature of calculation in finance.

In this chapter I want to argue for a different interpretation of the relationship between calculation and liquidity to the one offered by MacKenzie and other scholars working in the social studies of finance. The explanation of financial crisis as the failure of quantitative models includes a near direct attribution of agency to the models flattening out the subtle historical role that modelling has on

76   Contextualizing financial performativity

liquidity. If we look at the failure of modelling in light of the historical materialism of financial innovation, it forces us to consider causation of financial crisis in different terms to the simple failure of modelling as either a positive or performative endeavour, considering instead the contradictions inherent in modelling as transformation of the form of capital.

This chapter explores this line of argument with a particular focus on the work of probably the leading scholar on the social studies of finance, Donald MacKenzie. The sociologist Donald MacKenzie provided an account of the role aberrant risk calculation played in the credit crisis of 2007–08 in his paper *The Credit Crisis as a Problem in the Sociology of Knowledge* (2009).[1] The title of this working paper references an earlier paper by the sociologists Carruthers and Stinchcombe (1999) titled "Liquidity as a Problem in the Sociology of Knowledge". The act of renaming draws attention to a shift in the nature of liquidity in a securitised credit system as having an epistemological component, while at the same time implying explanation of the credit crisis as a liquidity crisis. It therefore illustrates the need to develop a new conceptual understanding of liquidity, in the historically specific form it took in the lead-up to the crisis, in terms of the calculation of risk.

It is interesting to note then, given MacKenzie's reference to liquidity in the title of his paper, that the version of MacKenzie's paper on the credit crisis published in the *American Journal of Sociology* vol. 116, No. 6 retreats from the conceptual discussion of liquidity in terms of performativity provided in his earlier paper focusing mainly on presenting the empirical detail of his research on the credit crisis. This is a pity because the revised article retreats from addressing the main conceptual issue that needs to be addressed to explain the credit crisis – the relationship between financial calculation and liquidity, in favour of describing the imperfect nature of financial engineering which enabled destabilising arbitrage opportunities to emerge. In fact, the words performativity and liquidity do not appear in the text of MacKenzie (2011) at all despite being the focus of his earlier working paper.

Given that the analysis of this book focuses on the relationship between risk and liquidity, it is more useful to analyse MacKenzie's earlier more conceptually focused work on performativity and the credit crisis (MacKenzie 2009 rather than MacKenzie 2011) that overtly attempts to grapple with the epistemological dimension to liquidity. This chapter critiques the shortcomings of the concept of performativity vis-à-vis the explanation of the credit crisis in order to illustrate how liquidity and the performativity of financial markets are inherently historical phenomena. This is to say that historical developments, as constituted by financial calculation in its role in commensurating hard to compare capital assets, is "performative" of liquidity rather than financial calculation.[2]

One of the interesting paradoxes in the work of MacKenzie (2009) relates to his use of the sociology of knowledge framework whereby, after describing the epistemological nature of crisis, he returns to description of a long list of means by which the flawed calculations were associated with a bubble. There is a gap between what MacKenzie can explain in terms of epistemology and the manifestation of the crisis in terms of liquidity dynamics. This presents a useful point

Contextualizing financial performativity 77

of entry to the question of how to understand liquidity and risk in the era of the derivative and securitisation that I will pick up on after describing the work of MacKenzie (2009) on the development of asset-backed securitisation in America.

Collateralised debt obligations

MacKenzie's work provides an innovative analysis of the technical details of the construction of financial instruments such as asset-backed securities (ABS) CDOs that emerged on the early 2000s and blew up in the financial crisis. MacKenzie emphasises the creation of the ABS CDO market, emerging through a process of convergent evolution to the collateralised mortgage obligation (CMO) via the development of CDS derivatives. In turn, the ABS CDO market merged with the CMO market when MBS were packaged into CDOs – a case of "interbreeding" between convergent species of financial instrument. The MBS and the CDO were both forms of securitisation constructed according to a similar logic of risk transfer, albeit initially developed in relation to different forms of debt using different risk transfer arrangements.

Mortgage securitisation was developed prior to the development of ABS CDOs. Mortgage securitisation was conducted by aggregating mortgage debts into a special purpose vehicle (SPV) otherwise known as a Real Estate Mortgage Investment Conduit (REMIC) that uses the interest payments on the aggregated debts as a source of yield on ownership of liabilities of the SPV. These liabilities are structured as fixed income securities that are designed to be sold to investors such as pension funds. The first type of security that showed a resemblance to the MBS involved in the financial crisis of 2007–08 was created in 1983 by Salomon Brothers and was the CMO. The tranche structure of the CMO was innovative because it provided a form of risk buffering called "overcollateralisation". This means that the volume of money to flow into the structure is higher than the volume in the underlying securities to take account of potential defaults. The excess volume would create a "residual" security, which was designed to behave as a buffer and would not normally receive payments unless the mortgage pool performed particularly well. This security would normally be held by the issuing firm. The value of this structure was that it protected the senior security holders from mortgage prepayments should interest rates drop and borrowers refinance cancelling their initial debt (Mason 2008a).

JP Morgan designed the first CDO to securitise loans it had issued to large corporations in 1992. The CDO is a form of securitisation structure that works on a slightly different logic to the CMO/REMIC structure using correlation modelling to manage risk rather than overcollateralisation. Correlation modelling mitigates risk through diversification. Hence, the first CDO "BISTRO" included the debts of 307 corporations, including a number of corporations in different industries who enjoyed AAA debt ratings (but no mortgages). The market for CDOs based on corporate debt preceded the development of the market for asset-backed (mortgage based) CDOs by nearly a decade. It wasn't until around 2001 that the ABS CDO market began to experience accelerating growth and to assume similar proportions to the corporate CDO market (MacKenzie 2009:38–40).

78 *Contextualizing financial performativity*

Financial instruments include an inherent risk to them in that they promise future income streams in exchange for principal payments of capital in the present. In Minsky's terms, they are "a money now for money later" deal (Minsky 1977:142). What is crucial to those investing in these instruments is that, as fixed income securities, MBS and CDOs deliver their expected yield. Yet because at their core these securities involve commitments to pay future, as yet unearned income, they are fundamentally risky and hence difficult to price.

There is a question of what anchors not only these instruments themselves, which I will discuss further shortly, but also the broader economic role they play; in particular, how they serve to link the present to the future. Up to the 1970s, it could be said that the Keynesian state connected the present with the future for the purposes of investment. The state managed macroeconomic aggregates and monetary aggregates to target stability over time. But with many of these roles now ceded to the market, the connection between the present and the future ceases to be an intentional policy agenda; instead it is more the unplanned consequence of a web of market practices including risk calculation.

MacKenzie identifies two different ways, or "meta-devices", participants can use to understand financial instruments such as securities and bonds and therefore confidently enter into exchange with some knowledge about their risk. The first meta-device MacKenzie describes is a "canonical mechanism" that transforms financial instruments into standardised and homogeneous commodities. Part of the production of canonical mechanism markets is the creation of public and open knowledge about the instrument. Carruthers and Stinchcombe (1999) argue that the government-sponsored enterprises (GSEs) were responsible for making the market for MBS into a canonical mechanism market through providing a government guarantee. Instruments that are defined by a canonical mechanism are traded in transparent and open markets organised with a double auction where bids are broadcast to all participants. This enables market participants to enter into exchanges with confidence about the qualities of the product that they are purchasing and clearly see its prevailing value in the market (MacKenzie 2009:11–12).

The second way that investors can learn and gain assurance about the qualities of a particular financial instrument is by reference to another epistemological "meta-device" – the risk rating system. The risk rating agencies have been operating since the beginning of the twentieth century providing assessments to investors about the creditworthiness of corporations. Their role in providing assurance about risk has been enshrined in legislation requiring pension funds to construct their portfolios in relation to certain risk benchmarks assessed by the ratings agencies. The ratings agencies also use a common risk management methodology derived from principles of academic finance including the capital asset pricing model and the Black-Scholes-Merton model, which many Wall Street banks and hedge funds use to manage their risk levels. Hence their assessments provide important practical inputs into a large range of investment and risk management decisions in the financial system (MacKenzie 2009:14–17).

The ratings agencies attributed ratings to MBS and CDOs by evaluating their structure, especially the model that the CDOs' designers used to construct the security comparing it against the rating agency's own benchmark model for CDOs. Rating the corporate CDO was relatively straightforward. There was a wealth of historical data in relation to the correlation between the debts of different corporations from the corporate bond market as well as correlations between the stock prices of different corporations in different industries to draw upon to form statistical inferences that defined risk. JP Morgan designed the CDO in light of this rich source of data on the value relations between corporations. They were confident that they could use these data to calculate the likely impact of defaults and build in appropriate risk layering to take account of these risks using correlation data to build diversification into the securities they designed (MacKenzie 2009:25–33).

However, although the financial engineers at JP Morgan and elsewhere eventually found a way to apply this structure to MBS, the meta-devices used had to be subtly different because of the specific character of mortgages and MBS. For example from the mid-1990s onwards the MBS market split into two markets, the prime and the sub-prime market. The prime market retained its definition as a "canonical mechanism market", while the sub-prime market, the market for risky mortgage borrowers, emerged through processes that defined it via various meta-devices associated with the risk rating system. The financial unit building an MBS typically performed modelling on the mortgages underpinning private label and sub-prime securities to quantify its risk using the Fair Isaac Corporation (FICO) credit score. From around 1996 onwards, managers of CMOs started to construct their securities taking into account the credit risk of the borrower, quantified using their FICO score. Riskier borrowers were generally charged a higher interest rate to compensate for the higher default risk they posed to lenders, a practice which formed the basis of the emergence of the market for sub-prime mortgages, i.e. mortgages issued to borrowers with a lower credit score (MacKenzie 2009, Poon 2009).

In fact, the mortgages that underpinned the CMOs produced prior to 1987 were mostly insured by the US government so that only a limited risk buffer was needed. The CMO allowed only three layers of tranching to be included. It was only with the introduction in 1987 of the REMIC, a special purpose vehicle used to warehouse, structure and then sell MBS, that tranching became more widespread and sophisticated (Ranieri 1996). Tranching enabled lenders to include riskier mortgages in the asset pools underlying their securitisations while maintaining AAA credit rating by including more sophisticated risk calculations and purchasing insurance on the riskier tranches (MacKenzie 2009, Poon 2009).

The market for MBS was a "canonical mechanism market" up until the introduction of the REMIC, which enabled investment banks to design more varied MBS structures. The mortgages included in CMOs were standardised mortgages issued on the basis of guidelines set by Fannie Mae and Freddie Mac which ensured that the mortgages were eligible to be insured by Ginnie Mae, receiving a government guarantee on the underlying mortgage payments should the borrower default on the mortgage. However, the flexibility of the REMIC necessitated that the ratings agencies play a larger role in the assessment of MBS. "Private label"

80 *Contextualizing financial performativity*

MBS, securitised by private financial institutions rather than the GSEs, were produced with the intention of delivering a certain yield while achieving a desired risk rating that provided some assurances about the quality of the underlying collateral (MacKenzie 2009:17–25).

In fact, sub-prime MBS and CDOs relied primarily on the meta-device of the risk rating system to make them knowable. MacKenzie states that the ratings and the MBS and ABS CDO securities were "co-produced" because the risk rating system was so important in facilitating their sale (MacKenzie 2009:22). If the mortgage pool, or collection of MBS, deviated in its characteristics from the benchmark pool of the ratings agencies, the designer would commonly purchase additional credit enhancement (insurance) to provide increased assurance about performance and hence yield of the underlying asset pool (MacKenzie 2009:22).

Interestingly, the production of risk ratings for ABS CDOs was actually done through the development of a "canonical mechanism" that defined the ABS CDO using sophisticated calculative techniques associated with trading over-the-counter (OTC) derivatives. This was because the ABS CDO – although functioning similar to an MBS – was constructed according to the logic of risk transfer. MacKenzie writes

> The derivatives team brought with them a crucial new tool and a different evaluation culture. The new tool was the credit default swap, an idea developed in the early 1990s at Bankers Trust, a bank that was characterised by its emphasis on viewing a financial instrument as a "bucket of risks" (as an interviewee involved put it), each component of which could be made into a tradeable instrument. Just as interest-rate swaps make the risk of interest rate movements tradeable, a credit default swap separates out the credit risk involved in lending and makes it into a tradeable instrument.
>
> (MacKenzie 2009:27)

The CDS on corporate debt became a "canonical mechanism market" by the late 1990s as the International Swaps and Derivatives Association standardised contracts and many investment banks traded CDS on hundreds of corporations (MacKenzie 2009:28).

A CDS is an OTC derivative, generally designed by an investment bank to enable its clients to diversify their credit risk. It enabled a financial unit that decided that it had too much of a certain type of risk, say exposure to the debt of the auto industry, to transfer some of the debt it owned from auto companies to another financial unit, exchanging it for debt for exposure to the debt of tech companies. Hence, both financial units were able to diversify their risks through the use of credit default swaps.

CDS are "synthetic" instruments in that they are not a real form of ownership of any underlying asset but rather a form of derivative that gives its holder exposure to price movements in the underlying asset (in this case, credit risk). Their synthetic nature is explicable in terms of their role in hedging.

These synthetic swaps were priced in a way that was similar to the Black-Scholes-Merton model for pricing derivatives using a related function called the

Contextualizing financial performativity 81

Gaussian Copula formula. The Gaussian Copula formula attributed the value of a synthetic CDO according to three variables, including the probability of default on the asset, the recovery rate for each asset and the credit correlation of the underlying income streams (MacKenzie 2009:29). These variables were therefore the key ingredients that helped to make the product knowable and hence manageable.

This formula could also be used for design purposes, enabling the derivatives desk to replicate the performance of a "cash" ABS CDO, giving its holders exposure to the performance of a pool of MBS or even another ABS CDO. This also meant that financial engineers could blend synthetic and cash CDOs to create new ABS CDOs. Synthetic CDOs were significantly faster to create because no MBS had to be purchased and packaged but rather just modelled. The CDS expanded the capacity of the CDO market. Instead of CDO managers having to buy loans or bonds for their asset pools, as in other forms of securitisation, they could simply sell protection on them via CDS, using the premiums they received from the swaps to pay the investors in the synthetic CDO securing diversification through synthetic means (MacKenzie 2009:28).

The "evaluative culture" associated with the trade in CDS was crucial to the development of ABS CDOs because it provided a solution to the empirical problem of how to price ABS CDOs. MacKenzie provides a detailed account of the technical difficulties involved in pricing ABS CDOs in an empirical fashion, which made it prohibitive, including the vast number of mortgage cash flows that needed to be accounted for. Given these difficulties, the market eventually moved towards adopting a method of valuation that was inductive, i.e. it used the Gaussian Copula formula, the model for pricing CDS and synthetic corporate CDOs, and worked backwards from this to attribute a price to all ABS CDOs, whether they were synthetic or otherwise. This technique included a "guesstimation" of the correlation between defaults in the underlying MBS to arrive at a valuation and risk rating for the overall CDO by plugging these inputs into the Gaussian Copula Formula (MacKenzie 2009:38–46). This type of correlation modelling on MBS had never been performed before given that it was irrelevant to prime MBS that were guaranteed by the GSEs. and the sub-prime market was newly emergent.

The problem was that the underlying assets of CDS and synthetic corporate CDOs are different from the underlying assets of MBS: the correlation coefficient of mortgage defaults turned out to be much higher: if one mortgage borrower defaults, it is more likely that others will default than is the case for CDS and corporate CDOs. This formula therefore provided an inaccurate calculation of the correlation of default in the underlying MBS that formed the basis of the CDOs, making the risks seems smaller than they actually were. It therefore generated unwarranted liquidity in the markets for the underlying securities that formed the basis of ABS CDOs, in particular, the market for sub-prime MBS and therefore sub-prime mortgages. The two meta-devices – the risk rating system and the canonical mechanism, the Gaussian Copula formula used to construct synthetic CDOs – which were supposed to make the financial instrument knowable, actually occluded accurate risk calculation rather than facilitating it, because of their

82 *Contextualizing financial performativity*

success in creating liquidity for the underlying assets of the CDO through, somewhat ironically, "more accurate" risk management[3] (MacKenzie 2009:51–60).

MacKenzie (2009:58–67) describes the failure of the CDO in terms of its apparent success at generating liquidity through risk calculation in terms of the concept of "performativity" or rather "counter-performativity". MacKenzie adopted the phrase "performativity", which had previously been theorised as a financial phenomenon by Barnes (1983) and Callon (2006), in relation to his findings from a previous study, *An engine, Not a Camera* (2006), about the price movements of derivatives upon the introduction of the Black-Scholes-Merton model for pricing derivatives. In his previous study MacKenzie interpreted financial models as "engines producing market behaviour and prices, instead of 'cameras' which merely depict what is ontologically given" (Engelen et al. 2010:9).

Counter-performativity occurs when the introduction of a model, instead of causing prices to tend towards its prescription, causes them to deviate away from the model because of some reflexive connection with the underlying subject of the model, thereby transforming the validity of the facilitating calculation. Alternatively a developing awareness of the effects of the model on prices can become a form of inside knowledge about the price dynamics of a commodity that can be "gamed", causing counter-performativity (MacKenzie 2009:67). This happens when, for example, market participants take positions on where they think the Black-Scholes-Merton price will move.

MacKenzie's conceptualisations here are important to note, taking us back to the starting point of this chapter, including its focus on risk as abstraction. MacKenzie illustrates how the pricing of assets does not work in a formulaic way, wherein the abstraction is not merely an abstraction, but treated as an ideal type – that is, concrete but representative. What I am seeking to do below is draw out the implications about evaluation as an issue that involves on the one hand thinking of risk as an abstraction, but on the other hand thinking about asset pricing assets in ways that see it as more than merely concretisations of the abstraction. Viewing it only as a concretisation of the abstraction creates a misunderstanding of what this type of abstraction actually is – a historical phenomenon (see the previous chapter that discusses the structure of arbitrage as generative of these types of abstractions).

In the later parts of his analysis, MacKenzie (2009) turns to a comprehensively detailed account of the mechanics of how these flawed calculations created a bubble. This makes his work a source of rich and comprehensive description of the crisis. But it reveals limitations too, for his mode of analysis is unable to spur any further conceptual insight into the nature of the crisis and liquidity beyond stating that the isolated error of calculation that he describes caused such enormous imbalances in the system. These problems in MacKenzie's analysis become the focus of the remainder of this chapter.

The identification of critique below is not to diminish the important contribution of MacKenzie (2009) to the understanding of financial calculation. The work of MacKenzie (2009) provides an astoundingly clear window into the technical dimensions of the crisis and a very suggestive conceptual discussion of

Contextualizing financial performativity 83

performativity. The implications of his analysis draw implicitly on the modern sociological dictum of the risk society, that making un-reflexive claims to quantitative knowledge about the world is fraught, that the world is broader than formal models and that the social scientist's role is to provide reflexivity to improve society's ability to deal with the complexity of modernity by highlighting any epistemological lacunas in our technical knowledge about the world. However, to fully appreciate how abstraction is not sociological but historical, we must move beyond MacKenzie's framework.

The problem with "particular" forms of explanation[4]

The problem with MacKenzie's account of liquidity as epistemological is that the explanation of liquidity as a systemic phenomenon, a property of the system as a whole, needs to extend from the totality to the particular rather than the other way around. For example, the problem with MacKenzie's sociological approach is that the burden of proof is enormous to verify that the cases he forensically investigates are not exceptions, but are indeed systemic. MacKenzie is seeking to explain a systemic event using a methodology that is averse to systematisation.

This problem in the construction of MacKenzie's argument can be expressed in terms of set theory. If a set is composed of a variety of other subsets, then explanation of a single one of the subsets cannot explain the character of the larger set unless it is also explained how changes in that set determine the behaviour and character of all the other subsets, thereby transforming the character of the larger set.

Nonetheless, MacKenzie (2009:71) is aware of this problem and claims that he is not attributing causation but is naming the character of one of the subsets relevant to the explanation of the totality. Yet his caution is belied by his ambitions for the discipline of sociology, and named in the title of his article, where he defines the problem of credit crisis as a problem in the sociology of knowledge rather than situates the problem of the sociology of knowledge in the credit crisis. MacKenzie's article should more correctly be called "sociology of knowledge problems in the credit crisis".

The reason for this quibble is that although MacKenzie (2009) provides some brilliant research, the problem with his conceptualisation occludes proper explanation by confusing the "universal" and the "particular". The sociology of knowledge problem needs to be solved in the context of a broader explanation of liquidity rather than the other way around.

Indeed, as the previous chapter argued, financial calculations do not have veracity because of predictive power but because the practice of financial modelling commensurates different forms of capital in order to make them into a form of liquidity. For the purposes of analysing liquidity, including the credit cycle and systemic risk, it is the role that the phenomenon of calculation plays in commensuration, in light of risk as a system of liquidity, that needs to be explored rather than the ways in which technical calculation is an inherently social and hence mutable phenomenon. The mutability of financial calculation is inherent

84 *Contextualizing financial performativity*

to the duality of effects of financial calculation in terms of its epistemology (risk measurement) and phenomenology (commensuration).

Emmanuel Derman, the physicist turned quantitative analyst turned financial epistemologist, notes that models are generally used for an accounting function rather than an exchange function, i.e. models are used "to turn . . . opinions about the future into an estimate of the appropriate price to pay today for a security that will be exposed to that imagined future" (Derman 2011:193). Hence, the significance of the practice of modelling is in enabling illiquid assets to be treated as liquid capital for the purposes of borrowing in the money markets. The holders of these instruments can bring forward the principal value of the asset should they experience a need for liquidity. This is a crucial part of the collateralised borrowing system for securities such as MBS, where there is not a large and active market for these securities outside of particular issues of MBS or ABS CDOs and hence the emphasis is on borrowing against these securities, or transferring their risks via CDS rather than reselling them.

Indeed, when we recognise the function of modelling in terms of generating liquidity through commensuration, it helps us to make sense of some of the contingency in MacKenzie's story of the construction of the model used to price ABS CDOs and his critique of the shortcomings of financial engineering as sociological. It reveals how calculative contingency was not the cause of the crisis but was rather a symptom of the crisis.

MacKenzie provides a detailed empirical account of the technical difficulties involved in pricing ABS CDOs: difficulties that made credible pricing prohibitive. The computing power needed to track the myriad layers of cash flows in a CDO in order to calculate the effects that different cash flow scenarios would have on price was gargantuan. Given these limits, the market eventually moved towards adopting a method of valuation that was inductive, i.e. it used the Gaussian Copula formula, the model for pricing CDS and synthetic corporate CDOs, thereby creating an abstract representation of the instrument's prices according to the principles of risk transfer, and worked backwards from this to attribute a price to all ABS CDOs whether they were synthetic (an abstract representation of the instruments) or actually linked to the cash flows from the underlying mortgages. This technique included a "guesstimation" of the correlation between defaults in the underlying MBS to arrive at a valuation and risk rating for the overall CDO (MacKenzie 2009:38–46).

The "guesstimation" involved made the risks in owning CDOs seem smaller than they actually were. It therefore generated unwarranted liquidity in the markets for the underlying securities that formed the basis of ABS CDOs, in particular, the market for sub-prime MBS and therefore sub-prime mortgages. The two "meta-devices", the risk rating system and the canonical mechanism, which the Gaussian Copula formula used to construct synthetic CDOs, while supposed to make the financial instrument knowable, actually occluded accurate risk calculation rather than facilitating it (MacKenzie 2009).[5]

But behind the apparent contingency and calculative enthusiasm associated with the adoption of the Gaussian Copula formula is the centrality of derivative-based

Contextualizing financial performativity 85

thinking in expanding the boundaries of the system of liquidity. The telling aspect of this story is the use of abstract calculation to incorporate assets with a complex structure into the system of liquidity and thereby make them liquid. The agency is, at least initially, in the spread of the form rather than the plight of predictions.

We could interpret the fact that derivative pricing techniques were used to price ABS CDOs, as making sense in light of the fact that in the last instance the most comprehensive and permanent way of making these securities liquid, i.e. getting them off-balance sheet and recapitalising, was in terms of risk transfer via CDS. The function of a credit default swap was similar to the repo market in that it enabled the holder of a security to pay a premium to swap the credit risk for cash, thereby transferring the risk onto another trading unit. The difference between the repo market and the market for CDS is that posting the securities in the repo market only moves them off balance sheet for a time, whereas a CDS should cover the risks in an ABS CDO for the life of the security.[6] The price of a CDO was therefore probably determined in relation to the means whereby it was made commensurate with money or other capital assets via risk calculation, reflecting the means whereby these securities were incorporated into the risk-based system of liquidity.

Similarly if we understand the adoption of the correlation from the corporate CDOs into ABS CDOs in light of the system of liquidity, it is not so confounding. A low correlation may have seemed reasonable to the designers of these securities given that the underlying incomes servicing the debt on CDOs were derived, to some extent, from the mortgage payments of labour whose employment source was probably roughly as diversified as various different corporations in different sectors of the economy were.

Furthermore, the main alternative measure of the correlation of ABS is their accumulation in portfolios compared with some approximation of beta and the price of the haircut in the money markets. ABS were being heavily accumulated in portfolios and the haircut in the money market for these securities was also low, suggesting that they were low risk. This suggested that low risk is important because the ratio between the haircut in the repo market and the premium in the CDS market could not have changed too much, in that the source of both of these prices is the risk of ABS CDOs. If these two quantities diverge, they are violating one of the central axioms of modern finance – "the law of one price" (Derman 2011:164–166). This would create arbitrage opportunities that would raise the price of the cheaper means of gaining exposure to ABS CDOs and lower the price of the more expensive means. Given that the price of the haircut was generally low during this period for AAA rated ABS, then it possibly made sense to impute a low correlation/premium for ABS CDOs.

In contrast to MacKenzie's cultural explanation of error (epistemology) the significance of the Gaussian Copula formula is that its design and implementation was so evidently conditioned by the system of liquidity as a derivative based system. The crisis therefore occurred on another level to epistemology as a problem of finding an anchor for commensuration between different forms of capital assets in light of the failure of the model to provide a basis for the capitalisation of ABS

86 *Contextualizing financial performativity*

CDOs in a way that was reflexive about the historical materialism of financial innovations in the system of liquidity.

This critique of MacKenzie's atomistic approach to explaining the technical causes of the crisis of 2007–08 illustrates that we need to develop a method of theorising the system as a whole at the same time as analysing the role of the form of the derivative or associated financial instrument in order to understand liquidity in the contemporary market system. Liquidity is performative of financial calculation and financial instruments.

What does this mean for MacKenzie's argument about the performativity or counter-performativity of financial models? It reveals a lack of a historical dimension to his argument. MacKenzie idealises performativity as an explanatory framework for contemporary financial collapse. However, given that liquidity is systemic, then it is only in the historical sense, in the transformation and development of the system of liquidity, that financial calculation could be performative of liquidity.

Performativity revisited

The argument of the chapter so far has looked at how MacKenzie framed the issue of performativity as opposed to liquidity. The issue that MacKenzie highlights in his analysis is that the epistemology of risk preceded its phenomenology. The ratings category and the pricing model were created prior to the actual ABS CDO as a financial product, leading MacKenzie to claim that financial calculation is performative (or counter-performative), implying that liquidity is epistemological. But this instance of performativity needs to be contextualised. What factors in the conjuncture framed the apparent performativity of financial modelling? The above section sought to invert MacKenzie's analysis by illustrating how liquidity could be considered to be performative of financial calculation.

It is worth exploring further how liquidity can be performative of financial calculation in the midst of the appearance of performativity of financial calculations generating liquidity. This is a historical problem. Financial calculation plays an important role in the contemporary financial system by constituting assets as risks in order to incorporate them into an abstract system of liquidity. Historically speaking, the fact that the reconstitution of assets as risks brings them into the orbit of a more mobile form of capital, thereby increasing their liquidity and ability to act as an effective store of wealth, cannot be extricated from the veracity of the predictions underpinning the constitution of these assets as risks. The transformation of phenomena, the act of commensuration, precedes quantification/abstraction and influences its veracity.

In the case of the performativity of the risk calculation, it is the historical process of transformation, the steady incorporation of assets into the new mode of evaluation of risks, as it occurs and spreads throughout the economy by the creation of new securities and derivatives and their exchange and valuation according to risk models, in which the agency in the system lies. The value of the parts, i.e. each MBS or CDO or CDS and the veracity of its constitutive calculations,

Contextualizing financial performativity 87

are by definition not independent of the systemic dynamics of the whole, i.e. the spread of liquidity through calculation as commensuration.

The capacity of the discourse of risk to increase values is typically claimed to be a result of the diversification of risks. However, the diversification of risks can, when viewed in terms of the historical materialism of the financial system, rather than from an organisational level as the most prudent means of constructing a portfolio, only be a dependent variable whose utility cannot be assessed in a way that is separate from the historical construction of assets in terms of risk. Prior to the act of diversification, there needs to be a historical process whereby capital is constituted as a risk that can then, only after this historical event of constitution as a risk, be utilised as a source of diversification. Diversification itself is a constructive historical process. Indeed, some financial economists now recognise that once an asset class is understood as a potential source of diversification, then it has lost its ability to actually perform diversification. The act of identifying something as a source of diversification presupposes its inclusion in the system of risks ultimately implying correlation. This suggests that it is the historical process of expansion of the sphere of risk rather than the isolated and atomised activity of financial units that include assets in portfolios as a source of diversification that is important to the dampening of risk and ongoing generation of liquidity (Bernstein 2012). It is useful to understand financial value as determined through an expansion of the sphere of risk itself rather than as a result of the everyday practice of risk calculation.

Another way of expressing this is to say that the modern system of liquidity poses a paradox. The paradox of liquidity is that it is impossible to tell the difference between whether an increase in liquidity is a result of the success or failure of risk management because in the initial phases of the introduction of new risk management technologies, given their role in commensuration, the effect on the market is the same – that the interest rate, as the discount against future volatility and credit risk, will tend to go down and consequently prices will tend to go up as it becomes cheaper to borrow – a situation which characterised the "great stability" in the lead-up to the crisis of 2007–08.

The veracity of risk calculation is profoundly historically contingent because whether or not risk management transforms a portfolio of capital assets into a more effective store of wealth is determined as much by the subsequent rate of introduction of financial innovations because the commensuration of risks ensures the continuation of liquid conditions ensuring retroactively that prior risk calculations retain the appearance of veracity and increasing sophistication of risk management as it is by the initial integrity of risk calculation given that value is defined in terms of historical transformation. Therefore, instead of attributing causation of liquidity crisis to isolated aberrant miscalculation of risk, in a way that tends to imply that the problems with these types of calculations can be addressed by socialising our viewpoint on them, it makes more sense to attribute causation of liquidity crisis to a breakdown in a historical process of transformation of the form of capital, that is, of 'financialisation' (Bryan et al. 2009).

The gap between the phenomenon of risk – the spread of the derivative form – and the accuracy of the quantification involved in the construction of the financial

88 *Contextualizing financial performativity*

instrument expresses the fact that financial calculations now have an inherent forward looking quality to them, and not just in the sense of pricing a calculable future, but also anticipating the future development of new innovations in order to maintain the integrity of calculations that underpin the transformation process. These calculations are reflexive in that they inherently assume the liquidity that is generated by the transformation of the system that they themselves help to orchestrate, and their use implies its projection into the future.

Conclusion

The question is not so much that the underlying predictions in the CDO were wrong: a problem of miscalculation. It could be argued that they are always inherently wrong given the limits of deductive rational knowledge in categorising the world and the self-referential nature of new financial instruments that were developed in the context of an economy subject to financial innovation. Instead it was as much a problem of as "historical development" understood as the transformation of the conjuncture in a way that facilitates the movements of value via the spread of relationships that facilitate intensified financial calculation and enable these calculations to appear right.

This means that Shiller (2008) is astute to say that the democratisation of risk management tools such as house price derivatives that are offered to mortgage borrowers may have helped to mitigate the crisis. These products may have helped to extend the program of financial innovation underpinning liquidity conditions. However, the significance of the development of 'democratising' products is not that they offer plausible solutions to financial crisis, given the increased calculative burden that they impose on households, but that they are an indication of the logic of how liquidity is generated on a systemic basis through financialisation as extending the boundaries of risk calculation. In this context, it is worth noting the brilliant insight of Mike Lewis' *The Big Short* (2010) – which tracked the hedge funds which "smelled the rot" and were able to successfully hedge against the crisis – is that he shows how the edifice of liquidity had become self-negating, i.e. that the construction of liquidity (successfully hedging against volatility) had come to involve an awareness of the fact that the system of liquidity did not have a foundation and should therefore have been shorted. Financial innovation ran up against the limits of its own internal contradictions.

The next chapter attempts to develop this picture of liquidity as successive waves of historical transformation via financial calculation. Chapter 7 characterises the issue of liquidity in the US financial system in the lead-up to the crisis of 2007–08 in these terms, identifying three phases of risk management. I then compare these phases of risk with the hedge, speculative and Ponzi finance described in Minsky's FIH in order to evaluate the usefulness of using Minsky's FIH in the analysis of the growth and collapse of the US sub-prime mortgage market. The analytical intention of this chapter is to show how Minsky's FIH can be considered to be immanent to modern finance.

Notes

1 This paper is now hard to find online, but can be located by searching with the wayback machine on MacKenzie's staff page at Edinburgh University. The paper is also presumably available from Donald MacKenzie (email: D.MacKenzie@ed.ac.uk), although it is no longer listed on his website http://www.sps.ed.ac.uk/staff/sociology/MacKenzie_donald.

2 The critique in this chapter may be considered slightly unfair to MacKenzie given that the restatement of his 2009 research in the *American Journal of Sociology* in 2011 is stronger and harder to criticize. However, dealing with his ideas as outlined in his working paper does help us to proceed further conceptually, including developing a better understanding of the concept of performativity as applied to financial markets. Hence the critique of MacKenzie's now withdrawn working paper is conducted in this chapter in order to extend and give new grounding to the concept of performativity that underpins much of his work.

3 In particular, a number of hedge funds such as Magnetar identified the problem and gamed the rating system. These hedge funds calculated that the yield on shorting the AAA rated tranches of CDOs would outweigh the loss they took on purchasing the residual layer of the CDO and the lower tranches. Hence these financial units facilitated the creation of a large proportion of the market for CDOs in light of the profitable possibilities of their failure. Indeed, many CDOs were constructed by investment banks in consultation with these hedge funds using particularly bad MBS tranches to pay a large yield upon their failure. The CDOs were sold to investors because of the large yield they generated in relation to their risk rating using the income from CDS premiums on upper tranche CDOs to synthetically replicate these tranches in other CDOs (Bernstein and Eisinger 2010, Lewis 2010).

4 I use the term "particular" in the Hegelian sense whereby Hegel argues that the particular must always be explained in the context of the universal, the totality (Levine 2009).

5 In particular, a number of hedge funds such as Magnetar identified the problem and gamed the rating system. These hedge funds calculated that the yield on shorting the AAA rated tranches of CDOs would outweigh the loss they took on purchasing the residual layer of the CDO and the lower tranches. Hence these financial units facilitated the creation of a large proportion of the market for CDOs in light of the profitable possibilities of their failure. Indeed, many CDOs were constructed by investment banks in consultation with these hedge funds using particularly bad MBS tranches to pay a large yield upon their failure. The CDOs were sold to investors because of the large yield they generated in relation to their risk rating using the income from CDS premiums on upper tranche CDOs to synthetically replicate these tranches in other CDOs (Bernstein and Eisinger 2010, Lewis 2010).

6 A debt instrument sold on a financial market may not have to be registered as a debt security up until 13 months, after which the money market contract needs to be registered as a debt security with the SEC rather than as a loan.

7 Recent financial instability in the US mortgage market

The three phases of risk

Many economists have noted how the description of Ponzi financial units in Minsky's Financial Instability Hypothesis (FIH) bears an uncanny resemblance to indebted sub-prime borrowers (McCulley 2009, Wray 2008). No income no job or assets (NINJA) loans common in the sub-prime boom placed borrowers in a position of accumulating debt offset only by the accumulation in the value of the asset they used the debt to purchase, to be realised when borrowers sell the property. This likeness to Ponzi finance implies that the borrowers in the housing market, or the US housing market as a whole, had at some stage moved through Minsky's other stages of finance, including hedge financing and speculative finance before becoming Ponzi financial units.

However, the movement through the categories of hedge and speculative finance, as propelled by liquidity dynamics, was not an obvious feature of the lead-up to the sub-prime crisis (Dymski 2010, Kregel 2008). The housing finance market is a peculiar fit with Minsky's work because leveraging to make position in a market where prices are going up depends on the invention of new forms of mortgage contracts and corresponding mortgage-backed securities (MBS) to enable the leverage cycle to proceed. Indeed, the quantitative processes of risk management inherent to these mortgage contracts are supposed to take into account that these cycles will occur and mitigate them with risk buffers and margins of safety (Kregel 2008).

Hence, with the development of securitisation, the institutional structure of housing finance was changed to the extent that a liquidity dynamic, conceptualised in terms of expanded cash flows between institutions as the Keynesian income multiplier kicks in warping expectations, no longer defined US housing finance. Instead, as explored in this book (see Chapters 1 and 3) and in other places (Bryan, Martin and Rafferty 2009, Jacobides 2005), it came to be characterised by sale of mortgage debt in markets as facilitated by the protection of *risk calculations* about the volatility of markets rather than processes that explained the formation of false expectations. On the surface it appears that the problem of explaining crisis in the US mortgage markets in 2007–08 involves addressing the error inherent to risk calculations that caused so many risky loans to be issued.

The previous chapter situated risk calculation within a system of liquidity in commensuration illustrating how this system conditioned risk calculations. This chapter explores this conditioning in more detail, focusing on the US mortgage market, arguing that it needs to be understood in terms of sequential movement through phases of risk management that are reminiscent of hedge, speculative and Ponzi financing arrangements. However, the drivers of these phases need to be reframed in terms of the construction of techniques of risk and arbitrage (commensuration) rather than monetary flows. These phases included risk screening, risk management and then a risk transfer phase.

It is important to note, however, despite the fact that I am describing these phases through reference to Minsky's cash flow taxonomy, that each of these phases had its own determinate constructive rationale that is not captured by Minsky's FIH. The resemblance that these phases bore to the stages in Minsky's FIH is in danger of being overstated, even though the trajectory or sequencing of these stages is familiar to it.

What I seek to do in this chapter is frame the ongoing relevance of the FIH to the crisis of 2007–08 in terms of a paradox – that it can describe the appearance of the forms (for example, speculative and Ponzi financial units) but not explain the processes of the crisis of 2007–08. This is because although liquidity dynamics are at play, they are immanent and appear through constructive processes associated with the arbitrage and commensuration of financial risks.

At issue is the question of whether Minsky provides a theory of crisis or, as some argue, just a description. The point of this chapter is to illustrate how risk should be at the forefront of analysis because risk is now the constructive component of liquid markets and, as Hegel would say, is a concept that should enjoy priority in terms of the explanation of the determinate historically located "being" of the financial system (MacKenzie 2006, 2009, 2011; MacKenzie, Muniesa and Siu 2007).[1] Thus understanding the development of markets, not just their moment of crisis wherein universalist theories of liquidity crisis become relevant as a way of describing market dynamics, therefore involves engaging with the way in which historically determinate forms of risk are generative of liquidity through the construction of markets for new financial products.

This raises the question of how to understand the role of idealist theories of liquidity crisis, such as Minsky's FIH, in explanation. The FIH was (and is) therefore (always) immanent to the collapse of the US housing market in that its vision of the phenomena that are typically involved with liquidity crisis was, in an empirical sense, accurate. However, explanation of the crisis must be a historically determinate application of these categories explaining how they emerged, that is, how these abstract universals were infused in the logic of the constructive discourse of risk. To rely solely on the FIH to explain contemporary financial crisis is to remain trapped in our efforts at interpretation on what Hegel would call "the plane of the abstract universal" including reliance on an outmoded theory of expectations and bubbles that dismisses the reality of risk management. If the theory is to be applicable, it needs to illustrate how its processes play through the constructive processes of risk.

92 *Instability in the US mortgage market*

The issue of identifying Ponzi finance units in the context of risk transfer

Before moving on to discuss the emergence of three phases of risk in the US mortgage market I want to explore how mortgages are situated in and conditioned by a system of liquidity. This illustrates the problem of applying a Minskyian analysis to contemporary instances of crisis by exploring the problem of the identification of Ponzi finance units in the context of risk transfer by considering the context in which the hybrid adjustable rate mortgage (ARM) emerged.

The hybrid ARM was the most popular product in the sub-prime market, constituting approximately 75 per cent of the market over the 2003–2007 period (Mayer et al. 2009:30). Although sub-prime mortgages such as the hybrid ARM have been identified as forms of Ponzi finance by some economists (see McCulley 2009, Wray 2008), they were different from the typical instance of Ponzi finance that Minsky described. The hybrid ARM was developed in the context of institutional and instrumental innovations – a system of risk transfer, which was designed to support capital asset values by managing market risks in a way that was intended to make even Ponzi finance useful and dependable.

In order to understand the relationship between Ponzi finance and financial innovation, it is useful to define a Ponzi unit and then consider how the existence of surrounding derivative markets transforms the meaning of the existence of Ponzi finance for the stability of the system. Indeed, the development of the relationship between the derivative markets and Ponzi finance illustrates the historical development of a new risk-based system of liquidity.

A Ponzi unit is defined by the fact that its internal sources of income, its earnings from operations, are inadequate to meet its liabilities, hence market moves in funding liquidity markets and asset markets determine its fate. For instance, a Ponzi unit cannot pay back interest or principal on its debt and must rely on rolling over larger amounts of debt to pay compounding interest in order to maintain its funding position. A Ponzi unit's profitability is then determined by whether it enjoys capital gains that will eventually enable it to make position paying back debt and interest while realising a profit (Minsky 2011).

Derivative markets transform the context in which Ponzi units are exposed to market moves, potentially making Ponzi finance more viable. What derivatives can do, in theory, is ensure that a Ponzi financial unit can hedge against adverse market moves while gaining exposure to positive market moves. The fact that it can hedge against negative market moves then makes capital gains more likely. This means that derivative trading can enable a financial unit to use equity finance, which Minsky (1986:213) held to be a buffer or margin of safety, more efficiently by making the assets that the equity is invested in a more effective and stable store of capital.

What this illustrates is that the mere identification of Ponzi finance in isolation from the surrounding development of the form of capital is not sufficient to the diagnosis of fragility. The issue of fragility cannot be diagnosed prior to the event of crisis by identifying the emergence of Ponzi financial units and thus

Instability in the US mortgage market 93

applying the FIH. The development of the risk transfer system is permissive of Ponzi finance, making it seem that liquidity crisis is constantly about to happen (is imminent). However, the actual determinant of the eventual occurrence of liquidity crisis, in the case of the crisis of 2007–08, was historically specific and located in the revelation of the system of risk transfer as contradictory, which then brought the potential for liquidity crisis to the fore.

The importance of these questions to Post-Keynesian economics is that it illustrates how Minsky's vision of liquidity crisis is immanent to modern finance. However, in order to ground this insight in an understanding of a theory of liquidity crisis that can be applied in a way that is appropriate to capturing historical specifics of the crisis of 2007–2008, we have to illustrate how risk was a form of liquidity, that is, how the historically determinate instances of crisis express the universal principle.

The two subsections below explore this issue in relation to the sub-prime crisis further by setting the issue out in terms of how the hybrid ARM was constructed in terms of risk transfer and then illustrating how the hybrid ARM was also a form of Ponzi finance, to which the potential of liquidity crisis was imminent. The focus then moves on to a discussion of the three phases of risk that illustrate how this type of Ponzi finance emerged in the US housing system in terms of the logic of risk construction.

The hybrid ARM as a form of Ponzi finance

The existence of Ponzi mortgages needs to be explored in the context of the development of derivative markets for associated risk that frame these mortgages very differently from their depiction as another instance of ad hoc folly with "funny money". These mortgages were actually an example of a rational innovation formulated drawing on the prevailing systemic logic.

Angelo Mozilo, the CEO of Countrywide, which was America's largest mortgage lender in the period 2004–2007, heralded innovative mortgages such as the hybrid ARM as the democratisation of finance. Urging faith in the industry's abilities to utilise risk, Mozilo called for the freedom to take a chance on extending leverage to low-income groups. Mozilo lamented that the industry had been much too slow to embrace technical risk management to encourage social inclusion, stating: "The industry has the greatest 17th century minds in the country. In a world that has changed dramatically, nothing in housing finance has changed" (Sichelman 2003).

Here, Mozilo presented the hybrid ARM as a means to more effectively achieve the societal goal of widespread homeownership through a form of "social innovation", a means of "liberating low income groups from the tyranny of earned income" (Froud et al. 2010). Indeed, Mozilo sought to focus the mortgage discourse on repayments, rather than "socking money away", as the basis of housing finance, arguing that it was meaningless to require targeted borrowers to come to the closing table with 10 per cent of the purchase price in cash, especially when

94 *Instability in the US mortgage market*

the money would come from a relative or some other third party and therefore serve as no indicator of their own creditworthiness. "It's often not their money anyway yet we put them through this torture. A down payment doesn't help the integrity of the loan at all" (Mozilo quoted in Sichelman 2003).

The hybrid ARM, the mortgage instrument by which Mozilo sought to democratise finance, was developed through the extension of derivative-based thinking to mortgage finance in the sub-prime market. The hybrid ARM contained a fixed rate period from 1–10 years at the beginning of the mortgage where the borrower paid a lower interest rate, making reduced payments on capital (or in the case of 60 per cent of Alt-A mortgages either interest only or negative amortisation) before the mortgage would reset to a floating rate, say 2 or 3 per cent above US Treasuries or the London Inter Bank Offered Rate LIBOR (Mayer et al. 2009:30–33). The spread above LIBOR represented payment of the principal that was often paid down across an extended loan period beyond 30 years (Mayer et al. 2009:39). The initial rate or repayment, at least to Alt-A borrowers (those who would otherwise be eligible for a conforming mortgage and hence aren't necessarily part of the sub-prime market) was at a discount of approximately 1 per cent on a traditional fixed rate mortgage, while for sub-prime borrowers, who were by definition generally subject to higher interest charges to compensate lenders for risk, the rate was roughly equivalent to a fixed rate mortgage to a conforming borrower (Mayer et al. 2009, Simon 2002).

Lenders marketed the ARM on the basis that it provided a way to reduce interest payments for a set period. Industry experts propounded that "hybrids make sense for people who expect to sell their homes or to pay off their mortgage [refinance] within a few years. A hybrid allows them to get the lower rates of an adjustable-rate mortgage without taking on the higher risks" (Simon 2002). These mortgages permitted the borrower to save a significant amount of money in the initial period as the following calculations, included in the *Wall Street Journal* in early 2002 show:

> At today's 7.33 per cent rate a borrower could expect to pay $1,375 a month on a $200,000 30 year fixed rate mortgage. But with a five one hybrid at 6.46 per cent, those loan payments would drop to $1,259. Over five years, the hybrid would cut interest charges by nearly $9,000.
>
> (Simon 2002)

However, the author and various industry experts also warned "holding a hybrid can be extremely painful if rates rise and borrowers don't move or pay off their loan as soon as planned" (Simon 2002). Hence, the extent to which this type of mortgage suited borrowers depended on their expectations of the future and the likelihood of prepayment. As one mortgage broker exclaimed, "we are a mobile society. We constantly move. The majority of 30 year loans are paid off by 5 years or 7 years. . . . [T]he ARM loan is a better deal to get a lower interest rate. I do that analysis every day for customers" (Rozens 2002).

These loans represented the emergence of a new norm that framed mortgage payments in terms of minimising the interest burden while encouraging borrowers

Instability in the US mortgage market 95

not to focus too much on how to build up equity to permanently eradicate debt. One professional from a large mortgage lender observed in 2005 that consumers "[were] becoming very much payment oriented. . . . I think more and more, we're going to be moving to interest only options. . . . [T]he customers out there are not concerned about socking money away by repaying principal through amortization" (Shenn 2005).

Sophisticated hybrid ARM loans were marketed as best suited to the financially literate, and the ads for these loans were peppered with examples of upper middle class people such as software engineers and semi-retired owners of manufacturing companies prospering by using these products (Shenn 2005, Simon 2002). Product developers at Countrywide home loans claimed "fixed-period ARMs are a smart solution for financially savvy first-time and move-up buyers who want to take advantage of low interest rates but still want a stable rate for a set period of time" (Finkelstein 2001).

However, despite the depiction of upper middle class borrowers in sales pitches, to whom these mortgages may have been initially marketed, these loans became increasingly popular with sub-prime borrowers from around 2003 onwards. The hybrid ARM was initially most popular amongst conforming borrowers, who wanted to access a larger mortgage principal, that is, as "jumbo Alt-A mortgages". But from 2003 onwards these mortgages were offered to sub-prime borrowers as a means of reducing down payments and as credit repair loans whereby borrowers could pay a low interest rate for a number of years, fixing their credit rating, before refinancing into a prime loan at a permanently lower rate (Mayer et al. 2009:33). This trend culminated in the development of the no-doc, no down payment, negative amortisation hybrid ARM that enabled borrowers to access credit for housing without any payment exposure to the house for a period of up to three years.

Gary Gorton, a consultant to AIG and professor of finance at Pennsylvania stated that the design of sub-prime mortgages, the vast majority of which by 2007 were hybrid ARMs, was unique in how they were designed to be refinanced and deliberately linked to house price gains (Gorton 2010:74–76). At the end of the low interest period, if equity was built up in the house, "the borrower could refinance to a lower loan to value ratio reflecting the embedded price appreciation" (Gorton 2010:68). The lender issuing the hybrid ARM under these circumstances was lowering underwriting standards to increase access to homeownership by effectively taking out an option on house price appreciation as a substitute for a down payment (Gorton 2010:61–115).

Hence, refinance was a design principle of these mortgages (and also a design principle of the consequent residential MBS which had a number of insurance and cash flow features that reflected the anticipated effect of refinancing on the mortgage pool underlying the residential MBS) (Gorton 2010:74–82). The innovation of the hybrid ARM lay with the way in which it constructed arbitrage opportunities for borrowers to leverage asset price gains in lieu of building equity through principal payments. The hybrid ARM encouraged borrowers to forgo equity. Indeed, the share of sub-prime originations with a piggyback second lien at origination

96   *Instability in the US mortgage market*

increased from 7 per cent in 2003 to 28 per cent in 2006 (Mayer et al. 2009:42). The new norm in mortgage design meant that from 2003 borrowers were not required to have a down payment to get a hybrid ARM. Consequently "the median combined loan to value ratio on sub-prime mortgages rose from 90 per cent in 2003 to 100 per cent for 2005–2007 originations" (Mayer et al. 2009:42).

The increasing prevalence of hybrid ARM mortgages had a profound effect on the duration of borrower's payment schedules. Reflecting the move towards treating the mortgage as a floating debt, the economists Mayer et al. (2009:39) wrote:

> by 2007, more than one-third of sub-prime 30 year mortgages had amortization schedules longer than 30 years, more than 44 percent of Alt-A loans allowed borrowers to pay only the interest on their mortgages, and more than one quarter of Alt-A loans gave borrowers the option to pay less than the interest due and thus grow their mortgage balances.
>
> (so called option adjustable mortgages)

Mortgage lenders had been remarkably successful in their efforts to encourage borrowers to drastically extend their repayment schedules and therefore increase the interest burden paid across the life of the loan, making borrowers cover the cost of carrying a large principal for longer.

Crisis dimensions of Ponzi mortgages

Having described the derivative logic behind the construction of the hybrid ARM, it is useful to explore the crisis dimensions to their construction in terms of the way they exemplified Ponzi finance. This helps to illustrate the way in which the FIH is immanent (though not determinant) to the logic of risk, a point that I will then expand upon in the following section on the development of different mortgages in terms of logics of risk management.

While the financial engineer Gorton's rationale of the hybrid ARM does have some logic to it, these mortgages were really different forms of finance to the traditional fixed interest loan. The differences meant that the borrower, not just the lender, carried additional risk. The hybrid ARM had a more sophisticated structure, with innovations that made it more akin to a form of corporate finance. This mortgage form placed borrowers in the position of managing a capital asset, which meant treating the principal of their mortgage as a "floating debt". Borrowers were placed in an analogous position to the treasuries of governments and corporations, who use short term finance to roll over their debts by issuing new bonds or corporate paper (Minsky 1986:95). As the above marketing of the hybrid ARM makes clear, the expectation was that this mortgage would operate similarly, with the borrower paying the interest only and rolling over the principal by selling or refinancing it at a later date to utilise the equity built up by asset price appreciation to pay back the principal (Finkelstein 2001, Rozens 2002, Simon 2002).

Floating the debt, however, was quite a radical innovation in mortgage design with very significant ramifications. Floating the debt effectively reduced equity payments, and hence potentially extended the life of the mortgage (as these mortgages have been shown to do) to manipulate the interest rate. The US economist and housing bubble expert Michael Hudson wrote

> A given monthly payment can carry radically different amounts of debt, depending on the rate of interest and how long those payments last. The purchasing power of a $1,000 monthly payment, for instance, nearly triples as the debt lingers and the interest rate declines.
>
> (Hudson 2006:40)

Although the monthly payments may be the same or lower, the result for the borrower of taking out a large loan using an interest only loan was significant. Despite the fact that these loans were marketed on the basis of periodicity, the marketing pitch neglected to mention how the borrower would build equity to provide a margin of safety in carrying the debt load, eventually paying off the loan nullifying the need to make payments in old age, if capital gains could not be assumed. Essentially, the borrower achieved a lower interest rate by implicitly betting that house price gains would continue enabling them to build equity through refinance.

The risk that borrowers take when they attempt to "float the principal" on the basis of short term finance is that there will be no capital gains when they refinance. In fact, an interest rate rise could jeopardise capital gains by dampening demand for housing. Borrowers were taking advantage of the fact that short term borrowing would be cheaper than long term borrowing, which includes more forecasting risk, and thus opting to ride the yield curve without any protection if future conditions confounded their expectations.

In fact, the problem wasn't just that borrowers had to depend on capital gains to build equity but rather that they would go backwards, further into debt, if there were no capital gains to be had. The hybrid structure of an initial fixed interest low rate period offered absolutely no value unless it coincided with capital gains. For example, assuming there are no capital gains in the fixed rate period, the borrower using a hybrid ARM had little incentive to refinance (unless the payment of the mortgage gave the borrower an improved credit rating which could earn him a cheaper mortgage if it helped him move into the prime bracket above a FICO score of 660). At the end of the term of the fixed rate period borrowers were likely to find themselves in a flat or higher interest rate environment (if we accept that high interest rates are correlated with low capital gains) where they would be trapped in the hybrid ARM mortgage. Their options in this case were to either continue with the ARM on a floating rate, often with compounded interest from the low interest period or attempt to refinance onto a fixed rate mortgage. There would be an incentive to continue with the existing loan because floating rate loans are cheaper than fixed rate loans. The goal would then be to pay off the loan in the allotted period, including compounded principal and interest payments, to avoid extending the life of the mortgage, which would mean incurring an additional period of interest payments. Alternatively, if they feared further interest rate

98 *Instability in the US mortgage market*

rises, they could refinance to a fixed rate mortgage at a higher base rate but with potentially lower total interest payments per period, hence lowering the average aggregate monthly payment by extending the life of the mortgage and therefore paying a greater lifetime sum in interest but at a lower rate.

In the latter option, borrowers end up getting less equity as a ratio of the sum of their interest payments so the incentive is actually to stick with the hybrid ARM mortgage if borrowers can scramble to make the higher payments and hope that interest rates fall or they can repair their credit record to an extent that will enable them to refinance onto a conforming loan. If there are no capital gains, borrowers are left with the hard reality that hybrid ARMs "back load" the payment schedule and refinancing extends the life of the loan.

This meant that to some extent, especially given the existence of prepayment penalties that kept borrowers in the loan during the low interest period, borrowers were trapped in these loans. The vast majority of sub-prime loans that were securitised, in fact 72 per cent, included prepayment penalties that lasted for at least the duration of the low rate teaser period, while this feature was uncommon in the conforming and Alt-A market (Mayer et al. 2009:30). The prepayment penalty was often approximately equivalent to about six months of interest payments (Mayer et al. 2009:37). Unsurprisingly, given this analysis, the two best predictors of mortgage default in relation to the crisis of 2007–08 were related to equity – whether a down payment was made and whether negative equity in the house had developed (Mayer et al. 2009:42–43).

Innovation processes moving the US housing finance market towards liquidity crisis: three phases of risk management

The discussion above deals with the appearance of Ponzi structures in the US housing finance system. However, as I have argued in this book, the FIH, understood as a universally applicable theory rather than a determinate analysis of the political economic context in which it was developed and applied, is inadequate to analysis of the development of Ponzi structures and the interpretation of their meaning in the US economy in the lead-up to the crisis of 2007–08.

In order to understand what explains the appearance of Ponzi structures and their significance we need to analyse how processes of risk management gave rise to particular types of arbitrage/commensuration that defined the form of capital, including the mortgage forms that could be offered. I am providing some preliminary research here towards this proposition, based on the interpretation of liquidity dynamics in earlier parts of this book, particularly Chapter 5, that risk based processes gain veracity in terms of enabling new types of arbitrage, thereby generating liquidity which underpins their risk assessments and pricing. The veracity of risk management as a form of capital is determined by its ability to produce itself, as a technique of risk management, by bringing about favourable new liquidity dynamics in terms of new logics of commensuration.

Below I analyse the development of risk as a form of capital in terms of three stages of development, including risk screening, risk management and risk transfer. These three phases of risk that are outlined below are historically overlapping and not necessarily distinct and exclusive of one another. Rather than thinking of these phases as historically closed, they should be more modestly understood as a somewhat, by necessity, conjectural interpretation of the dynamics that shaped the housing market in a way that moved it towards the growth of Ponzi structures in US housing finance. This approach to interpreting liquidity dynamics more adequately fits in with the explanatory framework for understanding the interaction between the veracity of risk calculation and the form of capital and liquidity outlined in this book, as well as making sense of the problem of locating liquidity dynamics in the emergence of forms of risk based finance in the US housing market.

Form of capital: risk screening

The "prime" or "conforming" mortgage dominated the US mortgage market in the 1990s and early 2000s, rising to prominence in the wake of the Savings and Loan crisis in the 1980s (Muolo and Padilla 2010). This mortgage was defined by the fact that the government or a private sector mortgage guarantor would guarantee the mortgage payments of borrowers in order to facilitate lending to these borrowers. Hence, mortgage payments were completed either by borrowers or by the state via government sponsored enterprises (GSEs) or an insurance company acting as guarantor on the mortgage (Green and Wachter 2005, Lea 1996). These institutions targeted their insurance towards moderate income borrowers who were judged as highly likely to pay back their mortgage as scheduled but not lending to borrowers who posed a high risk and hence were constituted by what Poon (2009) has called "risk screening" processes.

The US government predominantly implemented risk screening in the mortgage market through the creation of the GSEs – the Federal National Mortgage Association (FNMA, Fanny Mae), the Federal Home Loan Mortgage Corporation (FHLMC, Freddie Mac) or the Government National Mortgage Association (GNMC, Ginnie Mae), who were under charter from the US government to build new financial instruments and make them liquid in order to facilitate growth in the US housing market (Green and Wachter 2005:98).

Indeed, the GSEs played a central role in mortgage credit creation up until 2004. By 2003 the conforming mortgage market had grown to constitute 75 per cent of the overall mortgage market. The GSEs guaranteed or held 60 per cent of the conforming market (Green and Wachter 2005:99). However, from 2004 until 2007 their central role in the market was eclipsed by private sector innovators who were able to create more varied forms of mortgage credit and resulting MBS that were more effective in facilitating ongoing accumulation in the face of house price appreciation outside of the "affordable housing" pricing brackets that the GSEs were constrained to target by their charters (Coleman et al. 2008, Goodman et al. 2008).

Types of arbitrage associated with risk screening

The key to the growth of the GSEs in the 1980s and 1990s and the institutions associated with the securitisation of conforming mortgages, such as the investment

100   *Instability in the US mortgage market*

bank Salomon Brothers, was the development of the collateralised mortgage obligation (CMO), which made mortgage credit commensurate in risk with US government bonds while delivering a higher yield (Lewis 1989, Ranieri 1996). This incorporated mortgage credit more directly into capital market forms of credit. For instance, the first CMO was created in 1982 to overcome problems with "pass through securities", including their long duration and prepayment risk (Green and Wachter 2005, Lagesse 1987). Lewis (1989:160) writes:

> The CMO burst the dam between several trillion investable dollars looking for a home and nearly two trillion dollars of home mortgages looking for an investor. The CMO addressed the chief objection to buying mortgage securities, still voiced by everyone but thrifts and a handful of adventurous money managers: who wants to lend money not knowing when they'll get it back?

A CMO was a security that was tranched according to priority access to cash flows. The tranched structure of a CMO filters cash flows in a manner similar to the way champagne flows into a pyramid of champagne glasses stacked on a tray. For example the first glass – the security rated AAA by the credit rating agencies, which promises an interest payment say 1 per cent above LIBOR, has the highest priority access to cash flows and receives the first portion of interest payments as well as the first principal repayments until its principal has been repaid in full, whereby the next set of principal payments go to the next senior tranche of securities to guarantee their value (Lewis 1989:162).

The development of the CMO created arbitrage opportunities to investors in this new type of security. Indeed, Lewis Ranieri, the head of the mortgage trading desk at Salomon Brothers, writes that in the early 1980s when the market for MBS was getting up and running, the sales pitch of mortgage-backed securities relied on a parallel with Treasuries:

> I remember calling on Andy Carter, one of the great money managers of that day. In those days, single-A utility then was comparable to a junk bond today. "Andy," I said, "if I can swap you out of a single-A utility into a full-faith-and-credit, guaranteed timely payment government bond, would you do it?" He replied, "Hey stupid, of course I would." I then took out my Ginnie Mae certificate. In effect, I was offering him a treasury bond [risk] even yield with single-A utilities.
>
> (Ranieri 1996:36)

The yield on MBS backed by government guaranteed mortgages remained above the US government Treasuries rate up until the sub-prime crisis, providing significant risk adjusted value (Goodman et al. 2008).

The development of MBS created a number of other arbitrage opportunities for the GSEs themselves too. The GSEs arbitraged their perceived government guarantee in the money markets to access cheaper funding liquidity, which they used to hold their portfolio of mortgages. This generated a yield on the spread between their costs of funding in the short term money markets compared with the yield on their portfolio of mortgages (Schwartz and Order 1988).

Another important form of arbitrage associated with the development of securitisation of conforming mortgages was the arbitrage to mortgage banks (those banks that issued credit through the secondary mortgage market rather than using their deposit base, often by selling mortgages they originated to the GSEs) in terms of capital costs (Carlstrom and Samolyk 1995, Demyanyk and Loutskina 2012, Hill 1996, Jabłecki and Machaj 2009, Loutskina 2011). The 1988 Basel Accord forced banks to maintain higher capital ratios, creating incentives towards securitisation as a capital efficient means of generating credit (Jabłecki and Machaj 2009).

The development of techniques for securitising conforming mortgages also created arbitrage opportunities to mortgage borrowers, significantly reducing interest rates to borrowers who accessed credit through the GSE/securitisation channel rather than through the primary market (Kolari et al. 1998, Passmore 2005, Sirmans and Benjamin 1990, Torregrosa 2001).

The conforming mortgage underpinned by risk screening was a profitable instrument until, in 2004, the centre of gravity in the mortgage securitisation market shifted towards the shadow banks (mortgage originators, mortgage banks, investment banks, hedge funds) and away from the GSEs (Coleman et al. 2008). In 2004, the GSEs were forced to tighten their conforming mortgage standards following an accounting scandal. Furthermore house price appreciation moved an increasing proportion of the mortgage market beyond eligibility for conforming mortgages that were targeted at those on moderate incomes. The ability of sub-prime lenders to offer larger and more highly leveraged mortgages enabled them to capture an increasing market share from the GSEs (Goodman et al. 2008:8).

Form of capital: risk management

The distinctive feature of this form of capital was the way in which it used risk management as a constructive tool to replicate the performance of government bonds. However, this form of capital was quite distinct from agency MBS in the way it dealt with uncertainty. This form of capital permitted defaults. That is to say not all cash flows were guaranteed by the government. Instead they were assured by risk calculation and corresponding insurance and over-collateralisation measures (Poon 2009).

The sociologist Martha Poon (2009) provides a sophisticated analysis of the development of risk management as a constitutive discourse in the US mortgage market. It is useful to summarise this research because it provides a lot of insight into risk as a constructive discourse. What follows below is largely a summary of Poon's work supplemented by some additional research that I found useful to understanding the development of risk management practices in the mortgage market.

The use of risk calculation to price mortgages and construct subsequent securities was facilitated by a GSE policy decision made in the late 1990s about how

102 Instability in the US mortgage market

to use technology to measure and set up standards about consumer credit quality. The decision to rely on standards including FICO credit scores to screen mortgages for inclusion in agency MBS also facilitated the creation of the "sub-prime" market otherwise known as the "non-agency" or "private label" market, as including those mortgages issued outside of the GSE's standard based process (Poon 2009).

Indeed, in 1996 the GSEs decided to buy only those mortgages issued to borrowers with a FICO credit score over 660 termed "conforming" mortgages. The FICO credit score was produced by the Fair Isaac Corporation, a data-mining credit aggregator, who kept a database of consumers' credit history, including successful repayments, defaults and arrears. They produced a credit score indicating the likelihood that borrowers would repay a debt based on statistical analysis of their credit data. They required brokers to collect the FICO credit score and include it with the customer mortgage application along with other underwriting information including income, other assets, etc. (Poon 2009).

In effect the GSEs used their market power as the largest buyer of mortgage pools to introduce quality control via the FICO credit score to the market. The GSEs were set up and directed by charter to provide liquidity and quality assurance to the mortgage banking industry in order to increase access to "affordable housing" (Poon 2009:659). The GSEs developed automatic loan underwriting software and streamlined information forms to enable them to build the FICO credit score into their IT based decision-making processes. The GSEs provided their automatic underwriting program to the mortgage banking industry in order to replace a thick book of mortgage origination principles, which were only occasionally enforced by audit, and encourage the development of more efficient standardised information about mortgage pools (Poon 2009:661–662). Because of the GSEs' market position, their automated underwriting platform became the most widely adopted technical platform for underwriting mortgages, eventually forming the basis for how the industry not only screened good borrowers from bad borrowers, but how investment banks came to occupy a similar space to the GSEs evaluating risk and sorting mortgages to buy.

A side effect of the incorporation of the FICO credit score into assessment of borrower risk was that it generated a platform whereby sub-prime lenders could begin to undertake more detailed risk assessments of sub-prime borrowers in a way that was similar to the risk based pricing principles operating in the consumer credit card industry (Poon 2009). By around 1996 rating agency companies such as Standard and Poor's (S&P) had incorporated FICO credit scores into their statistical mortgage risk analysis program (LEVELS) and in 1999 they began actively urging companies to include FICO credit scores for their borrowers in the pools of mortgages they rated so that by 2003 the percentage of mortgage pools that included the FICO credit score was close to 100 per cent compared with 50 per cent of prime and 30 per cent of sub-prime in 1998 (Poon 2009:663–665). The mortgage risk programs that S&P developed used the FICO credit score to "stratify risk" to permit more "granular" pricing of mortgages to borrowers (Poon 2009:667).

Whereas the GSEs used the FICO score to do "screening", sub-prime mortgage companies used the FICO credit score to do "statistical lending" to achieve granular pricing of mortgages (Poon 2009:667). Poon observed that screening is a risk minimizing strategy in that it involves applying a standard, a "plimsoll line", above which the debt level is too heavy, whereas statistical lending is a risk management strategy that embraces risk and attempts to manage it. Risk management used the law of large numbers to underpin lending. It offsets the risk of a single mortgage by increasing the price, the interest rate, to a level that will allow lenders to achieve an aggregate profit across a large pool of similarly risky mortgages where the risk level is quantified using the FICO credit score. The interest rate for sub-prime borrowers was determined according to the level of risk indicated by a quantitative statistical analysis of the applicant's FICO score and deposit size (Raiter and Parisi 2004). The interest rate on sub-prime loans was determined in a different way to the interest rate for prime loans, which were set upon origination at a few per cent above the rate set by the Federal Reserve Board. This meant that somewhat paradoxically interest rates for people on a low income or people with a poor credit score often had a higher interest rate than for less "risky" borrowers, creating an incentive towards the emphasis in later mortgage forms of capturing asset price increases through refinancing.

Sub-prime mortgages were subject to a different underwriting technique reflecting the fact that they were developed for a different market from conforming mortgages. The demarcation between underwriting techniques had huge practical significance because it effectively determined the market for the loan. It determined whether the loan would be sent to the GSEs to be securitised or sent to Wall Street investment banks, which were the predominant buyers of sub-prime loans (as mentioned briefly above and discussed in more detail in the section below) to be securitised. The investment banks of Wall Street specialised in managing risk, performing a kind of alchemy using "tranching" to "overcollateralise" the mortgage-backed securities they created to give investors in the high order tranches greater security that the mortgage pool underlying the security would generate an expected yield (Fabozzi and Kothari 2007). The tranching of mortgage-backed securities ensured that the higher tranche MBS created by Wall Street on the basis of sub-prime loans were given AAA ratings by the rating agencies (MacKenzie 2011).

The introduction of the FICO credit score had significant implications for the non-agency MBS market, providing a way to use risk calculation as a constructive discourse in asset-backed financial products. Poon (2009) writes that the FICO score acted as a bridge between the products offered in the mortgage market and the products offered in the capital markets. By 2004, analysts concluded that the sub-prime mortgages were rationally priced according to the FICO credit score:

Examining the relationship between FICO scores and mortgage coupons (interest rates) from data in S&P's proprietary database of 9.3 million residential mortgages, the study concluded that rational risk based pricing had become more refined and more expansive since 1998. By rational they meant

104 *Instability in the US mortgage market*

that the interest rate of loans increase[d] as the FICO scores decreased, but also that "the coupon rate charged on the loan at origination [. . .] translated into true dollar costs over the life of the loan.

(Poon 2009:668)

This ability to calculate and manage risk enabled securitising firms to construct MBS with AAA credit ratings out of sub-prime mortgages (MacKenzie 2011, Poon 2009). Furthermore these products, like agency MBS, provided a higher yield than US government bonds while holding a supposedly similar level of credit risk (Fabozzi and Kothari 2007).

Types of arbitrage associated with risk management

The mortgage banks, investment banks and commercial banks (shadow banks) involved in the sub-prime market issued sub-prime MBS that received AAA credit ratings, similar to government bonds, while providing a significantly higher yield than government bonds and even prime MBS (Fabozzi and Kothari 2007, Lysandrou 2011b). These instruments therefore tended to increase in value, particularly in the low interest rate environment in America following the tech wreck in 2000 where high yielding instruments were hard to find (Adrian and Shin 2009)

The increasing value of the MBS through the early 2000s represented the fact that with the development of the sub-prime market in the late 1990s and consolidation in the early 2000s the shadow banks had found a way to replicate the GSE structure of arbitrage in a product market that the GSEs, by definition, could not access. The creation of sub-prime MBS opened up the various arbitrage opportunities involved in securitisation, similar to those the GSEs had tapped, but open to the shadow banks, including providing a higher yield to investors on risk compared with government bonds (Fabozzi and Kothari 2007), liquidity transformation (Loutskina 2011) and regulatory/capital arbitrage (Blundell-Wignall and Atkinson 2009). Indeed, these organisations competed by building their networks buying and creating agreements with mortgage banks, which had previously acted primarily as mortgage originators and servicers to the GSEs, in order to enable them greater access and control over the origination, warehousing, securitisation and distribution to investors of sub-prime mortgages (Muolo and Padilla 2010).

Form of capital: risk transfer

The development of the sub-prime market was notable for the extent to which it introduced risk calculation into the construction of asset-backed securities (ABS). However, it was the inclusion of the practice of risk transfer, and the focus on refinancing sub-prime mortgages, which enabled the development of Ponzi forms of housing finance (Gorton 2008).

Indeed, the hybrid ARM provided a way of allowing mortgage borrowers to trade capital gains for the requirement to pay interest, at least in the initial stages of the mortgage. The intention of this was to increase access to the housing market by enabling low-income borrowers not just to compensate lenders for risk, but to take risks themselves, which would then be hedged in the capital markets using credit default swaps (CDS) on the ABS created out of these mortgages.

On the surface it is easy to explain the financial crisis of 2007–08 in terms of the fact that the hedge on mortgage defaults, the CDS, was inaccurately priced (MacKenzie 2011, Tett 2009). This is obviously true, though as I have argued in the previous chapter, it is more of a descriptive statement than an explanatory statement.

The bigger issue is how this mispricing arose through historical processes whereby the concept of risk became baseless and self-negating. The prior chapter explored this issue, arguing that successive instances of liquidity-generating innovations came to condition risk calculations essential to the use of CDS for hedging mortgage defaults. This stemmed from the fact that the practices of risk calculation and risk transfer were themselves constitutive of an abstract form of liquidity as well as a form of analysis of risk. Ultimately, risk analysis understood as a subject was not separable from the object it was supposedly analysing given that it generated observer effects through its historical role in enabling the creation of new financial markets that transformed the financial system and the form of capital (see previous two chapters).

Indeed, the very structure of the hybrid ARM illustrates how liquidity had become constitutive of risk rather than appropriate risk calculation being facilitative of liquidity. For instance, the hybrid ARM enabled mortgage borrowers to take risk on capital gains. But capital gains were largely self-referential to the propensity of lenders to let borrowers take this risk. They were dependent on lenders' propensity to continue to lend to borrowers seeking capital gains and those borrowers' ability to refinance – that is to say on capital market conditions that borrowers were not well placed to be able to assess.

The structure of the hybrid ARM sought to use liquidity to get around the "margins of safety" implicit in calculating the risk premium according to the FICO credit score, that is, risk compensated interest payments. But without the payment of risk compensated yields, at least in the initial stages of the mortgage, the phenomenon of capital gains had no anchor. Investors, faced with a potential downturn, found it difficult to price assets based on these mortgages given that their yield was largely speculative (MacKenzie 2012). Indeed, when capital gains failed to eventuate for sub-prime borrowers and they realised that there was no value for them in the hybrid ARM contract, they ceased making mortgage payments (Mayer et al. 2009:46).

Types of arbitrage associated with risk transfer

Whereas the previous form of capital was more about risk construction, using this technique to create securities whose risk profile imitated government bonds while giving a more generous yield, this form of capital was about using a derivative logic to create liquidity through diversification of risks. The development of the

106 *Instability in the US mortgage market*

Gaussian Copula Formula (discussed in the previous chapter), which enabled the construction of ABS collateralised debt obligations (CDOs), created a secondary market for sub-prime MBS, particularly BBB rated tranches of sub-prime bonds (Cordell et al. 2012, MacKenzie 2011). The creation of the credit default swap made mortgage credit risk liquid across investment portfolios so that investors could manage risk not by evaluating substantive credit risk but through the abstract principles of risk transfer.

Indeed, prior to the development of the sub-prime ABS CDO and CDS, which became widespread in 2003–2005, sub-prime bonds were generally not liquid for investors (Mehrling 2011:126). Mortgage banks attempted to use baskets of derivatives that approximated their movement given that no direct hedge existed (see for example Veneits 2001). The extension of the ABS CDO market and CDS market to cover mortgage debt constituted the development of a substantively new way of generating liquidity for housing finance.

The effect of the development of the market for sub-prime CDO and CDS was to create an arbitrage opportunity whereby risk discounted BBB bonds could be packaged into AAA rated ABS CDO using the hedging possibilities afforded by the CDS market (Fabozzi et al. 2007). This tended to increase the value of all sub-prime bonds and ABS CDOs, discounting the cost of funding to hold them, creating a liquidity yield to investors who borrowed in the short-term money market to hold these bonds. This virtuous spiral created significant demand for risk as a way of generating a liquidity yield (Adrian and Shin 2009, 2010).

At the same time a number of investors were engaged in a different form of arbitrage (Bernstein and Eisinger 2010, Lewis 2010). These investors had identified that the pricing of CDS was flawed and found a way to short the ABS CDO market by buying naked CDS on the default risk of AAA rated tranches of ABS CDOs. These same investors, often hedge funds such as Magnetar, would buy the residual layers of ABS CDOs calculating that if the ABS CDO suffered defaults they would take a loss on the residuals that they held but the gain they made on the default of the AAA rated tranches of the ABS CDO would offset this loss (Lewis 2010, Tavakoli 2003:184–194, UBS 2008).

Contrary to the normal function of short selling, this type of shorting created liquidity in the underlying market without adding any new pricing information about "fundamental values" (Soros 2009). The market for short selling the ABS CDO market therefore contributed to the size of the bubble (Lewis 2010, Mehrling 2011).

Eventually there was a run in the money markets, the source of funding liquidity that hedge funds, investment banks and money market mutual funds used to hold ABS CDOs (Acharya and Schnabl 2010, Gorton 2010, Pozsar et al. 2010). This ended the possibility of making a liquidity yield by holding these positions and jeopardised the funding liquidity of many financial units holding ABS CDOs. When this form of arbitrage between funding liquidity and market liquidity broke down, it caused a negative spiral that drastically reduced the market liquidity of ABS CDOs, causing a liquidity crisis as well as a credit crunch as the value of these securities was written down (Brunnermeier 2009).

Conclusion: a reformulation of the FIH

The above illustration of stages of risk management suggests that the FIH captures something of the crisis of 2007–08, although we have to be very careful in determining what it is the FIH helps us to understand. The FIH does appear to go beyond the potential problem outlined in the introduction to this chapter, that is, that it is only explanation on the level of the "abstract universal". It somehow manages to describe the trajectory of the financial system that was characterised by the growing appearance of seemingly risky and fragile financial units in the lead-up to the crisis. However, it does not capture the actual processes and "being" of the crisis – the constructive dimension of risk management.

One interpretation of this conundrum that could be of benefit is to view the stages of Minsky's FIH, the hedge, speculative and Ponzi finance, as a theoretical description of how systems in which there are processes that habituate participants to risk can develop hidden systemic risks. The FIH expresses the contradiction of risk management in its "abstract universal form" in that mitigating risk, by definition, expands the amount of risk that can be taken. This interpretation accounts for the way that the FIH cannot capture the determinate nature of contemporary finance but can describe its path of development because it describes something of the inherent universal relationship between risk and liquidity if not the particular details of the historically located forms of risk. In this sense, risk management is a form of liquidity and the FIH – as a description of liquidity dynamics, is immanent (infused in) as well as immanent (about to happen) to modern financial techniques of risk management.

The last chapter follows on from this insight into liquidity as a historical process of transformation and development of the form of capital looking at reform proposals, including the work of Shiller (2004, 2008), in terms of a continuation of this process of risk transformation. The argument is that these "reforms" are only masquerading as such and should more accurately be understood as reconstitution of the dialectics of liquidity crisis described above.

APPENDIX C

The GSEs were actually only part of the consolidation phase of the risk screening system, which began prior to their construction. The risk screening system was first initiated by the US government when it created the Federal Housing Authority (FHA) to insure mortgages in 1936 in the context of the Great Depression. The intention of the government was to prop up the housing market by providing a guarantee to encourage investors to purchase mortgages (Green and Wachter 2005:95). The business of insuring mortgages turned out to be quite profitable and in the 1950s and 1960s a number of private companies, including the Mortgage Guarantee Insurance Company (MGIC), entered the market growing significantly into the 1990s, when they eclipsed the volume that the Government National

108 *Instability in the US mortgage market*

Mortgage Association (Ginnie Mae) insured before selling the mortgages to Fannie Mae or Freddie Mac (Green and Wachter 2005:95–97).

The government generally targeted insurance to the "conforming mortgages" of moderate income borrowers to encourage their participation in the housing market (Carrozzo 2004). The conforming mortgage was first instituted by the Home Owners Loan Corporation (HOLC). The HOLC bought defaulted mortgages from financial institutions using government funding and restructured borrowers' mortgages which were generally low loan-to-value ratio, short term non-amortizing debts, the interest rate of which was renegotiated and refinanced every 1–5 years. The HOLC restructured these mortgages to be long term high loan-to-value ratio, fixed rate fully amortizing loans (Green and Wachter 2005:95).

In 1938, the HOLC was disbanded and replaced by the Federal National Mortgage Association (Fannie Mae), which was created to boost the demand in the secondary investors market for FHA insured mortgages. In 1968 Fannie Mae was privatised and Ginnie Mae was created as government insurer to conforming mortgages. In 1970 the Federal Home Loan Mortgage Corporation (Freddie Mac) was created to provide competition to Fannie Mae in the secondary market to conforming mortgages focusing on buying mortgages from Savings and Loan associations (Green and Wachter 2005:95–99).

Note

1 MacKenzie does not invoke Hegel in his discussion of the constitution of financial markets. The point is rather that MacKenzie's work serves as an example of an investigation of the being, that is, the materialism (or lack thereof) of financial markets, arguing that they are at least partially conceptual and constituted by risk calculation.

8 Economics, regulation and capital

An assessment of some proposed reforms

In the wake of the financial crisis of 2007–08, a number of paradoxes are emerging in the way that economists are seeking to reconstruct the discipline of economics and their understanding of regulation. Economists and policy makers are, perhaps unconsciously, choosing to re-embrace the circumstances, structures and processes that led to the crisis rather than working to establish some sort of epistemic break from the ideologies, institutions and pattern of operations in which the crisis manifested itself.

The financial economist Robert Shiller (2004, 2008) has proposed house price derivatives, while banking economists (FSB 2009) have been working towards the introduction of pro-cyclical capital buffers to stabilise capital markets. These measures are indicative of how many economists are approaching the crisis as a problem of excess and hence seeking to moderate its dynamics through offsetting mechanisms. The risk is that these measures serve to shore up the underlying relationships that constituted important aspects of the process of the development of the current system of liquidity and reproduce them into the future rather than fix structural problems in the financial system.

I argue that when viewed in terms of how these ideas affect the form of capital that currently exists, we can see that reconstruction of the discourse of financial economics is in danger of serving as a source of ideas that facilitates further intensification of financial calculation and hence liquidity crisis. House price derivatives and pro-cyclical buffers are essentially innovations in the design and structuring of commodities, i.e. new forms of derivatives. I use Minsky's FIH in a critical way to show how these ideas if implemented could create similar dialectics of liquidity to that which was recently experienced in the lead-up to crisis. These ideas are deeply flawed because the conceptual frameworks from which they are drawn do not have a notion of the form of capital.

Economics of excess

Many interpretations of the causes of the financial crisis of 2007–08 are focused on excess. The popular understanding of the cause of the financial crisis is related to quantities – not enough regulation, leading to fraudulent behaviour; too much borrowing; overly inflated asset prices; irrational herd behaviour and pro-cyclical incentives in the financial system, etc.

110 *Economics, regulation and capital*

This language is significant in that it exemplifies how crisis demolished the pre-existing paradigm that economists used to understand the workings of financial markets based on the Efficient Market Hypothesis (EMH), where these excesses could not, by definition, occur (Fox 2009). The EMH holds that rationality, transparency of information and free price movements deliver a true representation of value and hence an efficient allocation of capital and systemic stability. The new consensus is that investment is harder to conduct on a rational basis than was previously thought given the prevalence of herding phenomena and pro-cyclical dynamics that undermine fundamental values (Bernanke 2009, Fox 2009).

The confession that markets may tend to instability and excess is appealing to those critical of the EMH who see more of a role for the state and welcome a change to the common refrain of conventional economists that the market generally knows best (Quiggin 2011, Stiglitz 2009, Wray 2008). These heterodox economists see equilibrium as a tarnished concept and welcome the opportunity for creative institutional re-design to admit new possibilities other than laissez-faire. The discussion of regulation is seen as an opportunity to begin evolution towards a more progressive financial system that places the emphasis less on speculative profits and leverage and more on the generation of productive new technologies, equality and economic development.

However, it is unclear whether the discourse of excess is a real epistemic break in terms of the underlying philosophy we use to understand and regulate the financial system, particularly in relation to liquidity. Although most commentators recognise that rational self-correcting markets are somewhat mythical entities, reform measures to economics as a discipline and practical regulation are still being guided by the notion of curtailing the excesses of the financial system of 2005–06 in order that the ideals of the efficient market may be realised through regulation, if not the inherent existence and unimpeded functioning of market processes. Many of the reform measures being put forward work towards developing a more rigorous institutional framework to discern excesses and aid the discovery of fundamental values, including better oversight, more information and more transparency, more markets to price and offset risks and larger capital buffers (Bryan 2009, Kroszner and Shiller 2011, Skeel 2010).

It could be that this discourse of excess which is now emerging out of economics encourages us to think only to a limited extent about regulatory reforms in terms of treading a path through regulation which affirms the belief in market processes but acknowledges that market processes were found wanting in the financial crisis (FC). From this perspective, regulation may not necessarily have the progressive connotations that many heterodox economists may wish that it contained. Regulation is, in this context, necessarily an attempt to constitute the sphere of private interests in a more rigorous way rather than expand social- democratic control over the market as the main institution of distribution and hence a site of struggle for economic justice (Watkins 2010). The status of the market in this respect is not really being challenged by reforms to economic thinking and the markets in the wake of the FC.

The present conjuncture is therefore interesting for the extent to which many economists have been forced to re-visit their assumptions underlying their

Economics, regulation and capital   111

ideologies and inquire about the manner in which real world financial markets actually work. This was particularly apparent in relation to discussion of nationalisation of the American banking system that occurred amongst prominent economists in May-June 2009 (Krugman 2009, Blodget 2009, Stiglitz 2009). Yet the results of the recent phase of existential questioning amongst the mainstream appears to be a shift in the nature of economics from being an attempt to create a positive inductive form of knowledge about economic processes starting at first principles towards including a constructive dimension that attempts to produce efficient markets through incorporating negative experiences of market processes, recognising the irrationality of markets that inspire the need for regulation to help the markets tend towards equilibrium. The ideal of the market has been tarnished, so it's up to regulators to give it a shine.

Hence, the dominant response to the financial crisis has not been to chart a new course but to transform the nature of economics as an intellectual project, to include constructive governance reasoning as inspiration for regulation. Robert Shiller, the behavioural economist at the head of a current push in the US to "humanise" financial markets by renovating the interface by which people interact with finance in light of behavioural principles of optimum choice conditions argues that

> [t]he free market is one of the most important inventions in human history. It is indeed an invention, and the invention takes the form of regulation and standards enforced by some form of government. Markets and government are thus inseparable, just as the functioning of markets has to change through time.
>
> (Kroszner and Shiller 2011:14)

Free markets remain the consensus model of economic organisation in the contemporary global economy, especially the Anglo-sphere, but the financial crisis has opened up the platform to other forms of economic theorising about how to achieve free markets.

The behavioural economics of Robert Shiller (2008) and Hyman Minsky's theories of financial instability and central bank policy (Minsky 1986) are both gaining attention in the search for conceptual tools to stabilise the system (Fox 2009, Kroszner and Shiller 2011, Mehrling 2011 and see for example references in Borio 2009). Both of these theories offer explanations for bubbles and insights into how to encourage stable growth.

However, the problematic of contemporary economic thinking on financial regulation discussed above, while being largely consistent with Shiller's ideology and political intentions, cuts against the grain of the theory of Hyman Minsky most acutely. Minsky's theory is an expression of the paradoxes of liquidity and an attempt to develop a structural hermeneutics that can conceptualise the nature of liquidity crisis in its historical dimension.

Adherents to Minsky's perspective thus find themselves being handed an intellectual victory on the one hand while suffering more political economic

112 *Economics, regulation and capital*

frustrations on the other as the policy discourse moves towards the reconstruction of pseudo free markets. This means that in order to avoid being handed only the meagre spoils of a thin intellectual victory in securing recognition that deviations from equilibrium can occur, progressive economists need to find a new way of conceptualising the crisis that goes beyond excess, that causes an epistemic break from the dominant market paradigm upheld by regulation, that includes an account of how markets and capital behave in a way that is materially different from conventional theory and will confound any repair efforts to "hammer" this paradigm back together in an ad-hoc way.

Solutions to excess

The discourse of bubbles and excess seems to be limited as a vehicle for progressive political economy, but before writing it off entirely we need to inquire as to how these limitations become binding. How are "bubbles" or deviations from "equilibrium" to be understood? What solutions are proposed to fix these excesses? Why is a focus on excess inadequate to the solution of these problems?

In fact, Shiller and Minsky conceptualise bubbles in radically different ways. Shiller, the financial economist with a background in the study of security prices, sees bubbles occurring as a result of an information cascade, whereas Minsky, the Post-Keynesian monetary theorist, at least as he is popularly understood, sees them occurring as a result of periodic excessive use of debt. For Shiller the solution is about innovation in the pricing of risk. The recommendations being drawn from a Minskyian perspective are about containment of debt and cyclical dynamics. The two perspectives are contradictory. Any effort to reign in the excesses of the finance sector based on a hybrid of these approaches is likely to face difficulties and may even reproduce some of the paradoxes of liquidity that Minsky (1986) theorised. Indeed, this becomes a plausible concern when we analyse the logic of implementation of solutions to excess in the case of house price derivatives and counter-cyclical buffers.

House price derivatives

Robert Shiller has been the most prescient mainstream economist to theorise bubbles in recent years. He included warnings about the technology bubble in his book *Irrational Exuberance*, including detailed information about the acceleration of American house prices in excess of historical trends in his second edition of the same title (Shiller 2005). He has been an influential voice guiding reform of the financial system in the wake of the crisis (Soros 2009). This section applies the "idealised theory – historicised reality" framework of analysis, which prior chapters in the book have exemplified, to Shiller's comments on recent financial instability.

For Shiller (2008) bubbles are a problem of rationality. The movement towards the truth, which comes about as a result of arbitrage in the EMH, is temporarily halted for an indeterminate amount of time as market prices come to represent

Economics, regulation and capital 113

"information cascades" rather than competing perspectives on value. Shiller outlines how bubbles consist of information cascades whereby

> [t]hose in a group disregard their own independent, individually collected information which might otherwise encourage them not to subscribe to a boom or other mass belief because they feel that everyone else simply couldn't be wrong. And when they disregard their own information, and act instead on general information as they perceive it, they squelch their own information. It is no longer available to the group and so does not figure in further collective judgements.
>
> (Shiller 2008:47)

Indeed, Shiller sees the solution to the sub-prime crisis as consisting of improved information infrastructure, presentation of existing information and economic choices in a way that is easier for lay people to digest and the democratisation of financial risk management tools through the creation of new products that are useful to people, not just financial institutions, so that they have an increased ability to identify and process risks (Shiller 2008:115–169). Shiller advocates for subsidised financial advice, a consumer product safety commission, improved financial disclosure and improved financial databases and better and more publicly available measurement indexes of growth. These measures will help to reduce the prevalence of irrational pricing in the financial system by making bubbles easier to identify as deviations from plausible trends and hence harder to rationalise.

Shiller proposes the development of a number of new markets to help people, not just financial institutions, to manage the risks they face. Shiller argues that derivatives facilitate risk management rather than risk avoidance and can therefore have the capacity to play a civilizing role in our society by encouraging people to take productive risks (Shiller 2008). Shiller argues for single-family home-price futures, which have recently been listed on the Chicago Mercantile Exchange but are in need of more liquidity to help them realise their potential. These futures enable house buyers to hedge against the risk of the value of their house declining. In a similar vein he also argues for continuous workout mortgages to low-income borrowers whereby repayments are indexed to income and house price growth. He also favours home equity insurance and livelihood insurance (Shiller 2008:157–169).

Counter-cyclical buffers

Various economists have been theorising ways to deal with the issue of liquidity and bubbles using the work of Minsky in order to manage liquidity in the credit system across the business cycle. One of Minsky's main claims was that the financial system is subject to periodic build-ups of hidden risk (Borio 2009a). Economists, regulators and policy makers now know they have to contend with the risks inherent in the credit cycle manifested in the interplay between asset prices and leverage (FSB 2009).

114 *Economics, regulation and capital*

Indeed, Minsky sought to evoke how the essential feature of "capitalism as a financial system" was that stability was destabilizing (Minsky 2011). He attempted to evoke this through his cash flow taxonomy in which he distinguished among three different financing techniques and their stance toward debt. Hedge financing units can pay off the interest and some of the principal from the income generated by their investments, hence they experience no uncertainty about the future. The present and the future are a continuum under their control. A speculative financial unit can pay only the interest and must roll over their debts depending on an expanded income in the future, or capital gains to generate profits and pay down their principal. Ponzi units, as noted above, cannot pay either the interest or the principal on their debts and must roll over debts depending on capital gains to stay solvent (Minsky 2011).

Minsky's theory of instability argues that the business cycle is determined by the endogenous dynamics of debt, that is, the price of credit risk as it manifests itself in the financial structure of financial units. The cycle starts when banks grow more confident in extending debt. The resulting growth from expanded debt use leads to additional growth in asset values, and lower risk premiums lead to higher leverage. As these pro-cyclical mechanisms kick in, the debt growth reaches a point where Ponzi financing units become increasingly prevalent. Ponzi units cannot service their debt with income, which are now by necessity floating debts subject to rollover, but rely on increasing asset values to cover this shortfall. Hence, Ponzi units are highly vulnerable to a decrease in asset values or a rise in interest rates. When this occurs, the financial system kicks into reverse as Ponzi units attempt to sell their positions in the market to make position on their debts leading to accelerating declines in asset values that begin to jeopardise the more stable units they have borrowed from, such as the banks, as growth in the economy stalls (Keen 1995:612).

The cash flow taxonomy was Minsky's way of capturing the modern manifestation of a liquidity crisis, in a banking system where financial units could buy funds and were not solely reliant on deposit funding, where a decrease in asset prices, an increase in interest rates or some obstruction in the money markets could cause speculative units to become Ponzi units and Ponzi units to face insolvency. The fate of speculative and Ponzi units was therefore not determined by the perspicacity of mangers but by money market conditions.

The Bank of International Settlements and the Basel committee convene the Financial Stability Forum, which includes policy makers from various central banks and financial regulators. This forum is a vehicle on which these member organisations can work together to take action on ensuring that post–financial crisis regulation is based around the undeniable fact of cyclical risk in the financial system. The *Report of the Financial Stability Forum on Addressing Procyclicality in the Financial System* (2009) includes recommendations that banks be required to develop counter-cyclical capital buffers (see also Borio 2009).

The intention is to impose a cost to leverage, thereby dampening pro-cyclicality in the financial system. The buffer also serves a dual function as a disincentive to leverage and an insurance scheme providing a larger cushion of safety during

Economics, regulation and capital   115

the downturn to cover write-downs on loss of income when Ponzi units fail to repay their debts to banks. This would help to prevent the banks themselves from becoming Ponzi units dependent on borrowings from central banks.

These measures were recently implemented in America and the UK via the _Dodd–Frank Wall Street Reform and Consumer Protection Act 2010_[1] in America and the _Financial Services Act 2012_[2] in the UK.

Contradictions in the underlying conceptual framework of these ideas

These two ideas appear to be conceptually consistent, on the level of intellectual discourse, as solutions to excess. They are both offsetting mechanisms that hedge against cyclicality. Yet I argue that they would be deeply contradictory if widely implemented in practice in a way that illustrates the links between financial innovation and financial instability, that is, the dialectics of liquidity crisis. These measures exemplify how financial instability is being addressed through processes that fail to realise that instability arises out of transformation of the form of capital, the core process in the generation of liquidity.

For instance, it is possible that Minskyian debt dynamics could arise in relation to the solutions that Shiller suggests. For example, to the extent to which house price derivatives and home equity insurance facilitate lower risk premiums, as lenders recognise that borrowers have transferred the risk associated with asset price deflation, the amount of equity and the interest rate on debt used to finance housing could be reduced. This would expand the amount of finance flowing into housing. The increased volume of finance flowing into housing would likely increase the capital value of housing and initially lower risk for both sides of the derivative trade on house prices, creating an effect that resembled a more efficient allocation of capital as EMH implies should occur when risk is more accurately priced, but is actually the beginnings of the upward phase in the credit cycle. A time could come when, given the expanded volume of investment, it becomes apparent that risk premiums have been discounted too far to cover the extended frontier of new investment made in conditions dissimilar to historical circumstances. At this point, those selling coverage would likely attempt to dump their positions that would create a glut in the market, causing these positions to be discounted. This would increase the cost of writing new coverage that would decrease the volume of investment in housing, which would affect capital values, creating a self-fulfilling prophecy of decreasing house prices. This would drag a higher number of options into the red, further decreasing their value and creating a collapse in the market as a result of the interaction of the market liquidity of these options and the funding liquidity for housing.

This picture, although admittedly only a plausible conjecture, indicates that Shiller's proposals may be flawed because despite their name, derivatives are not separate from the liquidity of the underlying asset and can influence its value, which exists in terms of the totality of relations in the financial system, not just as an independent atomised quantity. This point is crucial because it

116 *Economics, regulation and capital*

illustrates how a focus solely on excess, without understanding structural change through financial innovation, is flawed. Deviation from trend lines can occur as a result of the transformation of the underlying financial system in the way it constructs value.

If this is the case, then Shiller's advocacy of derivatives and rational markets, if implemented, could subject the economy to a peculiar problem. Shiller's enthusiasm for risk management technologies would have us striving to develop markets based on new information infrastructure and hedging tools that could ostensibly bring us closer to developing efficient markets, but the very act of implementing these markets would in fact take us further and further away from stability as liquidity dynamics in the secondary derivatives market interacted with funding dynamics in the primary market.

I do not want to argue that this will actually happen. There is a danger in Minskyian analysis and indeed crisis theory in general that the intellectual framework places its adherents in the position of constant anticipation of market collapse. The point I am trying to make is in relation to the coherence of reconstruction of economics as a discipline and the role of economics ideas in informing how value is constructed in the contemporary financial system – that as we have seen in relation to innovations, especially derivatives, innovation and regulations that inspire new innovations are deeply entwined with resolving the question "what is liquidity?" on a material level as well as on the level of intellectual discourse (Bryan and Rafferty 2006, MacKenzie 2006).

The problems with Shiller's idea suggest that we need to think carefully about the manner in which we understand bubbles. In fact, innovation and credit dynamics appear to be closely linked in this scenario in a way that Shiller would likely find counter-intuitive given his propensity for technical risk management. Hence, the focus of investigation needs to be deeper than excess and look into the instruments and innovations that constitute markets, i.e. of how liquidity is generated through new financial innovations such as securitisations and derivatives rather than in terms of the excesses of institutions, actors and asset prices.

Indeed, part of the argument of this book is that the financial crisis occurred as part of a process of transformation of the nature of capital flows that consequently affected credit dynamics. This is to say that the crisis manifested itself in credit dynamics that were a result of the structural transformation of finance from "a system of monetary processes into a system of commodity relations" (Bryan et al. 2009). Hence, we need to focus on understanding the qualitative nature of capital flows in terms of a history of forms that change in light of financial innovations rather than the changes in quantities of debt, leverage, growth and values.

Derivatives and capital

There is a further paradox inherent in dealing with this risk in the frame of hedging and counter-cyclicality. If we understand the contemporary development of capital in terms of extending the process of financialisation through hedging which forms the basis of the system of liquidity that led to the crisis, then it is clear that

Economics, regulation and capital   117

these ideas are a continuation of historical processes of the dialectics of liquidity crisis on both a theoretical level and potentially the shape of the conjuncture.

Indeed, the last crisis should not be understood as a cyclical phenomenon but as a systemic breakdown in the form of capital. Accordingly the measures arising from recent discourse in economics should be understood as reconstruction in a way that facilitates the reformation of capital along similar lines to the emergent system of liquidity that collapsed in the crisis of 2007–08.

For example, take Shiller's idea above, which was identified as being possibly subject to Minskyian dynamics if it becomes a widespread part of the market for mortgages. The only reason a home buyer would buy a derivative against their house price is if they wish to treat it as a source of wealth. The insurance is wasted money unless it enables the home-buyer to draw an offsetting income. Buying a derivative against a fall in the value of the house would enable the buyer to capitalise the house at a lower risk premium that would have the flow on effect of enabling them to increase the capitalisation of the house. If owners treat their house as a source of wealth, it means holding a floating debt against the house, i.e. engaging in a form of secured borrowing.[3] This is bad for households because they never build up any equity or cushion of safety. Hedging, understood in the context of the search for yield amongst a set of volatile investments, is very different from Minskyian hedge financing because it attempts to manage risk to enable accumulation rather than eradicate risk.

Managing risk implies leverage, especially in a system of secured borrowings, where the cost of capital is linked to asset prices. This means that uncertainty cannot be eradicated in a system of free price movements for collateralised borrowings, even with interest rate controls, because of what has been called the "upward instability of credit" (Mehrling 2011). This stems from the fact that most capital assets not only yield a direct income but include a "liquidity yield" as well, which can be understood as the possibility of capital gains, a derivative form of income (Minsky 1982a). Borrowers hold a floating debt against the value of an asset. Although hedging the capital gains should stabilise the value of the asset, this has consequences in terms of reflexivity because it could influence the carrying cost of the asset, the interest rate, because it adds security to lenders in a secured borrowing system. An apparent increase in the security of borrowings can cause a hidden build-up of risk because securing borrowings encourages a drop in interest rates that enable larger borrowings and hence increased sensitivity to interest rate changes later in the credit cycle (Borio 2009a).

The question is, are there parallels between hedging house prices and large banks taking measures to insulate themselves against cyclical risk? The problem is that although the regulators and large banks now recognise that there are risks in the credit cycle, they are attempting to deal with this issue through treating it as a "risk" – that is, through hedging techniques, not recognising that hedging itself is now a fundamental input of the credit cycle, i.e. part of how liquidity works in a securitised credit system where capital has a floating price.

Thus when banks adopt new measures in order to contain the pro-cyclical nature of the credit cycle by implementing counter-cyclical capital buffers and

118 *Economics, regulation and capital*

enhanced value-at-risk–based capital estimates in order to accumulate a larger buffer on the up-side of the cycle (see FSB 2009), this may eventually be offset by a corresponding reduction in the cost of capital in the money markets due to a perception that the problem of cyclical risk has been solved. This is likely to enable banks to increase their spreads and borrow more money on a short-term basis because it acts as a hedge against volatility and increases the security of its lenders.

In fact, securitisation was itself conceptualised as a capital preserving technology that enabled banks to manage their risk more effectively (Jabłecki and Machaj 2009, Minsky 2008). By moving many loans off balance sheet into special purpose vehicles, it was held that banks could reduce their exposure to credit risk and liquidity risk, thereby qualifying for cheaper funding in the money markets, which they then used to provide reserve lines of credit and bridging financing to SPVs which they managed (Blundell-Wignall and Atkinson 2009, Loutskina 2011, Schwartz and Order 1988). This suggests that shoring up capital buffers will not contribute to reducing the amplitude of the credit cycle.

It's difficult to get out of the loop because any innovation that works according to the logic of hedging facilitates the search for yield and is hence part of the reconstitution of the form of capital. The underlying problem is that it is difficult to use derivatives and option based thinking to ensure stability because on a systemic level they are also an important part of the form of capital.

Conclusion: observations on the paradoxes of reform of economics and economic policy

This chapter began with some reflections on the nature of economics, noting that the collapse of markets in the FC has not inspired a critique of markets as such but rather rethinking of the nature of markets as phenomena – they do not naturally emerge and work perfectly but must be framed by empirical study and intervention. This discourse treats the organisational form of markets as shibboleth but seeks to temper the excesses and shape the dynamics of asset prices in these markets through various offsetting measures.

The social formations of markets are therefore a sublimated part of these solutions. Economists have tended to devise solutions with an un-reflexive connection to the social formation in which they are to be deployed, not recognising that these solutions could serve merely to reconstitute the problems that have just been experienced.

The intention of this analysis is not to affirm predictions of further crisis, because this analysis of these ideas is really only a plausible conjecture dependent on their future uptake and degree of presence in the economy, but to make a methodological point about the nature of economic thinking as inherently constrained by the circumstances in which it is conducted.

This argument even applies to Minskyian economics as it is commonly understood in terms of debt dynamics. Understood in this way, Minskyian economics is a somewhat incomplete perspective in that it is mainly diagnostic: it identifies

Economics, regulation and capital   119

the problems of free markets and prescribes the solution to their crisis. It is therefore part of the same form of capital in that it invokes an ideal of stable markets, the attempt at realisation of which enables the continuation of the dialectics of liquidity crisis. It appears to be critical but is so descriptive and now so inherent to markets that it is part of the somewhat gothic creation that is the contemporary form of capital.

The contrast I have performed above, namely reading solutions to the crisis in terms of their effect on the conjuncture, reveals a paradox of the use of economic crisis theory, suggesting that the unintended side effects of theory itself are part of the object to be analysed. Indeed, the crucial issue is the analysis of the extension and development of the form of capital. However, this tends not to occur in a straightforward fashion but in terms of the implementation of new economic theories that aim at the resolution of problems in the previous form of capital.

Notes

1 See http://financialservices.house.gov/Dodd–Frank/.
2 See http://www.hm-treasury.gov.uk/fin_financial_services_bill.htm.
3 This proposition that innovation in managing volatility encourages mortgage borrowers to float their debts is explored in depth in relation to sub-prime mortgages in the previous chapter.

9 Conclusion

This book has explored the use of economic theory, particularly Minsky's Financial Instability Hypothesis (FIH), in the explanation of financial crisis focusing on the crisis of 2007–08. However, this exploration of the explanatory power of this theory to capture the events of 2007–08 ended up telling us as much about deep-seated issues with the use of theory in Post-Keynesian economics as it did about the event itself. The exploration of issues with the use of the FIH illustrated the importance of historicizing theory in order to understand crisis in a way that is appropriate to the particular historical details and form of capital that define it.

Crisis is not just an aberrant event to be explained but provides a standpoint from which to develop greater understanding about the uses of economic theories. This is because crisis provides material examples of the limitations of economic theory to understand and govern the economy. Indeed, this book interpreted the problem of crisis as a historical problem in that crisis illustrates how the objects of economics and finance – "liquidity", the "money supply" and "risk" – are continually in need of definition and re-definition according to historical developments.

Indeed, the most interesting and creative dimension of economic theory (indeed all theory) is precisely when theory does not exactly 'explain' and events do not exactly 'fit'. Indeed, while in much analysis there is an attempt (conscious or otherwise) to analytically 'bury' the mismatch, it is in the mismatch that theoretical and analytical innovation are to be usefully explored. This has been the abiding driver of analysis in this book.

The importance of the phenomena of financial crisis to economic understanding is slightly different to what Post-Keynesian economists, including Minsky (1972, 1986), have previously attributed to it. The argument that Minsky makes (and is common to heterodox economics in general) is that an understanding of economics that does not admit crisis as an important element is ignoring the real world workings of the economy and particularly the financial system. Post-Keynesians argue that the existence of crisis requires the development of theories that are adequate to the explanation of crisis.

However, what Minsky proposes is not so much a consideration of the issue of crisis itself and its implications for theory but using crisis as a rationale for theory. This book has explored how we need to go beyond this approach to crisis as testament to theory and consider the problems that crisis poses for the endeavour of theorizing the financial system itself. This approach promises to allow us to interpret and use theory in a way that engenders more understanding about both the nature of financial history – the development of the form of capital, and its relationship to economic theory.

Indeed, the consideration of crisis illustrates philosophical issues about the way the theories used in economics and finance relate to history. When we understand crisis, as a standpoint from which to interpret the functions of economics, we are entering into the domain of philosophy, particularly dialectical logic. This form of philosophy provides a way of understanding the historical issues with the use of abstract models and ideals for understanding the world. Dialectical logic involves historicizing the practice of theorisation to use the historical errors of economic theory to express insights about the development of the underlying object, that is, the form of capital.

Viewing economics from the perspective of the history of financial crisis acts as a spur towards a more radical pluralism, not just in terms of the need for heterodox economics but in terms of consideration of metaphysics (the nature of reality and causation), phenomenology (the historical logic of appearances), epistemology (the historical underpinnings of various forms of knowledge) and ontology (consideration of the various structures of experience and perspectives on history). What is needed is the development of new forms of historical reflexivity inspired by the experience of crisis and the insights it can give us into the limitations of economic understanding.

To some extent this is occurring in the mainstream of economics. In the wake of the crisis, conventional economists now advocate for "free markets" in a way that is reflexive of the apparent historical fact that free markets do not appear naturally. New regulations introduced in the United States in the wake of the financial crisis of 2007–08, such as Dodd–Frank display a commitment towards overtly regulating for the free market (see Appendix D at the end of this chapter for a description of the Dodd–Frank reforms to the US financial system).

The conventionally accepted explanation of the crisis that has now been embodied in Dodd–Frank regulations sees a growth in too-big-to-fail (TBTF) institutions as creating market failure that led to the crisis of 2007–08. In this view, the explanation of the crisis is conducted by identifying the obstacles to the emergence of the free market, that is, the factors that contribute to "market failure". The growth of TBTF institutions that could extract discounts on borrowings because of a perceived implicit government guarantee for their liabilities due to the implied threat of contagion and systemic breakdown and consequent likelihood of receiving a bailout from the central bank exemplified market failure. The ability to privatise the gains and socialise the losses introduced a "moral hazard" because TBTFs could avoid risk.

Indeed, the provisions in Dodd–Frank largely mirror Stiglitz's argument that ultimately regulators are to blame for enabling the growth of this type of market structure (Stiglitz 2009). US regulators took a hands-off attitude to monitoring the risk-taking activities of US financial institutions while on the other hand too often taking an active role in bailing out ailing financial institutions deemed TBTF. The

122 *Conclusion*

task therefore is to regulate the financial system in a way that facilitates appropriate risk taking.

From this perspective the event of crisis and consequent bailout creates a moment, a perspective, from which causation can be attributed. It reveals the crisis as an instance of regulatory failure in which the effects of the crisis, the bailouts, could be said plausibly to have caused the crisis retrospectively by setting up skewed incentives to take risk. Furthermore, the actions of the central bank and treasury in bailing out TBTF institutions also seems to reproduce the problem into the future by creating incentives for institutions to continue with this growth strategy.

The value of this explanation is that it posits a reflexive metaphysics and recognises the materialism of abstractions such as risk in the operation of the economy and the need to go beyond strictly mechanistic theories of economic causation towards understanding how the financial system can behave in a "reflexive" manner (Soros 2008; Stiglitz 2009, 2010). There is an advance in the understanding of the historical materialism of abstractions such as risk that was formerly held to be a largely positive and independent phenomenon in the economy. The coherence of the abstraction of risk and its ability to exercise a self-sustaining discipline on economic activity is now understood to be influenced by the regulatory system in which the conceptualisation and evaluation of risk is embedded.

However, the conceptualisation of the materialism of risk (which I discussed in Chapters 3–7) is still inadequately historical in the above account. Reflexivity comes after the fact and there is an assumption that an ideal risk profile can be constructed. There is not enough appreciation of how thoroughly historical the concept of risk is, with only the appearance of a rational construction, but a materiality as a form of liquidity stemming from historical transformation.

This deficiency means that Dodd–Frank reforms are interesting to consider, not so much as an example of the development of adequate metaphysics of the economy, but mainly for the extent to which they illustrate the importance of historicizing types of risk and liquidity, for the intention of regulation is to reconstruct a new, more resilient regulatory architecture to facilitate risk taking. In relation to Dodd–Frank reforms, regulatory measures and instruments that attempt to prevent market failure by removing obstacles to the identification and accurate pricing of risk could create a new form of liquidity that has value precisely because it abstracts from the problems of prior forms of risk.

Indeed, this book has looked at many similar moments in US financial history arguing that it is possible to interpret this dynamic whereby the subject (economics and economic policy) continually attempts to define and control its object, as influencing liquidity and the form of capital.

The contribution of this book

This book has attempted to go beyond the conceptual limitations discussed above, exploring the importance of crisis to economics using the consideration of crisis as a set of historical standpoints from which to move towards the analytical

Conclusion 123

objective of defining the form of capital and the associated determinants of liquidity while critiquing the inadequacies of economic theory to grasp these objects which they profess to take as their focus.

In regard to metaphysics of crisis and the associated issue of the epistemology of economic theories, this book has explored how the financial system can appear to behave mechanistically under the influence of positivist theories as Chapter 3 on Monetarism and Chapter 5 on the Efficient Markets Hypothesis illustrated. The Monetarists believed that the central bank need only control the money supply to secure stability. The financial economists believed that market participants need only compete in their conception of quantitative measures of risk in order to deepen the market to increase liquidity and stability. Both of these schools of economics are underpinned by a "scientistic" epistemology based on the testing of hypothesis, about the correlation of certain factors with inflation and growth in the case of the Monetarists and about risk correlations in the case of financial economists.

However, the appearance of the achievement of positive knowledge over the economy, which Monetarists such as Friedman (1966) claimed and is implicit in the methodology of financial economics, is generally a determinate and temporary effect of history. This book has illustrated how the development of the shape of markets (what I have called in this book the form of capital) came to confound both these positivist frameworks, partially as a result of the very influence of these theories on the historical dynamics of accumulation.

In this regard, Minsky's FIH provides an interesting alternative metaphysics that sees crisis as an emergent phenomenon that necessarily manifests itself as a result of the universal flaws of greed and systemic risk inherent to the market system. For Minsky these elements of the economy deserve attention over and above any fantasy of positive understanding and control of the financial system.

This Minskyian critique, although a useful alternative metaphysics, poses its own problems, though. This approach, considered on its own as a stand-alone theory, cannot provide a historically determinate account of crisis except as critique of these forms of positivism. But the act of critique locates Minsky's metaphysics in a particular conjuncture, historicizing it insofar as the Minskyian critique looks at fragility in existing financial relations, using this fragility as its analytical axis.

An analysis of the importance of critique to understanding and the consideration of the historical problems associated with the use of Minsky's theory in explanation of crisis have not been thoroughly conducted by Minsky or contemporary Minskyians in an adequate fashion because they are too eager to style their perspective as a positive theory or hypothesis. Heterodox economists interested in Minsky's work present it as an alternative to mainstream understanding, rather than a form of historicizing critique that potentially draws on more sophisticated philosophical concepts to express how the financial system develops.

I have explored these issues with Minsky's metaphysics of crisis in this book, arguing that the FIH can be better understood as immanent to modern finance. As illustrated in Chapters 4, 5, and particularly 7, which analysed the sub-prime crisis, the stages of Minsky's FIH, the hedge, speculative and Ponzi finance, are

124   *Conclusion*

dialectical descriptions of how systems in which there are processes that habituate participants to risk can often develop hidden systemic risks. The FIH expresses the contradiction of risk management in that mitigating risk expands the amount of risk that can be taken. Chapter 7 explored how to some extent it does not matter what type of risk is discussed, whether it be short-term loans in the money market or commodified risk such as derivatives. All are subject to the contradiction in their universal abstract form as risk, although the way this contradiction plays out will be historically specific. In this sense, risk management is a form of liquidity and the FIH is immanent (infused in) as well as imminent (about to happen) to modern financial techniques of risk management.

This book makes a contribution to our understanding of the epistemology of economic theory. It has focused on exploring the relationship between subject (theory) and object (the form of capital) arguing that Keynesian forms of economics and financial economics are mutually constitutive in terms of their respective effects on the form of capital. In practical terms this means that the actions of the central bank in providing lender-of-last-resort assistance to ailing financial institutions have historically tended to involve allowing new financial innovations to be accepted as forms of liquidity, providing a spur to financial innovation. In turn, these financial innovations, which are generally new forms of credit risk, tend to enable more efficient forms of arbitrage, giving rise to the visions of modern finance, that the more sophisticated conceptualisation of risk drives increases in liquidity and stability.

I argued in Chapter 5 for a way of making sense of these differing perspectives on the form of capital in terms of the way that these visions and associated economic policies and logics of market and price formation can be interpreted as being part of a structure of arbitrage in the US financial system. I argue that we can do this by reading Minsky's FIH as a historically determinate study of liquidity dynamics. This means re-interpreting Minsky's FIH in terms of the more fully developed processes and forms of arbitrage of the current financial system which the historical developments that Minsky was analysing eventually resulted in. Although this may appear teleological, it is not, because at the heart of the development of the US financial system and the liquidity dynamics that Minsky was analysing is a process of financial innovation whereby financial units arbitraged new, more flexible forms of capital against prior, less fungible forms of capital (Wojnilower 1980). The development of financial forms therefore tended to occur according to the need to find more streamlined ways of arbitraging prior forms of capital.

This book also included a "sociological interlude" (Chapter 6) that considered the epistemology of financial models by analysing explanation of the positivity of financial models as being indirectly positive, that is, "performative" (MacKenzie 2009). This section looked at the relationship between the epistemology of modelling and the phenomenology of risk. It argued that the discourse of risk can be understood as a way of commensurating the value of hard-to-compare assets. I interpreted the appearance of the performativity of financial models in terms of the ability of financial models to increase liquidity through commensuration. The

Conclusion 125

function of the discourse of risk is to make these assets easier to exchange for one another, thereby increasing liquidity. The power of the discourse of risk to construct value can be explained in terms of the historical process of transformation of the form of capital in terms of the addition of a new, more abstract, more mobile form of value. This form of value gave these models the appearance of performativity. However, given that the form of capital relied on transformation of older forms of capital, the liquidity that was created was inherently part of a historical process, and therefore unstable because it relied on the continuation of the process of transformation, past its own limits of viability, to retrospectively justify the attribution of increasing values.

Chapter 8 then looked at how the immanence of liquidity in risk means that efforts towards reconstruction of the form of capital, whether pursued with inspiration from theories about asymmetrical information (Stiglitz 2009), behavioural economics (Shiller 2008) or in terms of capital buffers (FSB 2009), are likely to reproduce the problem of liquidity crisis into the future. Indeed, the problem of liquidity crisis is inherent to capitalism in that it stems from the relationship between the standpoint from which economists and regulators develop and argue for their theories (ontology) and historical development of the form of capital.

All of the arguments in this book are based on the premise that the objective of scholarship should be to find a way to develop concepts and use them in a way that is adequate to providing an understanding of history. The argument in this book, about the immanence of Minsky's FIH to the crisis of 2007–08 and the nature of liquidity as an inherently historical phenomenon, indicates that we need to view economic theory through the prism of crisis, not just develop theories of crisis, in order to be able to use theory in a way that can help to develop an increased understanding about how to conceptualise the historical development of the form of capital.

APPENDIX D

Dodd–Frank regulation

Dodd–Frank is geared towards ensuring that the largest banks are curtailed in the extent to which they can take risk given that they are now manifestly TBTF (Acharya et al. 2010, Skeel 2010). It does this by seeking to increase the transparency of the financial markets to give regulators enough information to make a judgment about the effects of failure of a TBTF institution. It also seeks to curtail the likelihood of failure and extent of contagion that would ensue should the institution fail by building up firewalls between it and other institutions and internal capital buffers.

Dodd–Frank is specifically designed to cover "systemically important financial institutions" (SIFIs) formalizing the hitherto implicit category of TBTF. It subjects these institutions to various additional monitoring and capital and liquidity requirements. SIFIs are defined as banks over $50 billion in assets or a systemically

126   *Conclusion*

important non-bank financial institution as determined by the Financial Stability Oversight Council. Dodd–Frank gives the Federal Reserve the power to mandate an increase in capital buffers, the issuance of contingent capital or reduced reliance on short-term debt in order to guarantee liquidity.

These measures address the incentive for TBTF institutions to use leverage in a way that is pro-cyclical and creates systemic risk. In the lead-up to the crisis many of the largest US banks used the availability of cheap credit in the context of low short terms interest rates and cheap funding in the money markets to expand their borrowings associated with real estate. This created a virtuous spiral whereby the expanded credit led to growth in asset prices, which helped to facilitate leverage by ensuring that loans issued at the beginning of the cycle were easily paid off or refinanced as the value of the underlying asset increased. Indeed, liquidity, the capacity of the system to generate credit and leverage are integrally and pro-cyclically entwined in this way. Hence both asset holdings and leverage grew dramatically across the sector in the context of asset price inflation from 2000–2007 (Adrian and Shin 2009, FCIC 2010:65).

The governance provisions in Dodd–Frank are designed to make it easier for regulators to determine the risk of a bank's involvement in derivatives trading and connectedness to other institutions. The legislation includes various provisions moving many forms of derivatives trading onto exchanges. The law also now requires hedge funds to register with the SEC for monitoring and requires commercial banks to set up subsidiaries to trade derivatives so as to increase the transparency of their balance sheets. These measures make it easier for regulators to estimate the extent of counter-party risk in the derivatives markets.

These measures are designed to ensure that the US government is not placed in a similar position to the conundrum it was in when faced with the potential for failure of AIG. From late 2007 a number of CDOs protected by CDS issued by AIG began to be downgraded and counterparties demanded an increase in capital from AIG. At the same time, AIG's lenders demanded that AIG repay its loans which it had used to hold investments in MBS. AIG was significantly larger than Lehman Brothers, which the Fed had just allowed to collapse and there were more concerns about the exposure of large banks and money market mutual funds to AIG. AIG was the largest writer of CDS and its failure would have jeopardised confidence in the whole financial system given that nobody knew the extent of exposure that their counterparties had to AIG. Banks would have ceased to lend to one another for fear of counter-party risk (FCIC 2010:26–27).

An important part of the effort to simplify the banking system and reduce the growth of large complex financial institutions that are TBTF is contained in the Volker rule, which is reminiscent of Glass–Steagall to some extent in that it reintroduces a demarcation between commercial banking and investment banking. The Volker rule is intended to curtail the ability of commercial banks from conducting proprietary trading which involves trading as, or investing in, hedge funds above 3 per cent of the hedge funds capitalisation and 3 per cent of their own capital. The provisions under the Volker rule also regulate the interconnectedness

Conclusion 127

of those involved in the repo market, ensuring that they cannot lend to other institutions to which they already have up to 25 per cent exposure.

These measures are designed to prevent the build-up of hidden risks and interconnections in proprietary trading. This type of in house pro-cyclical securities trading caused Citigroup to take a $39 billion write-down on its ABS portfolio in late 2007 and early 2008, bringing the off-balance sheet hedge funds back onto its balance sheet to prevent failure (Laux and Leuz 2009). UBS was also forced to write down billions of dollars against its proprietary trading operations. The Shareholder Report on UBS's Write-Downs (UBS 2008:14, 22–23) provides a particularly clear description of how UBS came to write down a similar amount on its proprietary trading account. UBS held a large position in ABS CDOs in hedge funds that it had set up using client brokerage funds as equity. UBS hedged the middle tranches of its holdings using credit default swaps with AIG. It funded these holdings by posting these positions as collateral in the repo market. However, as sub-prime borrowers began to default on their mortgages, it was not only the middle tranches that experienced losses, which had been anticipated and were therefore hedged, but also the top AAA rated tranches of many ABS CDOs. This caused a liquidity crisis in the repo market as lenders sought a larger haircut to lend against AAA rated ABS CDOs. UBS was eventually forced by the run in the repo market to bring these positions onto their own books by providing financing to the hedge funds they had set up to continue to hold their ABS CDO positions.

The regulation also includes various other provisions less relevant to the TBTF problem, and hence I will not go into detail about them here, but relevant to the structure of markets such as increased consumer protection and education. It takes away responsibility from the Federal Reserve for consumer protection recognizing that the Fed's mandate is to generate stable growth, which can sometimes outweigh their priority or at least motivation to focus on consumer protection. It sets up the consumer protection bureau.

Overall, Dodd–Frank's strategic though unstated intentions are to encourage non-bank activity and herd risk taking on credit risk into the hedge fund sector where the institutions are generally smaller and can be allowed to fail without the risk of contagion. Dodd–Frank appears to be strategically designed to realise the market ideal, but just not in the banking sector until the megabanks have withered back down to a more manageable size.

Bibliography

Acharya, V. V. (2009). Manufacturing tail risk: A perspective on the financial crisis of 2007–2009. *Foundations and Trends® in Finance*, *4*(4): 247–325.

Acharya, V. V., Cooley, T. F., Richardson, M. P., & Walter, I. (2010). *Regulating Wall Street: The Dodd–Frank Act and the New Architecture of Global Finance* (Vol. 608). New York: Wiley & Sons.

Acharya, V. V., & Schnabl, P. (2010). Do global banks spread global imbalances? Asset-backed commercial paper during the financial crisis of 2007–2009. *IMF Economic Review*, *58*(1): 37–73.

Adrian, T., Estrella, A., & Shin, H. S. (2010). Monetary cycles, financial cycles, and the business cycle. *Staff Report, Federal Reserve Bank of New York* (No. 421).

Adrian, T., & Shin, H. S. (2009). The shadow banking system: Implications for financial regulation. *Staff Report, Federal Reserve Bank of New York* (No. 382).

Adrian, T., & Shin, H. S. (2010). Liquidity and leverage. *Journal of Financial Intermediation*, *19*(3): 418–437.

Althusser, Louis. (1981). "Marx's new science", in Bottomore, Tom (ed), *Modern Interpretations of Marx*. Oxford: Blackwell.

Althusser, Louis. (2005). *For Marx*. London: Verso.

Altman, E. I., & Sametz, A. W. (1977). *Financial Crises: Institutions and Markets in a Fragile Environment*. New York: John Wiley & Sons.

Argyrous, G. (2011). "The economics of the general theory", in Argyrous, G. & Stilwell, F. (eds), *Readings in Political Economy: Economics as a Social Science*, 3rd edition. Prahran: Tilde University Press: 164–171.

Austin, J. L. (1965). *How to Do Things with Words: The William James Lectures Delivered at Harvard University in 1955*. Oxford: Clarendon Press.

Baker, A. (2013). The new political economy of the macroprudential ideational shift. *New Political Economy*, *18*(1): 112–139.

Barberis, N., & Thaler, R. (2002). A survey of behavioral finance, NBER Working Paper 9222.

Barnes, Barry. (1983). Social life as bootstrapped induction. *Sociology*, *17*: 524–545.

Beiser, Frederick C. (2005). *Hegel*. New York: Routledge.

Beiser, Frederick C. (2008). *German Idealism: The Struggle against Subjectivism, 1781–1801*. Cambridge, MA: Harvard University Press.

Bernanke, B. (2009) Financial Reform to Address Systemic Risk. Speech At the Council on Foreign Relations, Washington, D.C. March 10, 2009. Available at https://www.federalreserve.gov/newsevents/speech/bernanke20090310a.htm?__hstc=2422639.913513 09f40c7c5d244ce0fc1171fa17.1404864000029.1404864000030.1404864000031.1&__hssc=2422639.1.1404864000032&__hsfp=1314462730. Accessed June 18 2010.

Bibliography 129

Bernstein, J., & Eisinger, J. (2010). The Magnetar trade: How one hedge fund helped keep the bubble going. *ProPublica*, April 9, 2010. https://www.propublica.org/article/all-the-magnetar-trade-how-one-hedge-fund-helped-keep-the-housing-bubble

Bernstein, P. L. (1993). *Capital Ideas: The Improbable Origins of Modern Wall Street*. New York: Free Press.

Bernstein, P. L. (1996). *Against the Gods: The Remarkable Story of Risk*. New York: John Wiley & Sons.

Bernstein, W. (2012). *Skating Where the Puck Was: The Correlation Game in a Flat World*. Efficient Frontiers Publications.

Beunza, D., & Stark, D. (2010). 'Models, reflexivity and systemic risk: A critique of behavioral finance' paper prepared for the workshop 'Reembedding Finance' Paris, May, *Available at* http://SSRN.com/abstract1285054. Accessed 1 May 2011.

Bhardwaj, G., & Sengupta, R. (2008). Sub-prime mortgage design. *Federal Reserve Bank of St. Louis Working Paper 2008–039E*.

Bitner, R. (2008). *Confessions of a Sub-prime Lender: An Insider's Tale of Greed, Fraud, and Ignorance*. Hoboken, NJ: John Wiley & Sons.

Blaug, M. (1975). Kuhn versus Lakatos, or paradigms versus research programmes in the history of economics. *History of Political Economy*, 7(4): 399–433.

Blundell-Wignall, A., & Atkinson, P. (2009). Origins of the financial crisis and requirements for reform. *Journal of Asian Economics*, 20(5): 536–548.

Bookstaber, R. (2008). *A Demon of Our Own Design: Markets, Hedge Funds, and the Perils of Financial Innovation*. Hoboken, NJ: Wiley & Sons.

Borio, C. (2004). Market distress and vanishing liquidity: Anatomy and policy options. *BIS Working Paper No. 158*. Available from SSRN at http://papers.ssrn.com/sol3/papers.cfm?abstract_id=781228. Accessed 28 March 2013.

Borio, C. (2009). The macroprudential approach to regulation and supervision. *VoxEU.org*, 14 April 2009. Available at http://voxeu.org/article/we-are-all-macroprudentialists-now. Accessed 30 June 2011.

Borio, C. (2009a). Ten propositions about liquidity crises. *BIS Working Papers No. 293*.

Borio, C., & Zhu, H. (2008). Capital regulation, risk-taking and monetary policy: A missing link in the transmission mechanism? *BIS Working Papers No. 268*. Available at http://www.bis.org/publ/work268.htm. Accessed 28 March 2013.

Brown, A. (2006). *The Poker Face of Wall Street*. Hoboken, NJ: Wiley & Sons.

Brunnermeier, M. K. (2009). Deciphering the liquidity and credit crunch 2007–2008. *Journal of Economic Perspectives*, 23(1): 77–100.

Brunnermeier, M. K., & Pedersen, L. H. (2005). Predatory trading. *The Journal of Finance*, 60(4): 1825–1863.

Brunnermeier, M. K., & Pedersen, L. H. (2009). Market liquidity and funding liquidity. *Review of Financial Studies*, 22(6): 2201–2238.

Bryan, D. (2009). Marketing opportunities from the global financial crisis. *Australian Review of Public Affairs*. April 2009. Available at http://www.australianreview.net/digest/2009/04/bryan.html. Accessed June 10 2009.

Bryan, D., Martin, R., & Rafferty, M. (2009). Financialization and Marx: Giving labour and capital a financial makeover. *Review of Radical Political Economics*, 41(4): 458–472.

Bryan, D., & Rafferty, M. (2006). *Capitalism with Derivatives: A Political Economy of Financial Derivatives, Capital and Class*. Houndmills, Basingstoke, Hampshire: Palgrave Macmillan.

Bryan, D., & Rafferty, M. (2011). Deriving capital's (and labour's) future. *Socialist Register*, 47: 196–223.

130   *Bibliography*

Bryan, D., & Rafferty, M. (2013). Fundamental value: A category in transformation. *Economy and Society, 42*(1): 130–153.

Callon, M. (2006). What does it mean to say that economics is performative? IDEAS Working Paper Series from RePEc, 2006.

Calomiris, C. (2007). Not (yet) a Minsky Moment. *American Enterprise Institute Report.* October 5, 2007. Available at http://www.aei.org/papers/economics/financial-services/not-yet-a-minsky-moment. Accessed 28 March 2013.

Carlstrom, C. T., & Samolyk, K. A. (1995). Loan sales as a response to market-based capital constraints. *Journal of Banking & Finance, 19*(3): 627–646.

Carrozzo, P. M. (2004). Marketing the American mortgage: The emergency Home Finance Act of 1970, standarization and the secondary market revolution. *Real Prop. Prob. & Tr. J., 39*(4): 765.

Carruthers, B. G., & Stinchcombe, A. L. (1999). The social structure of liquidity: Flexibility, markets, and states. *Theory and Society, 28*(3): 353–382.

Cohan, W. D. (2009). *House of Cards: A Tale of Hubris and Wretched Excess on Wall Street.* New York: Doubleday.

Coleman, M., LaCour-Little, M., & Vandell, K. D. (2008). Sub-prime lending and the housing bubble: Tail wags dog? *Journal of Housing Economics, 17*(4): 272–290.

Cordell, L., Huang, Y., & Williams, M. (2012). Collateral damage: Sizing and assessing the sub-prime CDO crisis. *Working Paper No. 11–30/R.* Federal Reserve Bank of Philadelphia.

Demyanyk, Y., & Loutskina, E. (2016). Mortgage companies and regulatory arbitrage. *Journal of Financial Economics,* 122(2): 328–351.

Derman, E. (2011). *Models: Behaving. Badly: Why Confusing Illusion with Reality Can Lead to Disaster, on Wall Street and in Life.* New York, NY: Free Press.

Dow, S. C. (2012). *Foundations for New Economic Thinking: A Collection of Essays.* Houndmills, Basingstoke: Palgrave Macmillan.

Dryzek, J. S., & Dunleavy, P. (2009). *Theories of the Democratic State.* Basingstoke, Hampshire: Palgrave Macmillan.

Dymski, G. (2010). Why the sub-prime crisis is different: A Minskyian approach. *Cambridge Journal of Economics, 34*: 239–255.

Edmunds, J. C. (1996). Securities: The new world wealth machine. *Foreign Policy,* 104(104): 118–133.

Edmunds, J. C. (2003). *Brave New Wealthy World: Winning the Struggle for World Prosperity.* London: Prentice Hall.

Engelen, E., Erturk, I., Froud, J., Leaver, A., & Williams, K. (2010). Reconceptualizing financial innovation: Frame, conjuncture and bricolage. *Economy and Society, 39*(1): 33–63.

Fabozzi, F., Goodman, L., & Lucas, D. (2007). Collateralized debt obligations and credit risk transfer. *Yale ICF Working Paper No. 0706.*

Fabozzi, F., & Kothari, V. (2007). Securitization: The tool of financial transformation. *Yale ICF Working Paper No. 07–07.* Available from SSRN at http://ssrn.com/abstract=997079.

Fama, E. (1970). Efficient capital markets: A review of theory and empirical work. *Journal of Finance,* 25(2): 383–417.

Fama, E. (1980). Banking in the theory of finance. *Journal of Monetary Economics, 6*(1): 39–57.

Foucault, M. (2008). *The Birth of Biopolitics: Lectures at the Collège De France, 1978–79.* Houndmills, Basingstoke: Palgrave Macmillan.

Bibliography 131

Fox, J. (2009). *The Myth of the Rational Market: A History of Risk, Reward, and Delusion on Wall Street*. New York: HarperBusiness.

Friedman, M. (1966). *Essays in Positive Economics* (Vol. 231). Chicago, IL: University of Chicago Press.

Friedman, M. (March 1968). The role of monetary policy. *The American Economic Review*, 58(1): 1–17.

Friedman, M., & Goodhart, C. A. (2003). *Money, Inflation and the Constitutional Position of the Central Bank*. London: Institute of Economic Affairs.

Friedman, M., & Schwartz, A. J. (1963). *A Monetary History of the United States, 1867–1960*. Princeton, NJ: Princeton University Press.

Froud, J., Johal, S., Montgomerie, J., & Williams, K. (2010). Escaping the tyranny of earned income? The failure of finance as social innovation. *New Political Economy*, 15(1): 147–164.

Gadamer, H. G. (2006). *Truth and Method*. London, UK: Continuum.

Gibson-Graham, J. K., Resnick, S., Wolff, R., Graham, J., & Gibson, K. (Eds.). (2001). *Re/Presenting Class: Essays in Postmodern Marxism*. Durham, NC: Duke University Press Books.

Godelier, M. (1972). "Structure and contradiction in capital", in Blackburn, Robin (ed), *Ideology in the Social Sciences*. Suffolk: Fontana Collins.

Goodman, L. S., Li, S., Lucas, D. J., Zimmerman, T. A., & Fabozzi, F. J. (2008). *Sub-prime Mortgage Credit Derivatives* (Vol. 159). Hoboken, NJ: Wiley & Sons.

Gorton, G. (2008). The sub-prime panic*. *European Financial Management*, 15(1): 10–46.

Gorton, G. (2010). *Slapped by the Invisible Hand: The Panic of 2007*. Oxford: Oxford University Press.

Green, R. K., & Wachter, S. M. (2005). The American mortgage in historical and international context. *The Journal of Economic Perspectives*, 19(4): 93–114.

Greenspan, A. (2007). *The Age of Turbulence: Adventures in a New World*. New York: Penguin.

Guerrien, B., & Gun, O. (2011). Efficient markets hypothesis: What are we talking about? *Real-World Economics Review*, 56(March): 19–30.

Hafer, R. W. (2001). What remains of monetarism? *Economic Review-Federal Reserve Bank of Atlanta*, 86(4): 13–34.

Hafer, R. W., & Wheelock, D. C. (2001). The rise and fall of a policy rule: Monetarism at the St. Louis Fed, 1968–1986. *Federal Reserve Bank of St. Louis Review*, 83(1): 1–24.

Hafer, R. W., & Wheelock, D. C. (2003). Darryl Francis and the making of monetary policy, 1966–1975. *Review – Federal Reserve Bank of Saint Louis*, 85(2): 1–12.

Hardt, M., & Negri, A. (1994). *Labor of Dionysus: A Critique of the State-Form*. Minneapolis: University of Minnesota.

Hegel, G. W. F., & Houlgate, S. (2008). *Outlines of the Philosophy of Right*. Oxford: Oxford University Press.

Hester, D. D., Carron, A. S., & Goldfeld, S. M. (1981). Innovations and monetary control. *Brookings Papers on Economic Activity*, (1): 141–199.

Hill, C. A. (1996). Securitization: A low-cost sweetener for lemons. *Washington University Law Quarterly*, 74(4): 1061–1116.

Jabłecki, J., & Machaj, M. (2009). The regulated meltdown of 2008. *Critical Review*, 21(2–3): 301–328.

Jacobides, M. G. (2005). Industry change through vertical disintegration: How and why markets emerged in mortgage banking. *Academy of Management Journal*, 48(3): 465–498.

132 *Bibliography*

Jameson, F. (1981). *The Political Unconscious: Narrative as a Socially Symbolic Act.* Ithaca, NY: Cornell University Press.

Jameson, F. (2010). *Valences of the Dialectic.* London: Verso.

Kaufman, H. (1986). *Interest Rates, the Markets, and the New Financial World.* New York: Times.

Keen, S. (1995). Finance and economic breakdown: Modelling Minsky's financial instability hypothesis. *Journal of Post Keynesian Economics, 17*(4): 607–635.

Keen, S. (2009). The global financial crisis, credit crunches and deleveraging. *Journal of Australian Political Economy, 64*: 22–36.

Kelly, M. G. E. (2009). *The Political Philosophy of Michel Foucault.* New York: Routledge.

Kendall, L. T., & Fishman, M. J. (1996). *A Primer on Securitization.* Cambridge, MA: MIT Press.

Kindleberger, C. P., & Aliber, R. Z. (2005). *Manias, Panics, and Crashes: A History of Financial Crises.* Hoboken, NJ: John Wiley & Sons.

Kolari, J. W., Fraser, D. R., & Anari, A. (1998). The effects of securitization on mortgage market yields: A cointegration analysis. *Real Estate Economics, 26*(4): 677–693.

Konings, M. (2011). "The global financial crisis", in Argyrous, G. & Stilwell, F. (eds), *Readings in Political Economy: Economics as a Social Science.* Prahran: Tilde University Press: 7–10.

Kregel, J. (2008). Minsky's cushions of safety: Systemic risk and the crisis in the US subprime mortgage market. *Public Policy Brief//Jerome Levy Economics Institute of Bard College* (No. 93).

Krippner, G. R. (2011). *Capitalizing on Crisis: The Political Origins of the Rise of Finance.* Cambridge, MA: Harvard University Press.

Kroszner, R. S., & Shiller, R. J. (2011). *Reforming US Financial Markets: Reflections before and beyond Dodd–Frank.* Cambridge, MA: MIT Press.

LaGesse, D. (January 23, 1987). CMOs, still dominant, may be headed for a fall. *American Banker, 151*(16): 8.

Laux, C., & Leuz, C. (2009). The crisis of fair-value accounting: Making sense of the recent debate. *Accounting, Organizations and Society, 34*(6): 826–834.

Lea, M. J. (1996). Innovation and the cost of mortgage credit: A historical perspective. *Housing Policy Debate, 7*(1): 147–174.

LeRoy, S. (1976). Efficient capital markets: A comment. *Journal of Finance, 31*(1): 139–141.

Levine, N. (2009). Hegelian continuities in Marx. *Critique, 37*(3): 345–370.

Lewis, M. (1989). *Liar's Poker: Rising through the Wreckage on Wall Street.* New York: Norton.

Lewis, M. (2010). *The Big Short: Inside the Doomsday Machine.* New York, NY: Allen Lane.

Lo, A. (2005). Reconciling efficient markets with behavioral finance: The adaptive markets hypothesis. *Journal of Investment Consulting, 7*(2): 21–44.

Lo, A. (2011). Reading about the financial crisis: A 21-book review. *Journal of Economic Literature, 50*(1): 151–178.

Loutskina, E. (2011). The role of securitization in bank liquidity and funding management. *Journal of Financial Economics, 100*(3): 663–684.

Lowenstein, R. (2000). *When Genius Failed: The Rise and Fall of Long-Term Capital Management.* New York: Random House.

Lysandrou, P. (2005). Globalisation as commodification. *Cambridge Journal of Economics, 29*(5): 769–797.

Bibliography   133

Lysandrou, P. (2011a). Global inequality as one of the root causes of the financial crisis: A suggested explanation. *Economy and Society, 40*(3): 323–355.

Lysandrou, P. (2011b). The primacy of hedge funds in the sub-prime crisis. *Journal of Post Keynesian Economics, 34*(2): 225–254.

MacKenzie, D. A. (2003). Long-term capital management and the sociology of arbitrage. *Economy and Society, 32*(3): 349–380.

MacKenzie, D. A. (2006). *An Engine, Not a Camera: How Financial Models Shape Markets.* Cambridge, MA: MIT Press.

MacKenzie, D. A. (2009). The credit crisis as a problem in the sociology of knowledge. *Working Paper November 2009.* Copies of this paper are available from https://web.archive.org/web/20100331233655/http://www.sps.ed.ac.uk/__data/assets/pdf_file/0019/36082/CrisisNew19.pdf . Accessed 29 November 2016.

MacKenzie, D. A. (2011). The credit crisis as a problem in the sociology of knowledge. *American Journal of Sociology, 116*(6): 1778–1841.

MacKenzie, D. A. (2012). Knowledge production in financial markets: Credit default swaps, the ABX and the sub-prime crisis. *Economy and Society, 41*(3): 335–359.

MacKenzie, D. A., & Millo, Y. (2003). Constructing a market, performing theory: The historical sociology of a financial derivatives exchange. *American Journal of Sociology, 109*(1): 107–145.

MacKenzie, D. A., Muniesa, F., & Siu, L. (2007). *Do Economists Make Markets?: On the Performativity of Economics.* Princeton, NJ: Princeton University Press.

Malkiel, B. (1987). "Efficient markets hypothesis", in Eatwell, John, Milgate, Murray, & Newman, Peter (eds), *The New Palgrave: A Dictionary of Economics,* 1st edition. Palgrave Macmillan.

Marx, K. (1976). *Capital: A Critique of Political Economy.* London: Penguin in Association with New Left Review.

Mason, D. L. (2004). *From Buildings and Loans to Bail-Outs: A History of the Savings and Loan Industry, 1831–1989.* Cambridge: Cambridge University Press.

Mason, J. (2008a). Cliff risk and the credit crisis. Available at SSRN: https://ssrn.com/abstract=1296250. Accessed August 15 2009.

Mason, J. (2008b). Structuring for leverage: CPDOs, SIVs, and ARSs. SIVs, and ARSs (October 17, 2008). Available at https://ssrn.com/abstract=1288051. Accessed August 16, 2009

Mason, J., & Rosner, J. (2007). How resilient are mortgage backed securities to collateralized debt obligation market disruptions? Available at SSRN: https://ssrn.com/abstract=1027472. Accessed August 16, 2009.

Mayer, C., Pence, K., & Herlund, S. (2009). The rise in mortgage defaults. *Journal of Economic Perspectives, 23*(1): 27–50.

McCulley, P. (2009). The shadow banking system and Hyman Minsky's economic journey. *Research Foundation of CFA Institute Report,* Vol. 2009. No. 5. Available at https://www.cfainstitute.org/learning/products/publications/rf/Pages/rf.v2009.n5.15.aspx. Accessed July 24, 2010.

Mehrling, P. (1998). The money muddle: The transformation of American monetary thought, 1920–1970. *History of Political Economy, 30*(Supplement): 293–306.

Mehrling, P. (1999). The vision of Hyman Minsky. *Journal of Economic Behaviour and Organisation, 39*: 129–158.

Mehrling, P. (2000). Minsky and modern finance. *The Journal of Portfolio Management, 26*(2): 81–88.

Mehrling, P. (2011). *The New Lombard Street: How the Fed Became the Dealer of Last Resort.* Princeton, NJ: Princeton University Press.

134   Bibliography

Meillassoux, Q. (2008). *After Finitude: An Essay on the Necessity of Contingency*. London: Continuum.

Merton, R. C. (2005). You have more capital than you think. *Harvard Bus. Rev., 83*(11): 84–94.

Mian, A. R., & Sufi, A. (2009a). House prices, home equity-based borrowing, and the US household leverage crisis (No. w15283). *National Bureau of Economic Research*.

Mian, A. R., & Sufi, A. (2009b). The consequences of mortgage credit expansion: Evidence from the US mortgage default crisis. *The Quarterly Journal of Economics, 124*(4): 1449–1496.

Miller, M. (1992). Financial innovation: Achievements and prospects. *Journal of Applied Corporate Finance, 4*(4): 4–11.

Minsky, H. P. (1957). Central banking and money market changes. *The Quarterly Journal of Economics, 71*(2): 171–187.

Minsky, H. P. (1972). An evaluation of recent monetary policy. *Nebraska Journal of Economics and Business, 11*(4): 37–56.

Minsky, H. P. (1975). *John Maynard Keynes*. New York: Columbia University Press.

Minsky, H. P. (1977). "The tendency towards Ponzi finance", in Altman, E. I. (ed), *Financial Crises: Institutions and Markets in a Fragile Environment*. New York: Wiley & Sons: 139–154.

Minsky, H. P. (1980). The Federal Reserve: Between a rock and a hard place. *Challenge, 23*(2): 30–36.

Minsky, H. P. (1982). "The financial instability hypothesis: An interpretation of Keynes and an alternative to 'standard theory'", in *Inflation, Recession and Economic Policy*. Brighton, Sussex: Wheatsheaf Books: 59–71.

Minsky, H. P. (1984). "Financial innovations and financial stability", in Brennan, D. (1984) *Financial Innovations: their impact on monetary policy and financial markets* – Federal Reserve Bank of St Louis. Boston: Kluwer Academic Publishers. 25–49.

Minsky, H. P. (1982b). "The financial instability hypothesis", in Wachtel, P. (ed), *Crises in the Economic and Financial Structure*. Lexington, MA: Lexington: 53–68.

Minsky, H. P. (1982c). *Can "It" Happen again?: Essays on Instability and Finance*. Armonk, NY: M. E. Sharpe.

Minsky, H. P. (1986). *Stabilizing an Unstable Economy*. New Haven: Yale University Press.

Minsky, H. P. (2008). Securitization. *The Levy Economics Institute of Bard College Policy Note 2008/2*. Preface and Afterword by L. Randal Wray. Available at http://www.levy institute.org/pubs/pn_08_2.pdf. Accessed 15 July 2009.

Minsky, H. P. (2011). "Financial instability hypothesis", in Argyrous, G. & Stilwell, F. (eds), *Readings in Political Economy: Economics as a Social Science*. Prahran: Tilde University Press: 233–238.

Minsky, H. P., & Wray, L. R. (2008). *Securitization* (No. 08-2). The Levy Economics Institute of Bard College Policy Note.

Mirowski, P. (2010). Inherent Vice: Minsky, Markomata, and the tendency of markets to undermine themselves. *Journal of Institutional Economics, 6*(4): 415–438.

Modigliani, F. (1988). The monetarist controversy revisited. *Contemporary Economic Policy, 6*(4): 3–18.

Moore, B. J. (1988). *Horizontalists and Verticalists: The Macroeconomics of Credit Money*. Cambridge: Cambridge University Press.

Muolo, P., & Padilla, M. (2010). *Chain of Blame: How Wall Street Caused the Mortgage and Credit Crisis*. Hoboken, NJ: Wiley & Sons.

Bibliography 135

Palley, T. I. (1993). Milton Friedman and the monetarist counter-revolution: A re-appraisal. *Eastern Economic Journal*, *19*(1): 71–81.

Passmore, W. (2005). The GSE implicit subsidy and the value of government ambiguity. *Real Estate Economics*, *33*(3): 465–486.

Patterson, S. (2010). *The Quants: How a Small Band of Math Wizards Took over Wall St. and Nearly Destroyed It*. New York: Crown.

Perez, C. (2009). The double bubble at the turn of the century: Technological roots and structural implications. *Cambridge Journal of Economics*, *33*(4): 779–805.

Pinkard, T. (1998). Hegel's hermeneutics (review). *Journal of the History of Philosophy*, *36*(2): 327–329.

Poon, M. (2009). From new deal institutions to capital markets: Commercial consumer risk scores and the making of sub-prime mortgage finance. *Accounting, Organizations and Society*, *34*(5): 654–674.

Postone, M. (1993). *Time, Labor, and Social Domination: A Reinterpretation of Marx's Critical Theory*. Cambridge, England: Cambridge.

Pozsar, Z., Adrian, T., Ashcraft, A., & Boesky, H. (2010). Shadow banking. FRB of New York Staff Report No. 458. Available at SSRN: https://ssrn.com/abstract=1645337.

Quiggin, J. (2011). "Regulating finance after the crisis", in Argyrous, G. & Stilwell, F. (eds), *Readings in Political Economy: Economics as a Social Science*. Prahran: Tilde University Press: 10–13.

Raiter, F., & Parisi, F. (2004). Mortgage credit and the evolution of risk-based pricing. *Joint Center for Housing Studies, Harvard University, BABC*, 04–23. Available at http://www.jchs.harvard.edu/research/publications/mortgage-credit-and-evolution-risk-based-pricing. Accessed May 5 2010.

Ranieri, L. (1996). "The origins of securitization, sources of its growth, and its future potential", in Kendall, L. T. & Fishman. M. J. (eds), *A Primer on Securitization*. Cambridge, MA: MIT Press: 55–70.

Rawls, J. (1971). *A Theory of Justice*. Cambridge, MA: Belknap of Harvard University Press.

Rebonato, R. (2010). *Plight of the Fortune Tellers: Why We Need to Manage Financial Risk Differently*. Princeton, NJ: Princeton University Press.

Redding, P. (1996). *Hegel's Hermeneutics*. Ithaca: Cornell University Press.

Schumpeter, J. (1928). The instability of capitalism. *The Economic Journal*, *38*(151): 361–386.

Schwartz, E., & Order, R. (1988). Valuing the implicit guarantee of the Federal National Mortgage Association. *The Journal of Real Estate Finance and Economics*, *1*(1): 23–34.

Shiller, R. J. (2004). *The New Financial Order: Risk in the 21st Century*. Princeton, NJ: Princeton University Press.

Shiller, R. (2005) *Irrational Exuberance*. Princeton, NJ : Princeton University Press, 2nd ed.

Shiller, R. J. (2008). *The Sub-prime Solution: How Today's Global Financial Crisis Happened and What to Do about It*. Princeton, NJ: Princeton University Press.

Silber, W. L. (1983). The process of financial innovation. *The American Economic Review*, *73*(2): 89–95.

Sirmans, C. F., & Benjamin, J. D. (1990). Pricing fixed rate mortgages: Some empirical evidence. *Journal of Financial Services Research*, *4*(3): 191–202.

Skeel, D. (2010). *The New Financial Deal: Understanding the Dodd–Frank Act and Its (Unintended) Consequences*. Hoboken, NJ: Wiley & Sons.

Snowdon, B., & Vane, H. R. (2005). *Modern Macroeconomics*. London: E. Elgar.

Soros, G. (1994) *The Alchemy of Finance : Reading the Mind of the Market*. Foreword by Paul Tudor Jones II. New York : J. Wiley.

136   Bibliography

Soros, G. (2008). *The New Paradigm for Financial Markets: The Credit Crisis of 2008 and What It Means*. New York, NY: PublicAffairs.

Stiglitz, J. E. (2009). Regulation and the theory of market and government failure. *Tobin Project Working Paper*. Available at http://www2.gsb.columbia.edu/faculty/jstiglitz/workingpapers.cfm.

Stiglitz, J. E. (2010). *Freefall: America, Free Markets, and the Sinking of the World Economy*. New York: W. W. Norton & Co.

Stilwell, F. (2002). *Political Economy: The Contest of Economic Ideas*. Cambridge, UK: Cambridge University Press.

Tavakoli, J. M. (2003). *Collateralized Debt Obligations and Structured Finance: New Developments in Cash and Synthetic Securitization*. Hoboken, NJ: Wiley & Sons.

Tett, G. (2009). *Fool's Gold: How the Bold Dream of a Small Tribe at JP Morgan Was Corrupted by Wall Street Greed and Unleashed a Catastrophe*. New York, NY: Simon and Schuster.

Thompson, E. P. (1978). *The Poverty of Theory and Other Essays*. London: Merlin Press.

Toporowski, J. (1999). *The End of Finance: Capital Market Inflation, Financial Derivatives and Pension Fund Capitalism*. London: Routledge.

Toporowski, J., & Tavasci, D. (2010). *Minsky, Crisis and Development*. Houndmills, Basingstoke, Hampshire: Palgrave Macmillan.

Varoufakis, Y., Halevi, J., & Theocarakis, N. (2011). *Modern Political Economics: Making Sense of the Post-2008 World*. Abingdon, Oxon: Routledge.

Watkins, S. (2010). Shifting sands. *New Left Review*, 61 January-February: 5–27.

Whalen, C. (2008). Understanding the credit crunch as a Minsky Moment. *Challenge*, *51*(1): 91–109.

Williams, J. (1986). *The Economic Function of Futures Markets*. Cambridge: Cambridge University Press.

Williamson, S. D. (2012). Liquidity, monetary policy, and the financial crisis: A new monetarist approach. *The American Economic Review*, *102*(6): 2570–2605.

Wojnilower, A. M. (1980). The central role of credit crunches in recent financial history. *Brookings Papers on Economic Activity*, *1980*(2): 277–339.

Wojnilower, A. M. (1985). Private credit demand, supply, and crunches – how different are the 1980's? *The American Economic Review*, *75*(2): 351–356.

Wojnilower, A. M. (2001). "Business cycles in a financially deregulated America", in Leijonhufvud (ed) *Monetary Theory as a Basis of Monetary Policy. International Economic Association (IEA) Conference Volume Series*. Basingstoke: Macmillan Press: 145–169.

Wray, L. R. (2008). Lessons from the sub-prime meltdown. *Challenge*, *51*(2): 40–68.

Wray, L. R. (2008a). Financial markets meltdown: What can we learn from Minsky? *The Levy Institute of Bard College Public Policy Brief Highlights No. 94A*.

Žižek, S. (2012). *Less Than Nothing: Hegel and the Shadow of Dialectical Materialism*. London: Verso.

Žižek, S. (2012a). A modest plea for enlightened catastrophism. *ABC Online*. July 11, 2012. Available at http://www.abc.net.au/religion/articles/2012/07/11/3543824.htm. Accessed 28 March 2012.

Organisational reports and congressional records

Financial Crisis Inquiry Commission. (2010). *Preliminary Staff Report, Governmental Rescues of "Too-Big-to-Fail" Financial Institutions, August 31, 2010*. See http://fcic-static.law.stanford.edu/cdn_media/fcic-reports/2010–0831-Governmental-Rescues.pdf.

Bibliography 137

Financial Crisis Inquiry Commission. (2011). *The Financial Crisis Inquiry Report: Final Report of the National Commission on the Causes of the Financial and Economic Crisis in the United States.* PublicAffairs, Perseus Books Group.

FSB. (2009). *The Report of the Financial Stability Forum on Addressing Pro-Cyclicality in the Financial System.* See http://www.financialstabilityboard.org/publications/r_0904a.pdf.

Secondary Market Operations of the Federal National Mortgage Association and the Federal Home Loan Mortgage Corporation. Hearings before the Committee on Banking, Housing and Urban Affairs United States Senate. Ninety Fourth Congress. Second Session. December 9, 10 and 13 (1976).

Torregrosa, D. (2001). *Interest Rate Differential between Jumbo and Conforming Mortgages 1995–2000.* Congressional Budget Office Paper May 2001.

UBS. (2008). *Shareholder Report on UBS's Write-Downs.* See http://www.propublica.org/documents/item/shareholder-report-on-ubss-write-downs.

Speeches

A Minsky Meltdown: Lessons for Central Bankers. Presentation to the 18th Annual Hyman P. Minsky Conference on the State of the U.S. and World Economies – "Meeting the Challenges of the Financial Crisis" Organized by the Levy Economics Institute of Bard College New York City by Janet L. Yellen, President and CEO, Federal Reserve Bank of San Francisco for Delivery on April 16, (2009). http://www.frbsf.org/our-district/press/presidents-speeches/yellen-speeches/2009/april/yellen-minsky-meltdown-central-bankers/.

Remarks by Chairman Alan Greenspan Technology and Financial Services before the Journal of Financial Services Research and the American Enterprise Institute Conference, in Honor of Anna Schwartz, Washington, DC. April 14, (2000). http://www.federalreserve.gov/boarddocs/speeches/2000/20000414.htm.

Magazine articles, journalism and online publications

Blodget, H. (2009). Roubini: Nationalizing banks is the best way to go. *The Business Insider,* 12 February 2009. Available online at http://www.businessinsider.com/roubini-nationalizing-banks-is-the-best-way-to-go-2009-2.

Blumberg, A., Davidson, A., & Glass, I. (2008). The giant pool of money. *This American Life.* NPR. Transcript available online at http://www.thisamericanlife.org/radio-archives/episode/355/transcript.

Elliot, B. S. (2004). Lenders push consumers into ARMs. *USA Today,* 27 April 2004: 4.

Finkelstein, B. (2001). What's hot, what's not. *Broker Magazine,* 7 December 2001, 3(6): 10.

Guha, K., & Luce, E. (2009). Greenspan backs bank nationalisation. *Financial Times,* 18 February 2009. Available online at http://www.ft.com/cms/s/0/e310cbf6-fd4e-11dd-a103-000077b07658.html.

Hagerty, J. (2004). For these mortgages downside comes later. *The Wall St Journal,* 5 October 2004: c1.

Hudson, M. (2005). The $4.7 trillion pyramid: Why social security won't be enough to save Wall Street. *Harper's Magazine,* April 2005, pp. 35–40.

Hudson, M. (2006). The new road to serfdom. *Harper's Magazine.* May 2006: 39–46.

Kendall, L. T. (1995). A time for retooling. *Mortgage Banking,* 56(1): 14.

138   *Bibliography*

Krugman, P. (2009). Banking on the brink. *New York Times*, Op-Ed., 22 February 2009. Available online at http://www.nytimes.com/2009/02/23/opinion/23krugman.html?_r=2.

Lanchester, J. (2011). The non-scenic route to the place we're going anyway. *London Review of Books*, 33(17): 3–5.

McDowell, E. (2004). To jumbo and beyond. *The New York Times*, 11 April 2004. RE1-2

Randazzo, A. (2009). The myth of financial deregulation: Government action caused the economic crisis, not the free market. *Reason Online*, 19 June 2009. Available online at http://www.reason.com/news/show/134238.html.

Rozens, A. (2002). Buyers dodge home price rise with adjustable loans. *Reuters News*, 5 April 2002.

Shenn, J. (2005). Gauging staying power of hybrid mortgages. *American Banker*, 13 January 2005, 170(9): 1.

Shostak, F. (2007). Does the current financial crisis vindicate the economics of Hyman Minsky? The Hyman Minsky theory does not explain the current financial crisis. *Ludwig von Mises Institute – Mises Daily*, 27 November. Available online at http://mises.org/daily/2787.

Sichelman, L. (2003). Mozilo: End downpayment requirements. *National Mortgage News*, 17 February 2003, 27(21): 21.

Simon, R. (2002). Mortgage financiers are high in hybrids. *The Wall St Journal*, 10 January 2002, C1.

Simon, R. (2003). The home loan that is still hot: Helocs. *The Wall St Journal*, 24 September 2003, D1.

Simon, R. (2004). Creative mortgages fuel home sales. *The Wall St Journal*, 16 March 2004, D1.

Soros, G. (2009). One way stop to bear raids. *Wall St Journal*, 24 March 2009. A17.

Veneits, K. (2001). Weak hedge takes hit at countrywide. *National Mortgage News*, 2 January 2001, 25(14): 3.

Index

AAA credit ratings 104
ABS (asset-backed securities) 10, 51–53, 68, 71, 77, 85, 104–6
ABS CDO market 77, 106
ABS CDOs 72–73, 80–1, 84–6, 106, 127
adaptive markets hypothesis 132
Alt-A mortgages 94–5
Althusser, Louis 5, 11, 14, 128
arbitrage 10, 49, 52, 60–74, 91, 98–9, 101, 104–6, 112, 124, 133
ARM (adjustable rate mortgage) 11, 92, 94, 97, 137
asset-backed securities *see* ABS

banker's view 22–25, 68
banking 34, 59, 130, 137–8
banking economists 48, 50–1, 53–4, 109
Beiser, Frederick 5, 12–15, 128
Black-Scholes-Merton model for pricing derivatives 80, 82
Borio, Claudio 48, 50, 52, 54, 71, 73, 111, 113–14, 117, 129
Brunnermeier, Markus 50
Bryan, Dick 55, 65, 68, 70, 87, 90, 110, 116, 129–30

canonical mechanism market 78–80
capital asset prices 19, 31, 39, 44–5, 64
capital buffers, counter-cyclical 114
capitalism 3, 5, 27, 125, 129, 135
capital markets 15, 27–8, 31–2, 51, 64–5, 103, 105, 135
CAPM (Capital Asset Pricing Model) 78
CDOs (collateralised debt obligations) 10, 52, 71, 75, 77–82, 84–6, 88–9, 106, 126
CDS (credit default swaps) 10, 19, 32, 51, 71, 75, 80–1, 84–6, 105–6, 126–7
CDS market 85, 106

central bank 8, 15–16, 19, 38–45, 56–8, 63, 111, 114–15, 121–4, 131
Citicorp 33
CMOs (collateralised mortgage obligation) 15, 77, 79, 100, 132
collateralised debt obligations. *See* CDOs
collateralised mortgage obligation *see* CMOs
commensuration 10, 28, 68–9, 71–2, 75, 83–7, 91, 98, 124
commercial banks 25, 29, 31–3, 64, 104, 126
conforming mortgages 94, 99, 101–3, 108, 137
contemporary financial crisis 2, 35, 46–8, 58, 60–1, 73, 91
cost of capital 24, 27–8, 117–18
Countrywide Financial 93, 95
credit crisis 76, 83, 133–4, 136
credit crunches 25–6, 30–1, 39–40, 45–6, 63, 73, 106, 129, 132, 136
credit cycle 41, 73, 83, 113, 115, 117–18
credit default swaps *see* CDS
credit risk 53, 65, 79–80, 85, 87, 104, 114, 118, 124, 127

dealers 51–3, 133
derivatives 9–10, 47, 49, 53–4, 69–72, 75, 80, 82, 106, 109, 113, 115–16, 118, 129, 131
Derman, Emmanuel 70, 84–5, 130
dialectical development 4, 14
dialectics 8, 11–15, 53, 58, 60, 132
DIDMCA (Depository Institutions Deregulation and Monetary Control Act 1981) 33
disintermediation 30–1, 40, 63
diversification 68, 77, 79, 87
DJIA (Dow Jones Industrial Average) 19–20
Dymski, Gary 9, 47, 90

140 *Index*

EMH (Efficient Market Hypothesis) 2, 10, 46–7, 49, 58, 60–2, 65–9, 72–4, 110, 112, 115, 123, 131, 133
equilibrium 19, 57, 60, 66
excesses, solutions to 112, 115

Fabozzi, Frank 103–4, 106, 130–1
Fama, Eugene 46, 66–7, 130
Fannie Mae (Federal National Mortgage Association) 79, 108, 135
FCIC (Financial Crisis Inquiry Commission 136–7
FDIC (Federal Deposit Insurance Corporation) 25, 29
Federal Reserve Bank 25–6, 33–4, 45, 50, 52–3, 99, 108, 126, 128–9, 131, 134, 137
Fed funds market 24
FHA (Federal Housing Authority) 107–8
FHLBB (Federal Home Loan Bank Board) 29, 31, 54
FICO (Fair Isaac Corporation) credit score 79, 97, 102–3, 105
FIH (Financial Instability Hypothesis) 1–3, 8–10, 17, 19, 21, 35, 48, 54, 60–1, 64–6, 90–1, 107, 120, 123–4, 134
financial calculations 9–10, 69, 75–6, 82–4, 86, 88, 109
financial crisis 1–4, 6, 8–11, 13–14, 16–17, 35–6, 47–9, 51, 60–1, 75–7, 109–11, 120–1, 128–29, 132–3, 136–8
financial economics 50, 54–5, 109, 123–4, 130, 132; based 46, 113
financial innovations 8, 17–19, 26–7, 29–32, 41–2, 53, 55–9, 61–2, 64–5, 70–1, 73–4, 86–8, 115–16, 124, 134–5
financial instruments 2, 10, 16, 18, 30, 51, 61, 63, 68–70, 74, 77–8, 80–1, 84, 86, 88
financialization 87–8, 116, 129
financial models 70, 86, 124
Financial Services Act 2012 UK 115
financial units 1, 18–19, 21, 38, 40, 43, 51, 54, 61–4, 70–2, 74, 80, 87, 89–92, 114
fiscalism 39, 41–2
floating rate instruments 30, 32–3
form of capital 4, 6, 27–8, 30, 42, 45, 62, 65, 67–8, 107, 109, 115, 117–18, 123, 125
Freddie Mac (Federal Home Loan Mortgage Corporation) 54, 66, 79, 99, 108
Friedman, Milton 36–44, 46, 123, 131, 135
FSF (Financial Stability Forum) 114, 137

funding dynamics 52, 116
funding liquidity, sources of 19, 31, 51, 54, 92, 106

Gadamer, Hans Georg 7, 17, 21, 131
Gaussian Copula Formula 81, 84–5, 106
Ginnie Mae 79, 99–100, 108
Gorton, Gary 95, 104, 106, 131
government bonds 39, 101, 104
GSEs (government-sponsored enterprises) 78, 80–1, 99–104, 107, 135

Hardt and Negri 5, 14, 25, 27–9
hedge funds 51, 61, 65, 71, 78, 88, 101, 106, 126–7
hedge unit 18, 38, 50, 61, 88, 90–2, 105, 107, 113, 115, 118, 123
hedging 49, 65, 71, 80, 88, 116–18
Hegel, Friedrich 12–14, 89, 91, 108, 128, 131, 136
hermeneutic circle 21
hermeneutics 7, 15, 30, 135
historical structure 60–74
historicity 1–2, 9, 13, 16–17
historicizing critique 2, 13–14, 46, 73, 123
HOLC (Home Owners Loan Corporation) 108
house price derivatives 11, 88, 109, 112, 115
hybrid ARM 92–8, 104–5

immanence 2, 7, 10–11, 14, 45, 61, 66, 88, 91, 93, 96, 107, 123–4
interest rate ceilings 25, 30, 33, 65
interest rates 17–18, 24–5, 27, 30–3, 39–40, 43–5, 50, 52, 63, 75, 77, 97–8, 103–4, 114–15, 117
investment banking 34, 126

Jameson, Fredric 13–15, 60, 132
JP Morgan 77, 79, 136

Kant, Immanuel 12, 15, 37
Kaufman, Henry 26, 30, 34
Keynes, John Maynard 2, 5, 7–8, 16–17, 19, 21–5, 27–8, 30, 41, 44, 46, 58–9, 134
Keynes's work 7, 17, 19, 21–2, 27
Kindleberger, Charles 2–3, 14, 132
Kregel, Jan 47, 58, 90, 132
Krippner, Greta 25–6, 29–34, 53, 63, 74, 132

lender of last resort 15, 19, 25, 41
Levy Economics Institute 134, 137

Index 141

liquidity 6, 8–11, 16, 22–5, 43, 45–59, 61, 69–77, 82–4, 86–8, 105–7, 113, 115–17, 122–6, 128–30
liquidity crisis 6, 8–9, 16–17, 19, 22–3, 26–9, 45–6, 48, 50–1, 53–8, 63–4, 69–70, 74, 91, 93
liquidity dynamics 7–8, 11, 17, 44–5, 51–3, 55, 57–8, 61, 65, 69, 71, 76, 90–1, 98, 124
liquidity preference 21–4, 27, 45, 67, 70
liquidity risk 118
liquidity yield 52, 65, 73, 106
LTCM (Long Term Capital Management) 9, 47, 49–53, 60, 66–7
Lysandrou, Photis 71, 104, 132–3

MacKenzie, Donald 10, 15, 50, 52, 56–7, 67, 71, 75–86, 89, 91, 103–6, 108, 116, 124, 133
Magnetar 89, 106, 129
market liquidity 18–19, 44, 49, 51–6, 64–5, 69, 72, 74, 106, 115, 129
market liquidity and funding liquidity 54, 72, 129
Marx, Karl 14, 128–9, 132–3
MBS (mortgage backed securities) 10, 16, 50, 54, 68, 71, 75, 77–81, 84, 86, 90, 99–100, 104, 126, 133
Mehrling, Perry 1–2, 6, 14, 16, 18, 24–5, 36, 38, 47–8, 50–60, 64–6, 69–71, 75, 106, 133
Meillassoux, Quentin 14–15, 134
metaphysics 38, 121, 123
MGIC (Mortgage Guarantee Insurance Company) 107
Minsky, Hyman 1–2, 7–9, 16–19, 21–48, 50–61, 63–6, 90–2, 111–14, 117–18, 120, 123–4, 130, 133–4, 136, 138
Minsky's critique of Monetarism 8, 35, 38, 42
Minsky's FIH (Financial Instability Hypothesis) 1, 3–4, 9, 17, 46, 53–5, 60–3, 65, 69, 88, 90–1, 109, 120, 123–5
Minsky's interpretation of Keynes 16, 21
modelling 75–6, 84, 124
Monetarism 2, 8–9, 14, 35–46, 57, 123, 131
monetary policy 37, 39, 131
money markets, short-term 24–5, 65, 106
money supply 8, 36, 38–44, 46, 120, 123
mortgage backed securities *see* MBS
mortgage banks 101, 104, 106
mortgage market 1, 99, 101, 103
Mozilo, Angelo 93

New Deal system 25–9, 32, 46

Palley, Thomas 35–6
performativity 10, 76, 82–3, 86, 89, 124
political economy 19, 128–9, 131–6
Ponzi units 18, 38, 54, 61–63, 88, 90–3, 104, 107, 114–15, 123, 134
Poon, Martha 101
Popper, Karl 37–8
positive economics 36–8, 42, 45, 131
Post-Keynesian economics 1–2, 14, 41, 93, 120

quantitative analysts 49, 84
Quantity Theory of Money framework 36

Rafferty, Mike 55, 65, 68, 70, 87, 90, 110, 116, 129–30
reflexivity 12–13, 54, 72, 83, 117, 122, 129
Regulation Q interest rate ceilings 25, 30, 33, 65
REIT (real estate investment trusts) 1, 19
REMIC (Real Estate Mortgage Investment Conduit) 77, 79
repo market 50, 70, 85, 127
risk-based system of liquidity 85, 92
risk calculation 47, 52, 57, 61, 69–70, 76, 78–9, 82, 85–8, 90, 99, 101, 103–5, 108
risk management 15, 68–70, 72, 87, 90–1, 96, 98, 101, 103–4, 107, 113, 124
risk screening 91, 98–9, 101
risk-taking channel 73–4
risk trading 47–50, 53, 55, 58, 61
risk trading system 9–10, 55, 71
risk transfer 15, 72, 84–5, 93, 98, 104–6

secondary market 24, 32, 54, 68, 71, 106, 108
securitisation 49, 53–4, 64, 68, 70, 75, 77, 79, 81, 101, 104, 116, 118, 130–2, 134–5
securitisation channel 64, 101
Shin, Hyun Song 50
SIFIs (Systemically Important Financial Institutions) 125
Silber, William 18, 30, 135
SIVs (Structured Investment Vehicles) 133
S&Ls (Savings and Loan Banks) 31–2, 53–4
Soros, George 54, 106, 112, 122, 135–6, 138
speculative units 18
SPVs (special purpose vehicle) 77, 79, 118
Stiglitz, Joseph 14, 110–11, 121–2, 125, 136
Stilwell, Frank 37, 128, 132, 134–6
subject and object 4–5, 12–13, 60

142　*Index*

sub-prime mortgage market 52, 73, 79, 81, 84, 92, 94–6, 102–5, 119, 127
synthetic CDOs 81, 84
system of liquidity 69–70, 72, 83, 85–6, 88, 91–2, 109, 116

TARP (Troubled Asset Relief Program) 50
TBTF (Too Big to Fail) 121, 125–6
tranching 79, 103

UBS 106, 127, 137
US housing market 11, 90–1, 99
US mortgage market 90–108, 128, 132–6

Varoufakis, Yanis 14, 37, 136
volatility 2, 29–30, 49, 51, 56, 61, 65, 70, 87–8, 90, 118
Volker rule 126

Wojnilower, Albert 19, 25–6, 28, 30–1, 33–4, 39–40, 44, 46, 53, 62–5, 68–9, 74, 124, 136

Yellen, Janet L. 137

Žižek, Slavoj 6, 11, 13–15, 74, 136